Lecture Notes in Computer Science 15930

Founding Editors

Gerhard Goos
Juris Hartmanis

Editorial Board Members

Elisa Bertino, *Purdue University, West Lafayette, IN, USA*
Wen Gao, *Peking University, Beijing, China*
Bernhard Steffen , *TU Dortmund University, Dortmund, Germany*
Moti Yung , *Columbia University, New York, NY, USA*

The series Lecture Notes in Computer Science (LNCS), including its subseries Lecture Notes in Artificial Intelligence (LNAI) and Lecture Notes in Bioinformatics (LNBI), has established itself as a medium for the publication of new developments in computer science and information technology research, teaching, and education.

LNCS enjoys close cooperation with the computer science R & D community, the series counts many renowned academics among its volume editors and paper authors, and collaborates with prestigious societies. Its mission is to serve this international community by providing an invaluable service, mainly focused on the publication of conference and workshop proceedings and postproceedings. LNCS commenced publication in 1973.

Marinos Ioannides · Eleanor Fink ·
Janet Anderson · Antonella Fresa ·
Antony Cassar · Sander Münster
Editors

3D Research Challenges in Cultural Heritage VI

DigitalTwin versus MemoryTwin

Editors
Marinos Ioannides
Cyprus University of Technology
Limassol, Cyprus

Eleanor Fink
International Cultural Heritage
Arlington, VA, USA

Janet Anderson
Visiting Professor, ELTE
Budapest, Hungary

Antonella Fresa
Promoter s.r.l.
Peccioli, Italy

Antony Cassar
Heritage Malta
Kalkara, Malta

Sander Münster
Friedrich-Schiller-Universität Jena
Jena, Germany

ISSN 0302-9743   ISSN 1611-3349 (electronic)
Lecture Notes in Computer Science
ISBN 978-3-032-05655-9   ISBN 978-3-032-05656-6 (eBook)
https://doi.org/10.1007/978-3-032-05656-6

© The Editor(s) (if applicable) and The Author(s), under exclusive license
to Springer Nature Switzerland AG 2026

This work is subject to copyright. All rights are solely and exclusively licensed by the Publisher, whether the whole or part of the material is concerned, specifically the rights of translation, reprinting, reuse of illustrations, recitation, broadcasting, reproduction on microfilms or in any other physical way, and transmission or information storage and retrieval, electronic adaptation, computer software, or by similar or dissimilar methodology now known or hereafter developed.
The use of general descriptive names, registered names, trademarks, service marks, etc. in this publication does not imply, even in the absence of a specific statement, that such names are exempt from the relevant protective laws and regulations and therefore free for general use.
The publisher, the authors and the editors are safe to assume that the advice and information in this book are believed to be true and accurate at the date of publication. Neither the publisher nor the authors or the editors give a warranty, expressed or implied, with respect to the material contained herein or for any errors or omissions that may have been made. The publisher remains neutral with regard to jurisdictional claims in published maps and institutional affiliations.

All rights reserved by UNESCO Chair on Digital Cultural Heritage at the Cyprus University of Technology

This Springer imprint is published by the registered company Springer Nature Switzerland AG
The registered company address is: Gewerbestrasse 11, 6330 Cham, Switzerland

If disposing of this product, please recycle the paper.

Preface

Recording cultural heritage, its transformation from the analogue to digital through 3D digitisation, modelling and documentation, has become a vital methodology. Using advanced technologies, such as photogrammetry, laser scanning, computer tomography, and multispectral imaging, heritage professionals can now create detailed digital 2D/3D representations of sites, monuments, and artefacts. However, a critical question arises: Is our goal merely to create Digital Twins, or to go further, toward Memory Twins?

Digital Twin: A Structure, Form, Function, and Technical Insight

The Digital Twin is a concept born in engineering (the automotive and aerospace industries) in the areas of Computer-Aided Design (CAD), Computer-Aided Manufacturing (CAM), and Computer- Integrated Manufacturing (CIM) in the 1970s and 1980s, it then found application in the architecture and civil engineering sectors, and is now widely used in the digital heritage/cultural informatics and e-humanities field. It refers to a high-fidelity, data-rich 3D model that mirrors a real-world object or site, enabling 2D/3D reconstruction, modelling, archiving, simulation, restoration, preservation, and monitoring. In the context of cultural heritage, Digital Twins are instrumental for:

- the creation of architectural designs;
- restoration planning and virtual reconstructions;
- structural diagnostics and preventive conservation;
- monument(s) and site(s) management systems;
- environmental and condition monitoring (GIS, etc.);
- tourism management systems; and
- enabling remote access and interaction.

These models provide a geometrical and technical insight – accurately replicating a site's form, structure, and current condition. Yet, while a Digital Twin shows *what* the object is, it does not always explain *why* it matters.

Memory Twin: Context, Story, and Cultural Significance

The Memory Twin has emerged as a profound evolution of the Digital Twin. It does not replace it, but extends it. While built upon the same technical foundation, the Memory Twin embeds within the 3D model the historical knowledge, the unique story, the cultural value, and, ultimately, the authentic memory and identity of the heritage asset.

It asks deeper questions:

- Why is this object named a "Monument", and why is it important?
- What stories or knowledge does it hold?

- Why must it be preserved for future generations?

The Memory Twin transforms the digital model into a value-bearing cultural artefact by integrating:

- historical narratives and scholarly interpretation;
- intangible heritage (rituals, memories, emotions);
- archival records, inscriptions, oral histories; and
- multilingual paradata, metadata and ethical context.

This holistic approach aligns with the FAIR (Findable, Accessible, Interoperable, Reusable) and CARE (Collective benefit, Authority to control, Responsibility, Ethics) principles, ensuring that digital documentation is both technically robust and ethically grounded.

Empowering the Memory Twin with ICT and XR

In the era of extended reality (XR) and the Metaverse, Memory Twins offer transformative potential. By combining precise 3D models with immersive storytelling, we can create experiential environments where artefacts, buildings, and monuments are no longer silent but act as accumulators of memory – they speak, interact, and teach.

Imagine:

- a ruined temple that narrates its own history in the voice of its ancient builders or owners;
- a museum object that tells of its cultural journey across centuries and continents; or
- a destroyed heritage site reconstructed in XR to teach peace, remembrance, and resilience.

In such immersive settings, Memory Twins do more than represent the past – they inspire the future. They serve as tools for education, empathy, innovation, and identity-building.

Conclusion

The Digital Twin gives us structure, form and function – but the Memory Twin gives us the story, meaning, and memory. It is not enough to preserve geometry; we must preserve identity. In a time when digital technologies offer new possibilities for heritage, the Memory Twin calls on us to use the full power of ICT not only to reconstruct the past but to connect it meaningfully to the present and the future.

Cultural heritage is not static; the Memory Twin acts as an accumulator of knowledge over time – a dynamic and expanding container of historical, cultural, and interpretive layers. In doing so, it becomes a cornerstone of a circular cultural economy, where lessons learned from the past inform the design of the future. This model allows us not only to preserve heritage but to activate it – transforming memory into a resource for innovation, identity, resilience, and sustainable development.

These digitally documented cultural objects – these accumulators of memory – become our lighthouses and semaphores. They illuminate the path forward, signalling through the noise of the present with the clarity of accumulated human experience. In preserving their stories, we equip ourselves to navigate the complexities of the future – guided by memory, grounded in history, and inspired by the enduring value of our shared heritage.

By documenting with accuracy, embedding cultural knowledge, and designing for immersive storytelling, we ensure that what we preserve today will speak clearly and powerfully to the generations of tomorrow – not only to remember, but to improve.

The papers included in this State-of-the-Art Survey were originally submitted and approved to the workshop organized by the UNESCO Chair on Digital Cultural Heritage during the EuroMed 2024 conference in Cyprus. The double-blind review of the 42 papers originally submitted was carried out by 24 experts in the domain of Digital Cultural Heritage. Further cooperation and research will remain critical to the development of 3D CH digitisation practice, guaranteeing that digital assets are credible and useful for future generations.

August 2025   Marinos Ioannides

Contents

Paradata, Metadata, and Data in the Digitisation of Cultural Heritage:
A Memory Twin Perspective 1
   Anthony Cassar

Generating Paradata by Asking Questions or Telling Stories 15
   Isto Huvila

IIIF 3D and Data Dimensions - Countdown on Collaborative Standards
for Sustainable Digital Heritage 25
   Ronald Haynes

Documentation and Scientificity of the 3D Reconstruction of Built
Heritage Models in the Age of GenAI 35
   Sander Münster

Representation and Preservation of Traditional Crafting Techniques 46
   *Xenophon Zabulis, Partarakis Nikolaos, Vasiliki Manikaki,
   David Arnaud, Noël Crescenzo, Arnaud Dubois, Ines Moreno,
   Juan José Ortega Gras, José Francisco Puche Forte,
   Valentina Bartalesi, Nicolò Pratelli, Carlo Meghini, Sotiris Manitsaris,
   and Gavriela Senteri*

3D and Annotations: The Memory Viewer as a Hub in the Semantic Web
for Cultural Heritage 58
   Øyvind Eide

The eArchiving Initiative and Long-Term Digital Preservation (LTDP)
of 3D Models 65
   Janet Anderson, Stephen Mackey, and Sven Schlarb

Introducing Scientific Reference Model and Critical Digital Model –
Methodological Approach in Hypothetical Source-Based 3D
Reconstruction of Built Cultural Heritage 77
   Piotr Kuroczyński and Fabrizio Ivan Apollonio

Developing the Core Data Model for 3D – Exploring Metadata
and Paradata Throughout Current 3D Infrastructure Projects 89
   Igor Piotr Bajena

Comprehensive Guide of the Benefits, Opportunities, Risks and Gaps in the Management of Cultural Heritage Digitisation. A Critical Literature Review 102
    Maria Drabczyk, Marco Rendina, Francesca Manfredini, Anastasia Dimou, Ruben Peeters, Jasper de Koning, and Jiri Svorc

Reviving Europe's Architectural Heritage: The CoVHer Project's Standards for 3D Digital Reconstructions 112
    Fabrizio Ivan Apollonio, Federico Fallavollita, and Riccardo Foschi

New Interoperable Solutions for Cultural Heritage Protection: The ANCHISE Toolset 125
    Axel Kerep, Valentina Vassallo, and Benjamin Omer

Heritage Buildings and Objects' Digitisation and Visualisation Within the Cloud (HERITALISE) 138
    Alan Miller, Catherine Anne Cassidy, Sharon Pisani, Mikel Borras, Drew Baker, and Jacquie Aitken

Florence4D's Interdisciplinary Workflow for Research-Based 3D Models: A Palazzo Medici Case Study 152
    Fabrizio Nevola, Anna McGee, and Luca Brunke

A Question of Competence, Quality & Infrastructure: The EUreka3D Initiative 163
    Valentina Bachi and Antonella Fresa

An Integrated and Open-Access Plugin for Uncertainty Assessment of the Hypothetical Virtual Reconstruction of Architecture 175
    Fabrizio Ivan Apollonio, Federico Fallavollita, and Riccardo Foschi

Author Index 189

Paradata, Metadata, and Data in the Digitisation of Cultural Heritage: A Memory Twin Perspective

Anthony Cassar(✉)

Heritage Malta Head Office, 35, Dawret Fra Giovanni Bichi, Il-Kalkara KKR 1280, Malta
digitisation@gov.mt

Abstract. This chapter explores the evolving role of metadata and paradata in the digitisation of cultural heritage and introduces the Memory Twin concept as a holistic framework that integrates both tangible and intangible dimensions of heritage. Drawing on historical milestones, technological advances, and European policy initiatives, it argues for a paradigm shift from data-centric to memory-enriched digitisation. The chapter presents insights from Heritage Malta's digitisation initiatives, highlighting challenges related to standardisation, context loss, and ethical issues in emerging technologies like AI. It emphasizes the need for certified frameworks for metadata and paradata to ensure transparency, reproducibility, and long-term preservation. The Memory Twin approach captures not only the form but also the meaning, memory, and cultural narratives embedded in heritage assets. By incorporating participatory practices and interdisciplinary governance, it advocates for a more inclusive, context-sensitive, and ethically responsible future in heritage digitization.

Keywords: MemoryTwin · Paradata · Metadata

1 Introduction

The digitisation of cultural heritage has made significant strides since the 1960s, largely propelled by continuous advancements in computing, imaging, and data management [1, 2]. Initial efforts during this period focused on creating basic databases to catalogue physical collections. By the 1980s, the introduction of digital imaging technologies enabled cultural institutions to produce visual records of manuscripts and artefacts, enhancing both documentation and accessibility [3]. The 1990s and 2000s marked a turning point, as innovations such as laser scanning and photogrammetry facilitated the detailed three-dimensional documentation of heritage assets, significantly improving preservation and research capabilities [4].

At the same time, major international efforts have highlighted the growing recognition of digitisation as a tool for cultural preservation and access. UNESCO's Memory of the World programme, launched in 1992, was established to protect and promote the world's documentary heritage by ensuring the long-term preservation and global accessibility of significant archives and library collections. Its aim was to combat the risk of collective amnesia and encourage the sharing of knowledge. Similarly, the launch of Europeana in 2008—now the largest digital platform for cultural heritage in Europe—has provided unprecedented access to collections from a wide range of cultural institutions across the continent, reinforcing the critical role of digital technologies in safeguarding heritage for future generations.

Since the early 2010s, the European Union has played a pivotal role in shaping digitisation policies that emphasize open access, interoperability, and the integration of artificial intelligence in restoration workflows. However, despite these efforts, new challenges continue to emerge, particularly regarding context, meaning, and the integration of intangible heritage as well as the lack of clear methodologies and standards to cover such data acquisition of Cultural Heritage especially in the area of 3D data acquisition.

As the Digitisation Unit at Heritage Malta, we have experienced significant advancements in technology that are profoundly transforming the ways in which cultural heritage is accessed, interpreted, and preserved.. But with all these powerful tools at our fingertips, another challenge is becoming more and more clear: it is not just about creating high-quality digital replicas. We need to make sure that what we capture digitally also reflects the full depth, meaning, and identity of the original object or site. It is about preserving the story, the context, and the soul of our heritage—not just its appearance—so that future generations can connect with it in a way that is authentic and complete. A more complete digitisation approach will allow us to understand the past but also learn for the future.

2 From Data Capture to Cultural Context

As 3D digitisation efforts continue to expand, much of the focus remains on capturing the physical characteristics of artefacts and sites. Technologies like LiDAR and photogrammetry have made it possible to produce highly accurate digital models, marking significant progress in both the preservation and accessibility of cultural heritage [5]. However, this technically oriented approach often fails to account for the contextual, social, and emotional dimensions that imbue heritage with deeper cultural significance.

At Heritage Malta, we frequently encounter the limitations of narrowly focused methodologies in data acquisition. A highly precise 3D scan of a statue or building, while technically impressive, often falls short of conveying the cultural context—the stories, rituals, and human interactions that truly define its significance. Much of this contextual information does exist, but is often siloed in separate departments, such as curatorial or conservation, where it is documented in ways that are not easily accessible to be integrated into digital representations.

This realization prompted us to seek ways to adopt more holistic documentation strategies that go beyond standard descriptive and administrative metadata. We have now started to actively incorporate Paradata— information that captures the decision-making processes, interpretative choices, and the rationale behind the creation of a digital surrogate. As it has been proven this approach not only enhances the authenticity and interpretive richness of digital objects but also fosters greater collaboration between departments, encouraging a more integrated and meaningful representation of heritage.

Yet, this shift exposed a deeper structural challenge: the lack of clear, widely adopted standards and methodologies for data acquisition in cultural heritage digitisation. This is particularly evident in the realm of 3D digitisation, where practices vary greatly in terms of resolution, file formats, capture protocols, and intended use. Without coherent frameworks, it becomes difficult to ensure interoperability, long-term preservation, and the ability for others to meaningfully reuse or reinterpret the data.

The integration of both the FAIR and CARE principles provides a comprehensive framework for responsible and meaningful digitisation of cultural heritage. The FAIR principles—Findable, Accessible, Interoperable, and Reusable—serve as a technical benchmark for enhancing the discoverability and utility of digital heritage assets [6]. However, in the field of 3D data, achieving true FAIRness remains challenging due to inconsistent documentation of contextual and interpretive information. This is where the CARE principles—Collective benefit, Authority to control, Responsibility, and Ethics—play a crucial role, bringing ethical considerations to the forefront, especially when digitising heritage that is community-held or culturally sensitive [7]. Together, FAIR and CARE ensure that digitisation is not only technically sound but also socially and ethically grounded. Additionally, while the CIDOC Conceptual Reference Model provides a robust semantic structure for documentation [8], its inconsistent application in 3D digitisation highlights the need for more unified and ethically aware data governance in heritage practices.

The challenge is compounded in the case of intangible cultural heritage [], where the subject matter is inherently dynamic, context-dependent, and often resistant to standardisation. Capturing the essence of a performance, ritual, or oral tradition requires flexible and culturally sensitive methodologies. Although the UNESCO 2003 Convention for the Safeguarding of Intangible Cultural Heritage offers a conceptual framework, the translation of its principles into digital documentation practices is far from straightforward, and varies widely across institutions and communities.

3 Towards Standards and Certification in Metadata and Paradata for Cultural Heritage Digitisation

To address the fragmentation and inconsistency observed in data acquisition practices, it is essential to strengthen the foundation upon which digitisation workflows are built: namely, the structured documentation of both metadata and paradata. These two elements serve as the twin pillars supporting not only the discoverability and interoperability of digitised heritage, but also its interpretive richness, scientific reproducibility, and long-term preservation.

Metadata plays a well-established role in the digitisation of cultural heritage, providing descriptive, administrative, and structural information that identifies and contextualizes digital objects. This includes essential data elements such as an artefact's title, creator, date, materials, provenance, and associated rights. To ensure interoperability, discoverability, and long-term accessibility, institutions rely on established metadata and ontology schemas. In the field of cultural heritage digitisation, several established metadata standards play a crucial role in ensuring the discoverability, interoperability, and preservation of digital assets. The Dublin Core Metadata Element Set, developed by the Dublin Core Metadata Initiative (DCMI), provides a widely adopted, general-purpose framework comprising 15 basic elements such as Title, Creator, Subject, and Date. For more semantically rich representations, the CIDOC Conceptual Reference Model (CIDOC-CRM), developed by ICOM's International Committee for Documentation, offers an ontology that supports complex historical and contextual relationships between entities. The Europeana Data Model (EDM), used by Europeana, is designed for multilingual and linked data aggregation across European cultural institutions. The Metadata Encoding and Transmission Standard (METS), an XML-based schema from the Library of Congress, enables the packaging of digital content alongside metadata. Finally, PBCore, an extension of Dublin Core developed by U.S. public media organisations, addresses the specific needs of audiovisual content management in broadcasting and archiving contexts. While metadata is vital for identifying and organising digital assets, it typically focuses on what the object is, rather than how it was digitally created or interpreted. Before meaningful reuse of 3D assets and digitised cultural heritage can occur, we must also ensure a deep understanding of the context, significance, and provenance of these assets. Without this foundation, there is a growing risk of misrepresentation—especially through AI-generated visualisations which, while visually compelling, may lack accuracy or authenticity. These outputs can inadvertently distort historical narratives, reinforcing the urgent need for comprehensive paradata and culturally informed documentation in all digitisation workflows.

This is where paradata becomes critical. Paradata documents the decisions, methods, and technical workflows that lead to the creation of a digital asset. It provides transparency into the data acquisition process: what equipment was used, what resolution was selected, what software processed the raw data, what interpretive choices were made during modelling or restoration, and even the conditions under which data capture occurred. While metadata preserves the object's story, paradata preserves the story of the digitisation process itself.

The absence of documented paradata in many digitisation initiatives has been repeatedly flagged as a barrier to quality assurance and reproducibility. As highlighted in the Study on Quality in 3D Digitisation of Tangible Cultural Heritage [9], most practitioners acknowledged that they either did not record paradata or lacked standardised mechanisms to do so. This creates blind spots in the digital lifecycle of heritage assets, leaving future users unable to assess the data's accuracy or understand the rationale behind its production.

Recognising this gap, there is a growing consensus around the need to develop standardised and certifiable frameworks for the documentation of metadata and paradata in cultural heritage digitisation. Such frameworks would serve multiple, interconnected purposes that collectively enhance the quality, reliability, and sustainability of digital heritage efforts. Firstly, they would enable consistency across projects by establishing common terminologies, formats, and levels of detail, ensuring that digitisation outputs from different institutions and countries can be more easily aligned, compared, and integrated. Secondly, by clearly documenting acquisition methodologies and interpretive decisions, these frameworks would foster greater transparency and trustworthiness, particularly critical for scholarly research and conservation work where the reliability of digital surrogates is paramount. Thirdly, well-structured metadata and paradata support long-term preservation and interoperability; as technologies continue to evolve, the availability of robust documentation ensures that digital objects can be migrated, reprocessed, or reused without losing essential contextual information. Moreover, a certification system built on these frameworks would introduce quality benchmarks, offering cultural institutions a means to validate their digitisation practices against international standards. Finally, such an approach would significantly advance the FAIR data agenda within the cultural heritage sector, ensuring that digital assets are not only findable and accessible, but also interoperable and reusable in meaningful and context-rich ways.

By incorporating both metadata and paradata into the digitisation workflow, institutions can more effectively meet the FAIR principles not only technically, but also contextually. While models such as CIDOC-CRM provide semantic grounding for metadata, their extension into paradata—especially in 3D digitisation—is still underdeveloped. Some initiatives have begun to explore paradata taxonomies, but widespread adoption remains limited due to the lack of consensus on what constitutes "sufficient" paradata, as well as the absence of user-friendly tools for its collection and integration. Ensuring high-quality paradata collection is essential in the digitisation of cultural heritage. Under the guidance of the UNESCO Chair in Digital Cultural Heritage, we have begun implementing structured methodologies for paradata documentation. These approaches are being applied both in our routine digitisation workflows and in the context of two Horizon-funded projects—**STECCI** (www.steccihorizoneu.com/) and **Heritalise** (https://heritalise-eccch.eu) where we are extensively involved in the digitisation work packages and hold primary responsibility for data acquisition activities.

At Heritage Malta, we are beginning to pilot internal protocols that document the scanning pipeline in detail, incorporating both technical parameters and interpretive decisions. This approach not only improves our internal workflows but encourages greater cross-departmental collaboration, as curators, conservators, and technologists contribute their expertise to a shared framework. Our long-term aim is to advocate for the formalisation of such practices at national and European levels, contributing to the development of certified standards for cultural heritage data acquisition, especially in emerging domains such as 3D digitisation and the documentation of intangible heritage.

As the field of digital acquisition of Cultural Heritage continues to evolve, the true value of cultural heritage digitisation will lie not only in the accuracy of its digital copy but in the meaningful recording of the context and processes that brought them into being. Metadata and paradata, when effectively standardised and certified, provide the foundation stones and structure necessary for a more holistic, trustworthy, and future-proof cultural record being developed through the Memory Twin.

4 Introducing the Memory Twin Concept

Building on the integration of data, metadata, and paradata, the Memory Twin concept is emerging as a transformative framework for cultural heritage preservation. Unlike conventional digital twins, which focus primarily on the accurate digital replication of physical objects, Memory Twins seek to embed the intangible cultural layers that surround those objects—rituals, stories, historical perceptions, and lived experiences. This approach recognises that heritage is not composed merely of artefacts or architecture, but of the collective memory that endows them with meaning [10]. In this sense, Memory Twins offer a more holistic and human-centered representation of cultural heritage.

The Memory Twin turns objects into artefacts and buildings into monuments. A recent example from our temporary exhibition *An Island at the Crossroads* at the Malta Maritime Museum brings this to life. Among the grander displays, one object stood out—a small, faded Angry Birds bouncy ball. On its own, it seemed insignificant. But once visitors learned it had been the only life-saving item a child carried during a dangerous sea crossing from North Africa to Malta, it took on a deeper meaning. It wasn't just a toy—it became a testament to identity, struggle, and survival. That is the power of the Memory Twin: giving space for stories that transform the ordinary into something unforgettable (Fig. 1).

The need to evolve metadata and paradata practices becomes even more urgent in light of this shift. Traditional documentation models—while effective in describing physical attributes and digitisation workflows—fall short when it comes to encoding the emotional, historical, and experiential dimensions of heritage. To fully realise the potential of the Memory Twin, we must extend our data frameworks to include new types of metadata and paradata that capture this cultural depth.

These extensions include narrative-driven metadata, which incorporates oral histories, storytelling, and user interactions that enrich the semantic layers of digital models. Equally important is the inclusion of experiential paradata—information that not only records how an object was digitised, but also how it was historically used, interpreted, and remembered by communities. In certain cases, the inclusion of multisensory data—such as ambient soundscapes, environmental conditions, or haptic interactions—can offer users a fuller, more immersive engagement with heritage objects and sites.

Promising models for this kind of integrated documentation already exist. The Holistic Heritage Building Information Modelling (HHBIM) approach, developed at the Politecnico di Milano and the Cyprus University of Technology, has begun to embed historical narratives and storytelling elements into traditional data frameworks, creating a structured pathway toward more layered digital reconstructions. This model offers a foundational architecture upon which the principles of the Memory Twin can be expanded.

The conceptual and emotional richness of the Memory Twin was perhaps most powerfully expressed during this year's EuroMed conference. Following the keynote speech on the opening day, a moment of particular resonance came from Prof. Marinos Ioannides, UNESCO Chair for Digital Cultural Heritage. In a vivid and elegant analogy, he asked us to imagine holding a tissue in our hands—representing a building or object that has been scanned and digitised, a conventional Digital Twin. But then, he invited us to dip the tissue into a cup of coffee. The coffee, he explained, symbolises memory—the emotions, stories, and intangible heritage that envelop the physical structure. Once the tissue absorbs the coffee, it is no longer just a neutral object; it becomes transformed. It is now a Memory Twin, infused with the cultural richness that transcends the physical and enters the domain of lived human experience.

This metaphor encapsulates the essence of what we must strive for in digital heritage practice. Our task is not simply to scan and preserve form—it is to preserve meaning. As we continue to expand the scope and sophistication of digitisation technologies, the

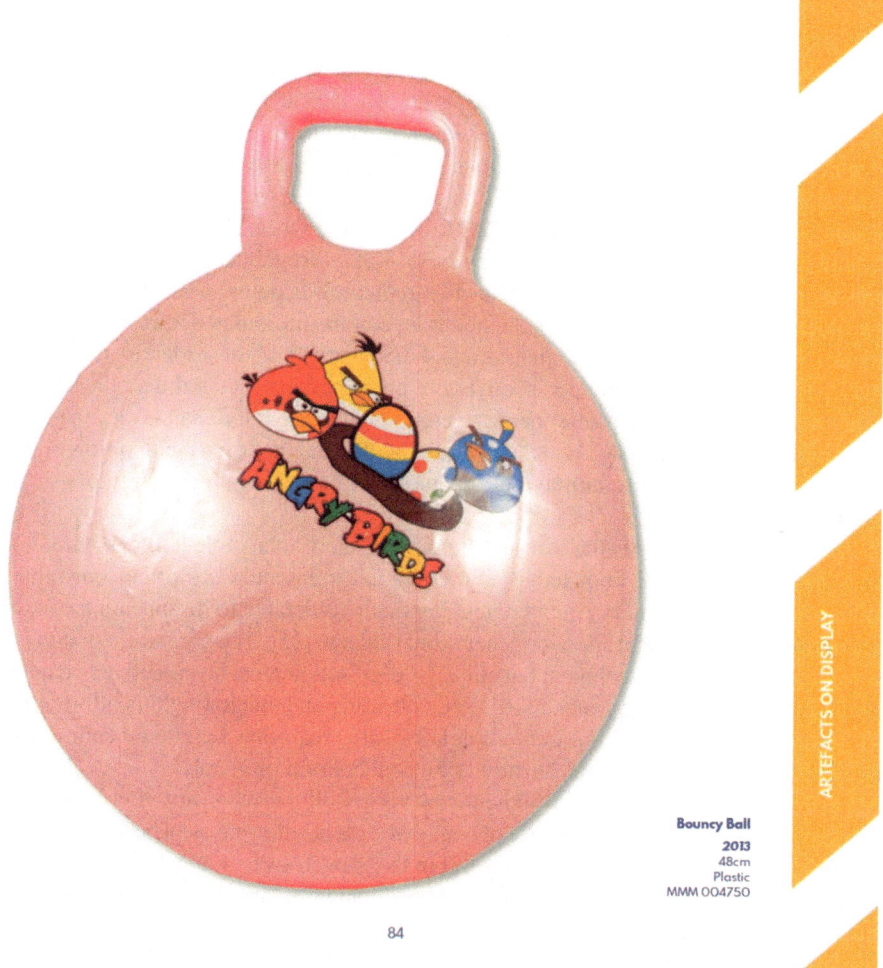

Fig. 1. This plastic toy ball meant for enjoyment served instead as a life saver for one of the many children that today cross the Mediterranean by boat in the search of a better life. https://emuseum.heritagemalta.mt/objects/294

real challenge lies in ensuring that we are also capturing the cultural narratives and emotional resonance that give heritage its enduring value. In doing so, we move beyond preservation for its own sake and toward the creation of digital heritage ecosystems that are alive with memory, capable of engaging present and future generations in a more profound and authentic way.

4.1 The Challenge of Digitising Identity

While digital tools such as 3D scanning, LiDAR, and high-resolution imaging can reproduce physical structures with exceptional fidelity [10], capturing the identity that those structures embody is far more elusive. Cultural identity is not fixed—it is dynamic, layered, and shaped by both personal and collective memory [11]. It is formed through lived experiences, emotional ties, historical narratives, and social practices that are often intangible, undocumented, and contested. This makes its integration into Memory Twins a task that is as much curatorial and ethical as it is technical.

One of the core challenges in digitising cultural heritage lies in the subjectivity of memory and interpretation. A single monument or site may carry vastly different meanings for different communities [12]. In Malta, the Queen Victoria monument in Valletta offers a clear example. Prominently located in Republic Square, it is seen by some as a historical marker of the British era—representing a time when Malta was part of a wider imperial framework and benefited from new institutions and infrastructure. For others, it symbolizes colonial domination and the silencing of Maltese identity in a central civic space. These contrasting perspectives are not anomalies—they reflect the broader reality that heritage is often dissonant, layered, and emotionally charged. Embedding such plurality into a Memory Twin requires thoughtful and inclusive methodologies that can capture and represent multiple interpretations without flattening them into a single narrative [13, 14] (Fig. 2).

Another critical issue is the loss and fragmentation of intangible heritage. Oral histories, rituals, traditional knowledge, and community practices are often transmitted informally and remain undocumented, making them vulnerable to disappearance in the face of modernisation, migration, or generational change [15]. The urgency to document these elements is not just technical but ethical—digitisation must be proactive in capturing these layers before they vanish [16]. Yet, collecting and integrating this information into digital representations is rarely straightforward, requiring long-term community engagement, trust-building, and sensitivity to local cultural protocols.

Furthermore, the question of authenticity versus digital reconstruction presents a philosophical dilemma. In the absence of complete data or when physical heritage is damaged or lost, digital reconstructions must fill in the gaps. However, this process involves interpretation, which may inadvertently impose contemporary values or perspectives onto historical narratives. This raises the issue of who decides what is reconstructed and how, and whether these decisions are made in consultation with the communities for whom the heritage holds meaning [17, 18].

Even in digitally rich environments, no amount of visual fidelity can substitute for emotional resonance. Without the stories, sounds, and lived connections that animate heritage in the eyes of its communities, digital representations risk becoming sterile simulations [19]. To navigate these complexities, the Memory Twin approach must adopt collaborative, community-based methodologies that prioritise inclusivity and shared authority [20] (Fig. 3).

Participatory practices—like co-curation, collecting oral histories, and collaborative storytelling—play a crucial role in ensuring that heritage is not just seen through institutional or academic lenses, but through the lived experiences of the people who shaped it. One powerful example of this is the oral history work we've carried out over the past three years with former Dockyard workers. By speaking directly with the men and women who spent their lives in the docks, we were able to document memories

Fig. 2. Statue of Queen Victoria standing in front of the National Library of Malta in Republic Square, Valletta

that would otherwise be lost—stories of daily routines, camaraderie, pride, and struggle. These personal accounts completely transform how we understand the digitised workshops, ship models, and tools in our collection. What might seem like static artefacts suddenly take on new life when connected to the voices of those who used them. That's why flexible metadata and paradata frameworks are so important: they allow us

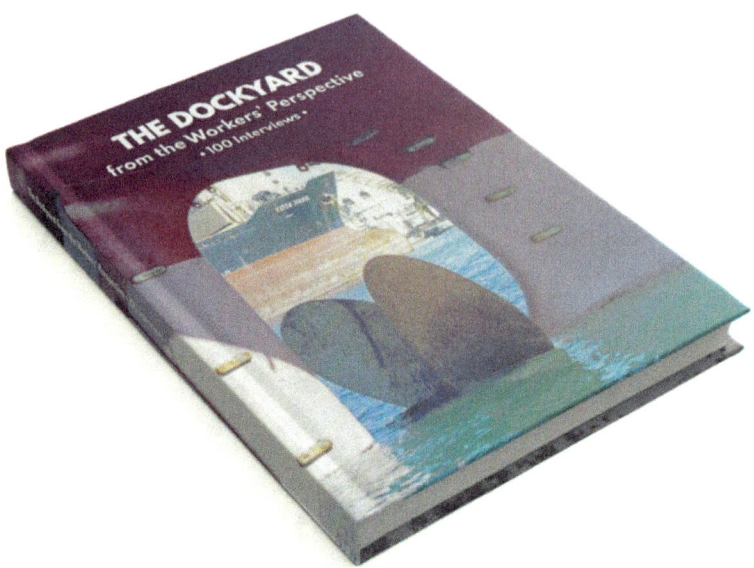

Fig. 3. *The Dockyard from the Workers' Perspective: 100 Interviews*—Over 200 h of oral histories from former Malta Dockyard workers, now available on Europeana, enrich digitised assets with lived experiences and cultural context.

to embed these overlapping, and sometimes even conflicting, narratives into the digital record. In doing so, we keep interpretation open and inclusive, reflecting the richness and complexity of cultural identity as it is truly lived and remembered.

4.2 Authentic Identity in Cultural Heritage

The concept of authenticity occupies a central place in cultural heritage discourse, particularly in relation to identity and representation. A foundational articulation of this can be found in the Nara Document on Authenticity (1994), which redefined authenticity as a pluralistic and culturally contingent concept. Rather than adhering to a singular, material-based definition—as had been dominant in conservation practices influenced by the Venice Charter (1964)—the Nara Document insisted that authenticity must be understood within the specific cultural context of the heritage in question. This includes factors such as "form and design, materials and substance, use and function, traditions and techniques, location and setting, and spirit and feeling" [21].

The shift from a universalist to a contextualist paradigm acknowledges that what counts as "authentic" is not a timeless essence inherent in the object or site, but a negotiated understanding tied to local cultural practices and social memory [22]. The document underscores that authenticity must be evaluated according to culturally specific sources of information, which can be oral, written, physical, or symbolic. These are foundational insights for contemporary critical heritage studies, as they challenge the dominance of expert-led narratives and open the door to community-defined interpretations of value and meaning [23].

This contextual and dialogic understanding of authenticity resonates strongly with the Memory Twin concept, which evolves from the Digital Twin model by shifting focus from geometric fidelity to experiential, affective, and narrative authenticity. Where Digital Twins excel in representing the physicality of cultural heritage assets through high-resolution 3D models and environmental data [24], they often replicate the object-centred biases critiqued by the Nara Document. In contrast, the Memory Twin seeks to capture and represent the plural and evolving relationships communities have with their heritage—relationships rooted in memory, emotion, performance, and reinterpretation.

This alignment is not coincidental. The Memory Twin takes seriously the Nara Document's insistence that "judgments of values and authenticity may differ from culture to culture, and even within the same culture". Rather than fix identity in a single authoritative narrative, the Memory Twin enables multi-vocal representations, allowing for the coexistence of conflicting, overlapping, or evolving memories and interpretations. This is especially important in contexts of dissonant or contested heritage, where identity is not about consensus but negotiation [25].

Moreover, the Memory Twin operationalizes the Nara principle that "responsibility for cultural heritage… Belongs, in the first place, to the cultural community that has generated it". It does this by incorporating tools that enable community participation, annotation, and curation, ensuring that digital representations are not imposed but co-produced. Through interactive storytelling, layered metadata, and support for oral and emotional histories, the Memory Twin gives agency back to the communities whose identities are entangled with the heritage being represented.

Authenticity in the Memory Twin, therefore, is not about verifying the originality of form or material. It is about reflecting lived experience, about capturing the processes through which identity is remembered, contested, and recreated. It aligns with the Nara view that the conservation of cultural heritage must be "rooted in the values attributed to the heritage" by the community itself. The Memory Twin thus offers a dynamic platform where memory becomes both the source and the substance of authenticity.

5 Conclusion

The Memory Twin concept offers a transformative approach through which we reconsider the digitisation of cultural heritage. It moves beyond the replication of physical form and proposes a more useful, authentic and complete model centred on the preservation of meaning, memory, and identity. This approach repositions digitisation not merely as a technical exercise, but as a cultural and ethical responsibility—ensuring that digital surrogates resonate with the communities and narratives they represent.

In the Maltese context, where history is densely layered into the national landscape, the act of digitising heritage extends far beyond conservation. At Heritage Malta, the objective is not only to safeguard artefacts from physical degradation, but to ensure that future generations can access and interpret them in a way that feels authentic and meaningful. The Memory Twin framework enables this by connecting tangible attributes to intangible dimensions—linking physical data with emotional, historical, and cultural context. In doing so, it also renders the immense responsibility of digitising the national collection for future generations more complete, ensuring that what is preserved is not only accurate, but resonant with memory and meaning.

Over recent decades, digitisation practices have progressed rapidly—from rudimentary cataloguing systems and flat image archives to sophisticated 3D reconstructions and metadata integration. These advances have greatly improved access, supported interdisciplinary collaboration, and contributed to international preservation efforts. Initiatives such as UNESCO's *Memory of the World* and Europeana have laid the groundwork for large-scale, interoperable digitisation. Yet, despite these achievements, significant gaps remain.

Chief among these is the continued dominance of object-centric approaches that prioritise fidelity of form at the expense of context and interpretation. Many digitisation efforts lack sufficient paradata, resulting in digital representations that are technically precise but culturally incomplete. Moreover, intangible heritage—rituals, stories, oral histories—remains marginal in many digital frameworks. To preserve heritage without its memory is to risk creating detached, sterile artefacts that no longer communicate their cultural significance.

The Memory Twin addresses these deficiencies by proposing a more integrated model of digital heritage. It retains the precision of conventional Digital Twins but expands their scope by embedding community memory, narrative, and interpretive depth. In this way, the Memory Twin is aligned with critical heritage theory and principles set out in the Nara Document on Authenticity, which recognises the plurality and cultural contingency of heritage values.

This shift necessitates new standards and methodologies. Digitisation workflows must incorporate robust and certifiable frameworks for both metadata and paradata—standards that support transparency, ethical accountability, and participatory input. Narrative metadata, experiential paradata, and community co-curation are essential elements of a more inclusive and human-centred approach.

Pilot initiatives at Heritage Malta are beginning to operationalise this vision. Cross-departmental protocols are being tested to capture not only the technical parameters of digitisation, but also the interpretive decisions and cultural narratives that give heritage its resonance. These practices, though still emerging, point to a future in which digital heritage is not merely archived but actively experienced.

Ultimately, the Memory Twin is not only a tool but a guiding philosophy. By placing memory—dynamic, plural, and lived—at the core of digital heritage, we can foster records that do not merely store information but sustain dialogue. This is the next frontier: heritage that is preserved with integrity and experienced with meaning.

References

1. Terras, M.: The digital classicist: disciplinary focus and interdisciplinary collaboration. In: Deegan, M., McCarty, K. (eds.) Collaborative Research in the Digital Humanities, pp. 83–100. Ashgate Publishing (2011)
2. Schreibman, S., Siemens, R., Unsworth, J. (eds.) A Companion to Digital Humanities. Blackwell (2004)

3. MacDonald, L., Quirke, M.: Cultural heritage imaging: a review of recent developments in cultural heritage imaging and analysis. Int. J. Digit. Libr. **22**(1), 47–66 (2021). https://doi.org/10.1007/s00799-020-00278-7
4. Ioannides, M., et al.: 3D documentation of tangible cultural heritage. Digit. Heritage Int. Congr. [DigitalHeritage] **1**, 131–138 (2013). https://doi.org/10.1109/DigitalHeritage.2013.6743720
5. Ioannides, M., Patias, P., Fink, E. (eds.) 3D Research Challenges in Cultural Heritage III: Complexity and Quality in Digitisation. Springer International Publishing, Cham (2023). https://doi.org/10.1007/978-3-031-35593-6
6. Wilkinson, M.D., et al.: The FAIR Guiding Principles for scientific data management and stewardship. Sci. Data **3**, 160018 (2016). https://doi.org/10.1038/sdata.2016.18
7. Carroll, S.R., et al.: The CARE principles for indigenous data governance. Data Sci. J. **19**(1), 43 (2020). https://doi.org/10.5334/dsj-2020-043
8. Doerr, M.: The CIDOC conceptual reference model: an ontological approach to semantic interoperability of metadata. AI Mag. **24**(3), 75–92 (2003). https://doi.org/10.1609/aimag.v24i3.1720
9. European Commission: Study on quality in 3D digitisation of tangible cultural heritage: Mapping parameters, formats, standards, benchmarks, methodologies, and guidelines. Publications Office of the European Union, Luxembourg (2022). https://op.europa.eu/en/publication-detail/-/publication/c0beb2b0-e21b-11ec-a534-01aa75ed71a1
10. Remondino, F., Campana, S. (eds.) 3D recording and Modelling in Archaeology and Cultural Heritage: Theory and Best Practices. Archaeopress (2014)
11. Ashworth, G.J., Graham, B., Tunbridge, J.E.: Pluralising Pasts: Heritage, Identity and Place in Multicultural Societies. Pluto Press (2007)
12. Tunbridge, J.E., Ashworth, G.J.: Dissonant heritage: The Management of the Past as a Resource in Conflict. Wiley (1996)
13. Smith, L.: Uses of Heritage. Routledge (2006)
14. Waterton, E., Watson, S.: Heritage and Community Engagement: Collaboration or Contestation? Routledge (2010)
15. UNESCO: Convention for the Safeguarding of the Intangible Cultural heritage (2003). https://ich.unesco.org]
16. Deacon, H., Dondolo, L., Mrubata, M., Prosalendis, S.: The Subtle Power of Intangible Heritage: Legal and Financial Instruments for Safeguarding Intangible Heritage. HSRC Press (2004)
17. Jones, S.: Negotiating authentic objects and authentic selves: beyond the deconstruction of authenticity. J. Mater. Cult. **15**(2), 181–203 (2010)
18. Avrami, E., Mason, R., de la Torre, M.: Values and Heritage Conservation. Getty Conservation Institute (2000)
19. Cameron, F., Kenderdine, S. (eds.) Theorizing Digital Cultural Heritage: A Critical Discourse. MIT Press (2007)
20. Giaccardi, E. (ed.) Heritage and Social Media: Understanding Heritage in a Participatory Culture. Routledge (2012)
21. ICOMOS: The Nara Document on Authenticity (1994). https://whc.unesco.org/events/gt-zimbabwe/nara.htm
22. Jokilehto, J.: Considerations on authenticity and integrity in world heritage context. City Time **2**(1), 1–16 (2006)
23. Harrison, R.: Heritage: Critical Approaches. Routledge (2013)
24. Forte, M.: 3D archaeology: new perspectives and challenges—the example of Çatalhöyük. Virtual Archaeol. Rev. **5**(10), 1–5 (2014). https://doi.org/10.4995/var.2014.4307

25. Logan, W.: Cultural diversity, cultural heritage and human rights: towards heritage management as human rights-based cultural practice. Int. J. Herit. Stud. **18**(3), 231–244 (2012). https://doi.org/10.1080/13527258.2011.632873

Generating Paradata by Asking Questions or Telling Stories

Isto Huvila

Department of ALM, Uppsala University, Uppsala, Sweden
isto.huvila@abm.uu.se

Abstract. Paradata types and the practices of using and generating paradata intersect and influence each other. This chapter inquires into their linkages and how diverging paradata generation strategies lead to paradata that function differently despite the occasional similarities of paradata artefacts. The discussion draws from a comparison of two major strategies of paradata generation, one based on requesting input from researchers through asking them to provide answers to specific questions, and another on asking them to provide narrative descriptions of their activities. While generating paradata through asking questions might help to address the needs of structured and technically interoperable paradata, storying can contribute better to conveying an in-depth understanding of practice. The key question is, however, that instead of merely focusing paradata artefacts, for the usability of paradata, it is vital to consider how the documentation is induced and made.

Keywords: paradata · narratives · prompting · processes · practices · generation

1 Introduction

Earlier studies point to a broad diversity of information – paradata – that conveys understanding of practices and processes underpinning the making of different types of research materials, including digital 3D visualisations [1,2]. Similarly, a large number of practices relating to generation and use of such information have been identified (e.g., [3–5]). What remains under-researched so far is, how the practices of generating and using paradata intersect.

This chapter draws from on-going research on paradata creators and users paradata preferences to interrogate two major strategies of paradata generation, one based on requesting input from researchers through asking them to provide answers to specific questions, and another on asking them to provide narrative descriptions of their activities. The aim of the chapter is to elucidate on the linkages of paradata generation strategies, generated paradata, and user needs and preferences. Through discussing examples and differences of the two approaches—including conversational agents and structured metadata of the first, and data narratives and argumentation chains of the second—and their outputs, and contrasting them to findings on the preferences of paradata creators and users, the chapter sheds light on showing how they are closely linked and how the approach of generating paradata is intimately related to resulting paradata and its usability for specific purposes.

2 Types of Paradata

Previous research has identified a wealth of different types of documents and artefacts that can function as paradata and different types of paradata with distinct functions. They range from textual and visual depictions to for examples names of methods, procedures, or tools encoded in formal metadata [5,6]. Börjesson and colleagues [7] identify *scope paradata* (information on what the documented entity, e.g. data or 3D model, covers and not), *provenance paradata* (concerning the origins of the documented entity), *methods paradata* (explaining methods and methodological decisions relating to the generation of the documented entity), and *knowledge organisation and representation paradata* (concerns how the documented entity is structured and communicated). In another text, Börjesson et al. [4] further distinguish *knowledge-making paradata* concerning information on how knowledge is turned to the documented entity, for example, research data or a 3D visualisation, and *knowledge organisation paradata* that documented how the knowledge is organised and represented in paradata, for instance, using keywords selected from controlled vocabularies, visual cues, or narratives developed according to particular guidelines.

As Börjesson et al. [7] emphasise, paradata types are linked to information needs relating to specific aspects of processes of, for example, generating research data or 3D visualisations. They link the above discussed categories to corresponding information needs. In parallel, it is possible to draw connections between various uses of paradata to types of useful information. Huvila et al. [3] show how a need to understand technical means and steps of producing artefacts requires detailed information on data collection procedures and tools, need to understand the contexts of their making and prior use requires corresponding information on uses and versions of artefacts, and producing formally correct aggregations of artefacts requires detailed information on standards used in their generation. Further, sometimes it can be relevant to know the credentials of those who created artefacts for assessing their trustworthiness, and sometimes formal methods used in the process that requires detailed references to methods literature, procedures and tools. The pertinence of specific types of paradata depend on how it is used and for what purposes [8], in practice the task in hand (cf. [9,10]), and what Huvila has termed *epistemic distance* between the those originally enacting a practice and those who try to understand it by using paradata ([11]; see also [12]).

3 Modes of Generating Paradata

Besides inquiring into paradata types, the recent research on paradata generation practices has identified how researchers generate paradata and paradata-like information using a variety of approaches. The practices have differences but also elements that are common to multiple strategies or modes of paradata generation. Partly, paradata generation always happens in a temporal relation to the documented practices. Juneström and Huvila [13] distinguish prospective, in situ and retrospectives modes of creating paradata before, during and after the documented actions take place (see also [14,15]). Prospective paradata generation produces typically different types of plans for intended activities that to different degrees correspond with the realised actions. In situ paradata can consist of, for example, notes written during an activity, photographs and recordings (e.g., video, sound, movement) that capture a selection of aspects of what is happening. Schenk and Reuß [6] present further examples derived from survey research, many of which are relevant to processes of generating 3D visualisations as well, including geographical coordinates (where generation and data capture happens), device paradata, and automatic timestamps. In contrast to prospective paradata generation, according to Juneström and Huvila [13], retrospective paradata generation focuses on generating documentation of past activities, for example, by encoding paradata in formal metadata or narrative descriptions.

In parallel to having different temporal modes of coming into being, paradata emerges through parallel modalities of stabilising practices and processes. Huvila suggests that there are two major modalities of how this happens through embodiment and inscription [16]. *Embodied* paradata refers to features that are informative of practices that is an intrinsic part of other entities, for instance, tools, participants or outputs of activities. Examples of embodied paradata include technical features of 3D visualisations that are indicative of how they were constructed, features of tools that steer the practices of making visualisations, and experience, skills and track record of 3D modellers that can help to understand how they probably worked. A second epistemic mode of paradata are *inscriptions* that are, to a varying degree, consciously produced instances of documentation. This category covers written accounts, photographs taken for capturing practice, and diverse structured forms of documentation, for example, formal metadata.

Trace and Hodges [17] make a further distinction between *paradata for transparency* and *paradata for explainability* when discussing how different forms of paradata can contribute to algorithmic accountability. Paradata for transparency consist of the evidentiary record of practices and processes whereas the latter refer to specific artefacts constructed (or possible construct) on the basis of the first category of paradata.

Finally, Rainey et al. [18] distinguish *objective* and *subjective* paradata, that is (in practice, relatively) uncontroversial observations of activities, and personal interpretations and experiences. By suggesting that it is at least to some degree possible to categorise specific instances and types of paradata as distinctly subjective or objective, the proposition underlines how paradata can be approached epistemologically from both positivist and interpretivist perspectives with corresponding modes of paradata generation and use geared towards capturing and utilising in part objectivist observations and in part subjectivist perceptions of activities. The same fault line has been observed in empirical research as a tension between emphasising either standardisation or flexibility in documentation [8,19].

4 Asking Questions and Telling Stories

In addition to categorising modes of paradata generation in terms of their temporal relations to documented activities, outputs, or subjectivity, paradata generation – similarly to knowledge creation in general – can be based on categorisation or narrativisation, or to use Ingold's term, 'storying' [20]. The both have been extensively researched in the anthropology and sociology of knowledge (e.g., [21,22]). Even if it is admittedly possible to categorise and narrate using a plethora of different methods, in broad terms, the two modes are aligned with interrogative and narrativising modes of elicitation of knowledge, in practice, asking questions and telling stories. Questions and answers result in categories whereas telling stories generate storied knowledge. Considering agency of paradata-making, asking questions is an audience or facilitator-driven 'pull' -oriented method of generating paradata whereas storytelling, even if prompted, a creator-driven 'push' strategy.

The both can take many forms. Questions can be asked in an interview or using a survey questionnaire but also more indirectly through providing a set of guidelines, for example, a standard that stipulates what types and forms of information should be provided. In parallel to prompting answers by using fixed lists of questions or a relying on a human interviewer, rapidly developing conversational user interfaces (chatbots) provide new opportunities to automate and adapt such processes.

Similarly to how many possible strategies to ask questions exist, stories can be told in many forms [23]: in written and oral stories, comics, performances, videos and immersive multidimensional presentations. Stories can told by humans – either individuals or groups – but similarly to asking and answering questions, also storytelling is often facilitated by technologies from simple writing and drawing aids to complex visualisation, text, speech and image generation techniques (e.g., [24,25]).

Both asking questions and storytelling have been applied in diverse forms in data documentation. Data stories and data storytelling has been identified as a potentially powerful approach to make datasets understandable for diverse audiences [26]. As per paradata, it seems though that so far the inspiration for advocating different approaches appears to stem frequently from parallels of how narratives and structured data have been found useful in general rather than from a systematic work towards identifying or developing dedicated approaches that are particularly fitting for eliciting paradata (cf. e.g., [13]).

From the perspective of their practical implications, the key question with the diverse modes of paradata generation – not least to understand differences between storying and asking questions – is how they link to resulting paradata. Similarly to the temporal modes of paradata generation, also asking questions and telling stories influence generated paradata and what it is good for, or more precisely, what specific uses the paradata affords and constraints. Applying them results in to a certain extent divergent manifestations – for example, written text, formal metadata or images – but considering the observations on that specific forms of paradata can be useful and used for multiple purposes (e.g., [3,8]), it is apparent that the links between the modes of generation and resulting paradata are more complicated. A written narrative of an activity can be an answer to a question or an unprompted storification, similarly to how both answers and storied paradata can have multiple other manifestations than a written narrative.

5 Paradata Modalities as Social Genres

The complexity of how different manifestations of paradata, what ends up being documented and how, and how it is generated and useful means that instead of focussing on individual media forms, generation processes and uses, paradata generation and its implications need to be approached more broadly. Different meaningful types of paradata unfold as *modalities* comparable to how Krueckeberg and colleagues frame the notion of memory modalities as 'arrangements of how memories are and how they are made and conditioned' [27]. Analogously, diverse forms of paradata can be described as arrangements of how paradata is, how it is made and conditioned. Such arrangements further incorporate the ways how they are used or acted upon. Rather than being categories of literature or information akin literary genre theory, they form social genres, typified forms of social action as per Miller's [28] social genre theory.

The theoretical move from focusing on paradata as a particular material form of data allows us to approach it as a functional entity. Paradata is relational and processual from its making to its taking as paradata (see [16,29]) in each particular situation rather than a singular thing or product. A particular piece of paradata is not understandable in isolation, for example, as a narrative or set of formal descriptors. They become meaningful only as types of social action that incorporate how and when they were conceived, what forms they take, and how and what types of actions they afford and constrain. Much similarly to solving epistemic hurdles of scholarly work in general [30], understanding each of them requires engaging with and committing to a specific common ground and its genealogy through time and in parallel becoming proficient in its particular reflexive language [30–32] that makes it possible to figure out and commune how that particular type of paradata modality works. Further, while the outspoken ambition with paradata would be to *represent* past practices for facilitating understanding and reuse of, for instance, 3D visualisations, archival records or research data, paradata is not a mirror or a finding aid (cf. [33,34]). It is generative, however, not alone but rather together with a plethora of other things – including those we typically term 'sources', 'research material', 'tools', or for example 'methods'. Putting and keeping such assemblages that include information appropriable as paradata together allows us to generating adequate understanding of things and their underpinning processes to a degree that enables, for example, their meaningful reuse across contexts.

6 Matching Paradata Needs and Generation Approaches

The major practical implication of the theoretical reformulation of the paradata concept as modalities is in how it can help to understand why a particular piece of paradata works or fails to work as it does. As a consequence, it can also provide stratagems to matching of paradata needs and different approaches to paradata generation. With different approaches to creating paradata leading to distinct outcomes (i.e. paradata), it is critical to choose an approach that affords generating documentation that is likely to match future needs.

Both studies of paradata needs and earlier research on how information sources types can be to a certain extent linked to tasks [9] and criteria of work success [35] suggest that partial mappings between paradata manifestations and their relevance for specific uses are possible. However, at the same time, the usability of many paradata manifestations spans over individual uses [7] suggesting that manifestation alone might not be enough to estimate the usefulness of paradata. Other indicators, like the intention of paradata creators to produce paradata for specific uses might appear promising, as long the difficulty to anticipate user needs [14] and the plentiful opportunities to extract useful paradata from research outputs and documentation produced without intention to produce paradata [4] are ignored.

In contrast, considering how paradata works in practice as a modality, it seems plausible to suggest that the moment when paradata is produced in relation to what it documents and whether it is a result of specific prompts (answers to questions) or storying are much more promising starting points to make projections of its usefulness and usability in specific tasks. Combined with a comparable, adequately nuanced understanding of paradata users' needs to use paradata, for example, to understand the scope of documented assets, their provenance, methods and decisions related to their making, and their representational structure and organisation [7], it is possible to establish a set of facets that covers major aspects of paradata from its making to how it is appropriated for diverse expected and unanticipated uses. The baseline is, however, the moment and mode of generating paradata as crucial determinants of the epistemic affordances and constraints of paradata. Earlier research of data creators and users paradata preferences points to differences in what is documentable and what makes processes understandable [3].

In practical terms, considering what asking questions and storying does for paradata and what types of paradata needs have been identified so far, it is possible to pin down certain points of confluence sumamrised in Table 1. The diverse uses of paradata identified by Huvila et al. [3] point to the presence of the parallel needs of formal technical information (e.g., names of methods and tools, credentials) and information that provides context and understanding (e.g., underpinnings of decisions, descriptions and reflections) that correspond to a certain extent with the subjective/objective distinction of Rainey et al. [18], however, probably rather than *being* subjective or objective per se, in practice pertaining to how sometimes paradata needs to be *framed* as descriptive and oriented to helping in sense-making, or definite, oriented to providing unambiguous answers to direct questions. Indicative of how framing of information is central to how it is elicited are the differences identified between research data makers' and managers' preference for information a kin formal questions and answers that is straightforward to generate and manage, and data reusers' leaning towards storied descriptions that help to understand and reuse datasets in practice [3]. An exemplary task relating to descriptive framing is understanding how and why a 3D visualisation was made. A correspondingly illustrative example of the second type of definite task is how to make a 3D visualisation searchable and findable through formal queries in a digital database.

Table 1. Characteristics of the modalities paradata and paradata making through asking questions and telling stories.

	Asking questions	Telling stories
Approach	– Paradata user or data manager driven – Pull-oriented	– Data and paradata creator driven – Push-oriented
Methods (examples)	– Interview – Survey – Guidelines – Protocols	– Written stories – Oral stories – Comics – Videos – Digital immersive stories
Generating actor (examples)	– Human interviewer – Questionnaire – Conversational agent	– Human storyteller – Technical aids – Text, speech, image generation
Generated paradata	– Answers to specific questions – Structured and standardised – Technically interoperable	– (Relatively) open-ended – (Relatively) unstructured – Contextually pertinent
Facilitates	– Findability – Machine readability – Technical reuse	– Understandability – Human readability – Contextually anchored reuse

The crux is that the both require different type of paradata. Even if answers to formal definite questions can often be extracted from narratives and structured keywords can help to make sense, choosing an approach geared towards generating particular type of paradata makes it more likely that the resulting documentation is useful. Acknowledging this, being aware of the implications of paradata generation approaches to paradata itself and communicating them to paradata creators can help to ensure that the resulting paradata is more informative and meaningful in its use. Without a clear understanding of how the generated paradata is intended to be used and for what purposes, there is an apparent risk that paradata creators do not fully understand what they are expected to do, why and how that leads to poor answers and uninformative narratives (cf. [26]). For comprehensive documentation, multiple approaches are needed. They can also be combined and packaged together. For example, Bowker and Star have speculated of the possible usefulness of wrapping formal data descriptions in informal ones [36]. However, explaining paradata creators that the aim of writing a narrative description is to help others to understand the process of generating a 3D visualisation and assigning particular types of descriptors that indicate, for example, what formal standards were used, who participated in the making of the visualisation, or how, what tools were used is to make the visualisation findable online can be expected to lead to a more informative, comprehensive and meaningful paradata.

7 Conclusions

The kernel of the present overview of the diverse modalities of paradata and paradata generation is to shed light on how the making and being of paradata are linked and how this linkage has implications to what can be achieved with a particular piece of paradata. Similarly to how the media of paradata affects its usability for specific tasks, the mode of generating paradata through prompting – asking questions – or storifying it as a narrative leads to different types of paradata with different affordances and constraints to its use. Asking questions might in most cases help to produce more complete, standardised and in a technical sense interoperable paradata but not necessarily descriptions that help to understand the described practice or process. Even if superficially similar, two paradata artefacts – for example, written descriptions or diagrams – might not necessarily function similarly if they are results of different kinds of practices of making.

This means that instead of focusing on producing particular types of paradata artefacts – formal descriptors, written descriptions or images – it is vital to consider how the artefacts are induced and made. Rather than thinking of paradata as things, it might be more useful to approach it through considering different modalities of paradata akin social genres. The focal point is not the paradata artefact but the totality of a particular kind of social action, which ties together what paradata conveys of particular practices and processes, how a specific type of paradata itself is a typified practice, and how it itself influences, enables and constrains future practices.

Acknowledgements. This work has received funding from the European Research Council (ERC) under the European Union's Horizon 2020 research and innovation programme grant agreement No 818210 as a part of the project CApturing Paradata for documenTing data creation and Use for the REsearch of the future (CAPTURE).

References

1. Huvila, I., Andersson, L., Sköld, O.: Perspectives on paradata: research and practice of documenting data processes. Knowledge Management and Organizational Learning. Springer, Cham (2024)
2. Bentkowska-Kafel, A., Denard, H., Baker, D. (eds.): Paradata and Transparency in Virtual Heritage. Ashgate, Farnham (2012)
3. Huvila, I., Andersson, L., Sköld, O.: Patterns in paradata preferences among the makers and reusers of archaeological data. Data and Inf. Manag. **8**(4), 100077 (2024)
4. Börjesson, L., Sköld, O., Friberg, Z., Löwenborg, D., Pálsson, G., Huvila, I.: Repurposing excavation database content as paradata: an explorative analysis of paradata identification challenges and opportunities. KULA: Knowledge Creation, Dissemination, and Preservation Studies **6**(3) (2022) 1–18
5. Huvila, I., Sköld, O., Börjesson, L.: Documenting information making in archaeological field reports. J. Documentation **77**(5), 1107–1127 (2021)
6. Schenk, P.O., Reuß, S.: Paradata in surveys. In: Huvila, I., Andersson, L., Sköld, O. (eds.) Perspectives on Paradata: Research and Practice of Documenting Data Processes. Knowledge Management and Organizational Learning. Springer, Cham (2024)
7. Börjesson, L., Huvila, I., Sköld, O.: Information needs on research data creation. Inf. res. **27**(Special Issue) (2022) isic2208
8. Huvila, I., Andersson, L., Sköld, O., Liu, Y.H.: Data makers' and users' views on useful paradata: priorities in documenting data creation, curation, manipulation and use in archaeology. Int. J. Digit. Curation **19**(1), 1–24 (2025)
9. Dodson, S., Sinnamon, L., Kopak, R.: Mapping the relationship between genres and tasks: a study of undergraduate engineers. J. Am. Soc. Inf. Sci. **75**(12), 1380–1397 (2024)
10. Kumpulainen, S., Keskustalo, H., Zhang, B., Stefanidis, K.: Historical reasoning in authentic research tasks: mapping cognitive and document spaces. J. Am. Soc. Inf. Sci. **71**(2), 230–241 (2019)
11. Huvila, I.: Information-making-related information needs and the credibility of information. Inf. Res. **25**(4) (2020) paper isic2002
12. Borgman, C.L., Groth, P.: From data creator to data reuser: distance matters. Harvard Data Science Review (2025)
13. Juneström, A., Huvila, I.: Categorizing methods and approaches for generating and identifying paradata. (forthcoming)
14. Huvila, I.: Improving the usefulness of research data with better paradata. Open Inf. Sci. **6**(1), 28–48 (2022)
15. Huvila, I., et al.: Paradata: documenting data creation, curation and use. Cambridge University Press (forthcoming in 2025)
16. Huvila, I.: A paradata reference model. In:Huvila, I., ed.: Paradata: Documenting Data Creation, Curation and Use. Cambridge University Press, Cambridge (forthcoming in 2025)
17. Trace, C.B., Hodges, J.A.: The role of paradata in algorithmic accountability. In: Huvila, I., Andersson, L., Sköld, O. (eds.) Perspectives on Paradata: Research and Practice of Documenting Process Knowledge, pp. 197–213. Springer International Publishing, Cham (2024)
18. Rainey, J., et al.: Exploring the role of paradata in digitally supported qualitative co-research. In: CHI Conference on Human Factors in Computing Systems, New Orleans, ACM (2022) 1–16

19. Huvila, I.: Being formal and flexible: semantic wiki as an archaeological e-Science infrastructure. In: Zhou, M., Romanowska, I., Wu, Z., Xu, P., Verhagen, P. (eds.) Revive the Past: Proceeding of the 39th Conference on Computer Applications and Quantitative Methods in Archaeology, Beijing, 12–16 April 2011, pp. 186–197. Amsterdam University Press, Amsterdam (2012)
20. Ingold, T.: Being alive: essays on movement, knowledge and description. Knowledge and Description. Routledge, London, Essays on Movement (2011)
21. Bruner, J.: The narrative construction of reality. Crit. Inq. **18**(1), 1–21 (1991)
22. Law, J.: On the subject of the object: narrative, technology, and interpellation. Configurations **8**(1), 1–29 (2000)
23. Page, R. (ed.): New Perspectives on Narrative and Multimodality. Routledge, New York (September (2009)
24. Chang, Y.T., Chen, S.C., Li, T.Y.: A computer-aided system for narrative creation. In: 2013 IEEE Symposium on Computational Intelligence for Creativity and Affective Computing (CICAC),pp. 40–47 (2013)
25. Han, A., Cai, Z.: Design implications of generative AI systems for visual storytelling for young learners. In: Proceedings of the 22nd Annual ACM Interaction Design and Children Conference. IDC '23, New York, ACM,pp.470–474 (2023)
26. Mosconi, G., Karasti, H., Randall, D.: Designing a data story: an innovative approach for the selective care of qualitative and ethnographic data. In: Burkhardt, M., et al. eds.: Interrogating Datafication: Towards a Praxeology of Data. transcript Verlag, Bielefeld, pp. 207–230 (2022)
27. Krueckeberg, J., Tran, Q.T., Zengenene, D., Tzouganatou, A., Huvila, I., Koch, G.: Memory modalities: explorations into the socio-material arrangements of the past at the present for the future. In: Koch, G., Smith, R.C. (eds.) Future Memory Practices, pp. 119–138. Routledge, London (2024)
28. Miller, C.R.: Genre as social action. Quarterly J. Speech **70**(2), 151–167 (1984)
29. Huvila, I.: Making and taking information. JASIST **73**(4), 528–541 (2022)
30. Kockelman, P.: The art of interpretation in the age of computation. Volume 1. Oxford University Press (2017)
31. Lucy, J.A.: Reflexive language and the human disciplines. In: Lucy, J.A. (ed.) Reflexive Language: Reported Speech and Metapragmatics, pp. 9–32. Cambridge University Press, Cambridge (1993)
32. Jakobson, R.: Six Lectures on Sound and Meaning. MIT Press, Cambridge, MA (1981)
33. Lehtonen, M.: Maa-ilma: materialistisen kulttuuriteorian Lähtökohtia. Vastapaino, Tampere (2014)
34. In: Introduction. Ashgate, Farnham (2011) 1–20
35. Huvila, I.: Information sources and perceived success in corporate finance. JASIST **61**(11), 2219–2229 (2010)
36. Bowker, G.C., Star, S.L.: Sorting Things out: Classification and Its Consequences. MIT Press, Cambridge, MA (2000)

IIIF 3D and Data Dimensions - Countdown on Collaborative Standards for Sustainable Digital Heritage

Ronald Haynes

University of Cambridge, Cambridge CB2 1TN, UK
rsh27@cam.ac.uk

Abstract. The expanding considerations of intangible as well as tangible cultural heritage, and memory twins along with digital twins, has extraordinary potential for adding more human aspects to digital heritage, if we can find ways to express it in a common and supported framework. In a related way, the IIIF (International Image Interoperability Framework) [1] provides a vital model for a communal approach to successfully developing and adopting a framework for pairing essential data and metadata, shared via documented APIs and expressed within a clearly-specified manifest, a document structured in a JSON-LD file. Similarly structured documentation for essential paradata may in future complement extensive digital collections using IIIF to enable sharing, extending and blending collections globally.

Complementing the impact of the IIIF in 2D and Audio/Video (A/V) digital collections around the world, the IIIF 3D Technical Specification Group (TSG) has a road map to draft standards for 3D content, incorporating established open web standards, to complement and expand the potential of all IIIF-based collections worldwide. Engaging with specialists and representatives across user communities, international and standards bodies, the TSG are expanding options for better data sharing across institutions, to help overcome barriers for sustainable digital collections.

The planned changes to the IIIF Presentation API specification [2] will enable display and creative presentation of 3D resources using IIIF tools. Draft examples of updated IIIF Presentation documents encoding 3D resources, and related viewers that support these documents to display 3D web content, highlight enriched ways of storytelling and interacting by combining 3D, 2D and A/V.

Keywords: 3D Data · 3D Digital Documentation · Metadata · Cultural Heritage · Digital Twin · Memory Twin · Paradata

1 Introduction

The paths our cultures take, in pursuit of innovation and the interchange of ideas and industry, often includes sharing, critiquing, improving, and repeating the cycle for overall mutual benefit. Along with creative flexibility, part of this innovation process usually involves mutual constraints, whether by intention or habituation, design or necessity. There are times when such constraints are key factors fuelling innovation, where limitations in some areas lead to more and enhanced capabilities in other areas of our creative enterprises. Standardisation of the components of productive processes can be just such an enabling constraint which leads to much greater outcomes, in terms of productivity, maintainability, and often profitability.

For example, there is an credible and curious connection between a key measure of horse-drawn carriages, including ancient Roman chariots, and the evolution of the automobile, by way of the development of standard-gauge railway [3]. The ruts that formed in ancient roads, including from various horse-drawn carriages, lead to prudent standardisation of the wheelbase and generally the carriages placed on top of them, based in part on the carriages needing to fit a horse (at least one) as well as people side by side. The ruts common in roads from years of similar cart travel required wheels and axels of new carriages to be built conforming to the width, to avoid rapid damage and breakage.

Following the development of the railroad, and the initial use of the same type of carriages, the carriagemakers also helped in the development of the automobile. Before road could be renovated, and long before pavement, it was prudent to start with a wheelbase that could fit in and survive the roads and ruts, much as needed for the horse-drawn carriages.

Standardisation helped accelerate automobile evolution, including with Ransom Olds founding Oldsmobile in 1897 and pioneering the assembly line using identical, interchangeable parts, enabling thousands of cars to be produced by 1903. Henry Ford introduced the famous Model T in 1908, and from 1913 introduced a moving assembly line using standardised parts and lowering the price nearly 50%, creating an iconic mass-produced and widely affordable vehicle. These families of pioneers and products share innovations through a kind of inheritance often enabled by creative constraints and effective standardisation, often building on others, and many more potentially benefitting from the sharing.

Museums are vehicles for ideas; we build them to share with future generations. For the cultural heritage areas, the collections and curations in the GLAM sector, the galleries and libraries, archives and museums, standardisation can be a means of preserving and promoting the rich materials of these memory institutions. Given popular planning and some products developing the idea of building a meaningful metaverse, and much like lessons from train and automobile development, standardisation can bring stability as well as innovation, and interoperability can ensure sustainability.

For widespread evolution of museums in a shared virtual or metaverse setting, effective interoperability can enable growth, with the means to connect and share digital collections more widely, bringing enduring options for reciprocal resilience for all involved. Sustainable standards and persistent storage systems are needed to enable reliable and readily shareable digital collections in the present, in addition to ensuring preservation of collections well into the future.

2   IIIF - The International Image Interoperability Framework

IIIF, the International Image Interoperability Framework, provides a robust model for sustainable interoperability, bringing together shared expertise in a collaborative community for successfully developing and adopting a framework for pairing essential data and metadata, shared via documented APIs and well expressed within a clearly-specified manifest, a document structured in a standardised way to complement the data file.

What makes IIIF work is the increasing ease of access to the world's images and audio/visual files, whether for general interest or specialist research purposes. Open standards provide this access to high-quality objects online and at scale, with rough estimates of over a billion objects available online as of this writing. There is a global community [4] developing and implementing the IIIF APIs, backed by a consortium of leading cultural institutions, ensuring the freedom to work across barriers and the continued rapid growth of materials. For researchers this offers the ability to examine, compare, annotate, and share. For developers it provides efficiency, without vendor lock-in. For leaders it is practical, widely shareable, and cost-effective. The key combination is of community, standards, software, and collections all working together.

IIIF is "a way to standardise the delivery of images and audio/visual files from servers to different environments on the Web where they can then be viewed and interacted with in many ways." [5] IIIF uses open Web standards, such as the Web Annotation Data Model specification [6], which together define how modern Web browsers work, placing objects on a 2D canvas and enabling richer functionality such as deep zoom, multi-file comparison, data ordering and structure, transcriptions and translations, and various types of annotations. The flexibility of the combinations results in more modular rather than monolithic results (Fig. 1).

IIIF ensures all these elements work consistently, enabling portability of and connection to materials across institutional and international boundaries. This is accomplished through the use of APIs (application programming interfaces), which are collaboratively developed in a widespread community of shared effort and expertise, to define specifications for software systems to reliably communicate and exchange data. The two main interface specifications are the Image API, which can deliver the digital objects to sites in a variety of optional sizes and other transforms, and the Presentation API, which conveys key details in a special file called a manifest, noted above, to accompany the objects and enrich viewing capabilities (Fig. 2):

> The Presentation API attaches basic metadata and structure to digital objects, defining how they appear in viewers. It does this via the Manifest, a JSON file which bundles up all the different elements of an IIIF object (such as a single image, or a series of images) with basic metadata (like title, description, and rights information) and structural information (such as page order) [5].

A IIIF manifest is a structured document that describes a digital object and how it should be presented. A manifest can be human written or machine-generated (or both) and is specified to complement the HTML, the basis of Web documents, with the programmable capabilities of the JSON-LD format.

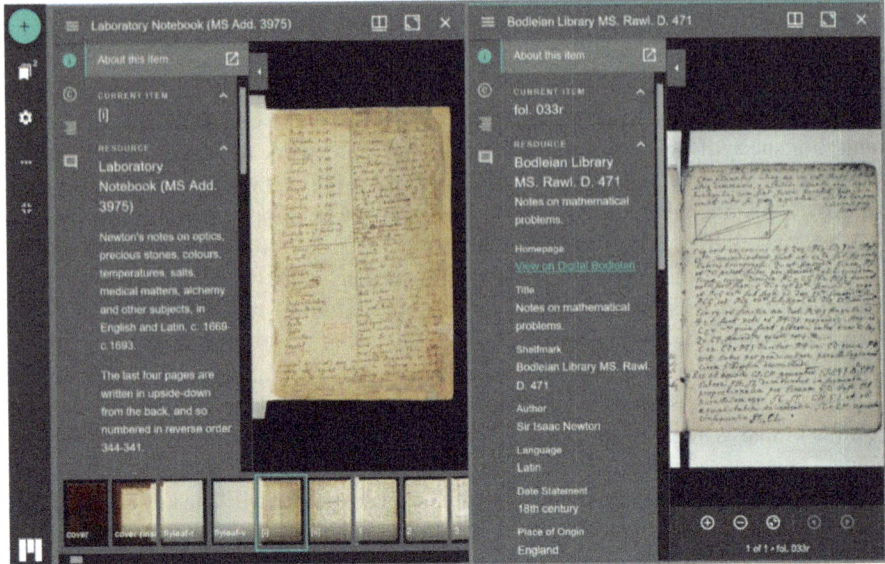

Fig. 1. IIIF example of side-by-side viewing of Newton's notebooks from separate collections, Cambridge Digital Library [7], Digital Bodleian [8]

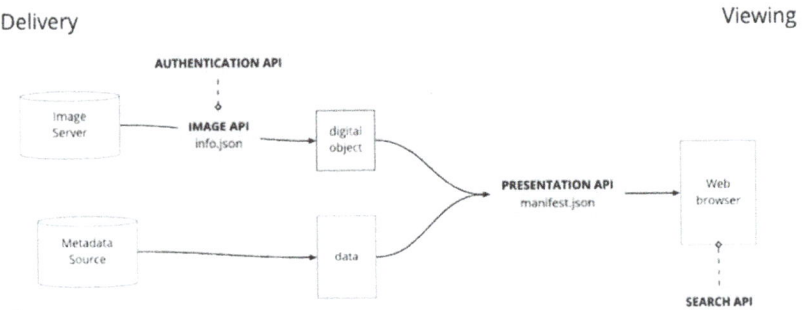

Fig. 2. How the core IIIF APIs work together (additional APIs shown with dotted lines) [5]

JSON [9] is the JavaScript Object Notation, a technical standard based on a subset of the long-established JavaScript Programming Language standard. It is a widely used lightweight data-interchange format, which is text-based and easy for humans to read and write, while also easy for machine instructions to be generated and followed. JSON-LD [10] is JSON for Linking Data, a standardised method of encoding linked data using JSON, structured to be more easily interlinked with other data, local or remote, to extend capabilities and become more effective for combining objects and content from otherwise disparate systems (Fig. 3).

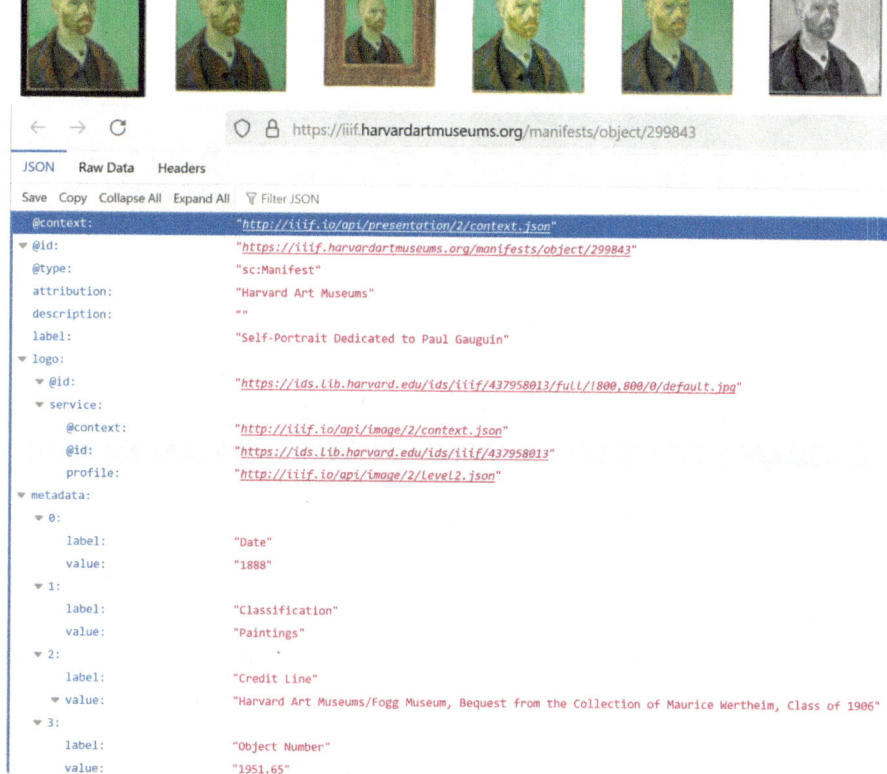

Fig. 3. Example display options of Van Gogh's Self-Portrait Dedicated to Paul Gauguin [11], available from the accompanying IIIF manifest [12], Harvard Art Museums

3 IIIF for 2D - Expanding for 3D

Complementing the impact of the IIIF in 2D and Audio/Video (A/V) digital collections around the world, the IIIF 3D Technical Specification Group (TSG) [13] has committed community representation and a road map [14] to draft standards for 3D content, incorporating additional and established open web standards, to complement and expand the potential of all IIIF-based collections worldwide. Engaging with specialists and representatives across user communities, international and standards bodies, the TSG are expanding options for better data sharing across institutions, to help overcome barriers for sustainable digital collections (Fig. 4).

The planned changes to the IIIF Presentation API specification will enable display and creative presentation of 3D resources using IIIF tools. This includes the introduction of a 3D scene as a new virtual container, with a boundless (infinite) usable space, stretching in all directions, which also brings a need to define orientation (which way is 'up'). While the IIIF canvas has its origin point in the top left corner of the 2D space (x = 0, y = 0), the 3D scene has its zero or origin point in the centre (x = 0, y = 0, z

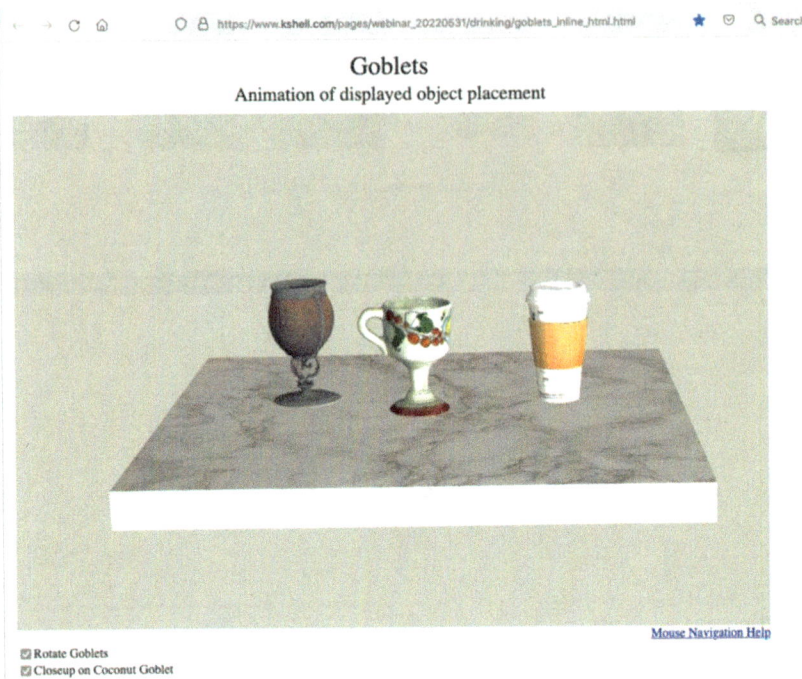

Fig. 4. Example experiment of visual annotation, navigation, and combined assets from multiple sources and file formats in a single scene, Vincent Marchetti [15]

= 0) and for technical orientation () is within a right handed coordinate space (positive Y-axis is up, positive Z-axis is forward) (Table 1).

Table 1. Selected 3D sources (for reference)

3D Collection	Link	Notes
Digital Repository of Ireland	https://dri.ie	
Europeana	https://www.europeana.eu	ee also: https://eureka3d.eu
MorphoSource	https://www.morphosource.org	research-oriented
National 3D Data Repository	https://3d.humanities.science	France
Sketchfab	https://sketchfab.com	https://www.fab.com – to replace?
Smithsonian 3D	https://3d.si.edu	

Orientation is of course important when working with a single object in a scene, however it has particular importance when working with more than one object, so that some are not upside down or backwards or otherwise misaligned (relative to each other). Like a canvas, a scene can contain more than one object, although adding 3D to 2D and A/V and annotations, however in addition it is planned that existing canvases can be added to a scene as well. This should make it simpler to combine existing scanned paintings and other collection materials with recreations of rooms, current and previous, e.g. to help present digital twins of former palaces or existing galleries (without having to rescan the 2D assets already available) (Fig. 5).

Fig. 5. Infinite Canvas, multi-dimensional experimental interaction with images, video, 3D, with object and section zoom, video playback, 3D rotation of viewer plane (Left-Click + Drag), Edward Silverton [16]

Draft examples of updated IIIF Presentation documents encoding 3D resources, and related viewers that support these documents to display 3D web content, highlight enriched ways of storytelling and interacting by combining 3D, 2D and A/V. When placing (also known as 'painting') objects into a 3D scene, which along with labels and comments is considered a kind of annotation process, new options particularly for such scenes include at least one camera, and light. The 'painting annotations' can also be used for placing in the scene 3D models, as well as 2D canvas, and if helpful for another 3D scene inside the initial scene (i.e. nested scenes, or a main scene with one or more sub-scenes).

Positioning of any content will be handled via an identified 3D point (pointSelector) along with operations indicated with transforms (e.g. translate, rotate, scale). In a scene, many objects can be position and operations can be handled in a kind of freeform manner, or optionally in a more planned or constrained way. For instance, commenting annotations can be linked to camera views, such that selecting one comment after another could change the view presented, perhaps to look under or behind a model.

Many other, and more advanced operations for making changes in a scene are possible through the use of Content State [17], another IIIF API which provides an effective way to refer to Presentation API resources, for instance to initialize the view of a model, and then guide the move to additional pre-planned views in the scene, perhaps through selectable commenting annotations. Content state details can be included in the manifest, and can optionally enable modifications to a scene, such as with interactions to select and hide or reveal statues or other objects. These capabilities for instance will enable the creation of guided tours through a virtual space such as a gallery or museum hall containing multiple objects to be curated and shared accordingly (Fig. 6).

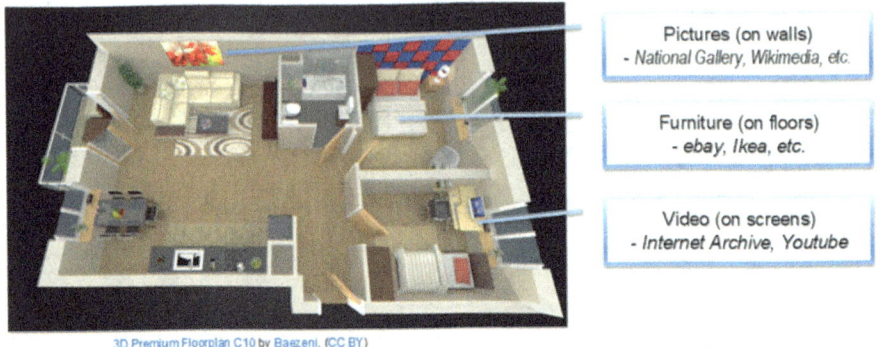

Fig. 6. Imagined (near) future of a metaverse made by interoperability, based on 3D Premium Floorplan C10 by Baezeni (CC-BY) [18]

4   Next Steps – IIIF 3D, Paramaterising Paradata?

From 2022 the IIIF 3D TSG has met nearly every 2 weeks on Zoom, complemented by a set of focussed in person meetings, to propose and discuss specification proposals, testing with technical demonstrations, and exploring related topics directly relevant to future 3D additions to the IIIF Presentation specification. The meetings are open, and new members are welcome.

At the IIIF Annual Conference 2025, 2–5 June in Leeds, UK, the TSG plans to share a release candidate for the 3D-enabling Presentation API 4.0 specification, along with demonstrations and discussion. That too is open, all are welcome, and updates will be widely shared. In addition, the follow up to the discussions and engagement with the details presented will help refine the release candidate, and resulting further updates are planned for later in the year.

Like all intricate projects, the specification is expected to continue to evolve, especially as the community supporters committed to help, by piloting the specification with their collections, will provide vital feedback. Along with other adopters, this will combine to further the development and provide good examples to help others more widely adopt the new specification, continuing the iterative improvements.

Since IIIF typically pairs a data file with a manifest file with meaningful metadata, including from a collection, this has proved to be a powerful and practical means to help extend and blend collections and cultural communications around the world. While the specification of the content of the manifest is well defined, and compliance is key to shareability and sustainability, there is room for extending and adding extra information where useful, such as where beneficial for local system features and integrations.

Parallel to this, there is long-standing and renewed interest in how to connect and keep track of paradata, considered as details about how the data connected to the object was collected or created, or details about how the object is used, or perhaps what the object has meant or means to different people and/or in different times. Notably, in the expanding considerations of intangible as well as tangible cultural heritage, there seem to be similar concerns for recording similar paradata. So too are the similar concerns in the emergence of memory twins to complement digital twins. All of these developments have extraordinary potential for adding the more human aspects to digital heritage, especially if we can find ways to express them in a common and supported framework.

At EuroMed2024 questions were raised as to whether structured documentation, perhaps similar to the manifest created for IIIF metadata, might be collaboratively crafted to be suitable for essential paradata. If it is possible to add interoperability to the development of the memory twin, we may want to consider whether we can collaboratively craft a kind of 'paramanifest'. Suggestions for collaborative consideration included how Memory Twin could include intangible heritage, whether paradata can be specified to be more interoperable, and how a 'paramanifest' might complement a IIIF metadata manifest?

Initial discussion about the potential for considering such an approach for the future, perhaps to complement the extensive digital collections using IIIF to enable sharing collections globally, suggested it was worth additional attention. Further discussions are planned with specialists in the areas of paradata and memory twin, and the author hopes that all involved will be able to share more in a future gathering and subsequent publication.

Acknowledgments. Many thanks go to fellow IIIF 3D group Co-Chairs Julie Winchester <julia.m.winchester@gmail.com> from MorphoSource and Duke University, and Edward Silverton <ed@mnemoscene.io> from Mnemoscene, who with fellow IIIF 3D group developer Vincent Marchetti vmarchetti@kshell.com helped provide key material for this article, along with all the longstanding input and creative discourse with our many other colleagues in these collaborative 3D developments.

Special thanks go to Marinos Ioannides <marinos.ioannides@cut.ac.cy> and Drew Baker <drew.baker@cut.ac.cy> from the Cyprus University of Technology and the colleagues from the Digital Heritage Research Lab, for the continuing encouragement, collegiality, and inclusive engagement in building a larger collaborative community, which will help make IIIF 3D and the related practical standards a reality.

Special mention goes to colleagues in the Cambridge Digital Library, Cambridge Museums and related collections, Cambridge Digital Humanities, the Darwin 3D project group, and the Cambridge 4D community.

Disclosure of Interests. The author has no competing interests to declare that are relevant to the content of this article.

References

1. IIIF, International Image Interoperability Framework. https://iiif.io. Accessed 08 Mar 2025
2. IIIF Presentation API 3.0. https://iiif.io/api/presentation/3.0. Accessed 08 Mar 2025
3. Standard-gauge railway, Wikipedia. https://en.wikipedia.org/wiki/Standard-gauge_railway. Accessed 08 Mar 2025
4. IIIF Community Map. https://iiif.io/community/map. Accessed 08 Mar 2025
5. IIIF How It Works. https://iiif.io/get-started/how-iiif-works. Accessed 08 Mar 2025
6. Web Annotation Data Model specification. https://www.w3.org/TR/annotation-model. Accessed 08 Mar 2025
7. Cambridge Digital Library. https://cudl.lib.cam.ac.uk. Accessed 08 Mar 2025
8. Digital Bodleian. https://digital.bodleian.ox.ac.uk. Accessed 08 Mar 2025
9. JSON, JavaScript Object Notation. https://json.org. Accessed 08 Mar 2025
10. JSON-LD, JSON for Linking Data. https://json-ld.org. Accessed 08 Mar 2025
11. Self-Portrait Dedicated to Paul Gauguin, Van Gogh, Harvard Art Museums. https://harvardartmuseums.org/collections/object/299843. Accessed 08 Mar 2025
12. Manifest for Self-Portrait Dedicated to Paul Gauguin, Harvard Art Museums. https://iiif.harvardartmuseums.org/manifests/object/299843. Accessed 08 Mar 2025
13. IIIF 3D Technical Specification Group. https://iiif.io/community/groups/3d/tsg. Accessed 08 Mar 2025
14. IIIF 3D Technical Specification Group Charter. https://iiif.io/community/groups/3d/tsg-charter. Accessed 08 Mar 2025
15. Goblet, Animation of displayed object placement. https://www.kshell.com/pages/webinar_20220531/drinking/goblets_inline_html.html. Accessed 08 Mar 2025
16. Infinite Canvas. https://infinitecanvas.vercel.app. Accessed 08 Mar 2025
17. IIIF Content State API 1.0. https://iiif.io/api/content-state/1.0. Accessed 08 Mar 2025
18. 3D Premium Floorplan C10, Baezeni. https://skfb.ly/A8Mo. Accessed 08 Mar 2025

Documentation and Scientificity of the 3D Reconstruction of Built Heritage Models in the Age of GenAI

Sander Münster[✉]

Friedrich-Schiller-Universität Jena, Leutragraben 1, 07743 Jena, Germany
sander.muenster@uni-jena.de

Abstract. For more than 30 years, digital 3D modelling and visualization technologies have been widely used to support research and education in the humanities, especially but not exclusively for historical architecture. This article is proposed to highlight core concepts and challenges of documentation of 3D models of built heritage and particularly of 3D reconstructions as usually hand-modelled digital representations of no more extant or never realized buildings and cityscapes. This article is proposed to (a) highlight core concepts of documentation of 3D reconstructions, to (b) highlight technologies and particularly AI-based approaches for automatically generating 3D reconstructions of built heritage from multimodal data and (c) to discuss and assess their documentation.

Keywords: Urban history · cultural heritage

1 Introduction[1]

For more than 30 years, digital 3D modelling and visualization technologies have been widely used to support research and education in the humanities, especially but not exclusively for historical architecture. Despite the immense efforts spent on the establishment of information technologies and in particular 3D technologies as digital 3D modelling, and visualization as daily use tools for researchers in humanities, the current situation is still ambiguous. On the one hand, humanities researchers frequently use a wide scope of digital tools for information search, communication, publication, and research support (e.g., reference management or personal organization) [5, p. 28]. There is also a huge number of projects investigating and utilizing those technologies in various settings. On the other hand, the use of digital tools for research work differs widely between the individual sub-disciplines of humanities, and development of that field is driven by language and textual related disciplines like linguistics or edition studies.

A major challenge is to document the 3D modelling with regards to its results and workflows. This takes usually place via data, metadata and paradata.

---

[1] Parts of this article has been published in [1–4].

This article is proposed to (a) highlight core concepts of documentation of 3D reconstructions, to (b) highlight technologies and particularly AI-based approaches for automatically generating 3D reconstructions of built heritage from multimodal data and (c) to discuss and assess their documentation.

2 Core Concepts and Challenges of Documentation[2]

Investigating documentation principles is a core topic of library and information studies (LIS) [9]. **Philosophy of documentation** is related to information conceptualization as models and theories [10, 11], e.g., classification [12], information creation [13], and information behaviour [14]. As a methodological approach, documentation behaviour is primarily investigated using empirical methods described above [9]. Specifically for the documentation of scientific processes, **scholarly** publication has had established principles for a long time. With regards to the documentation of digital processes and via digital means, there are numerous guidelines of overarching relevance [e.g. 15, 16]. The technical classification of research results is usually practiced via metadata and paradata. The process and principles for developing metadata schemes are formalized [17] via the **request for comments approach** widely used for technical standardization [18].

2.1 Documentation Strategies

Documentation strategies address the preservation of knowledge, and are thus linked to transparency, reproducibility, and portability. These objectives entail clarification of "included sources, decisions, workflows, possible misinterpretations and methodology" [19]. Internally, this helps project partners with safeguarding and communicating their contribution. Externally, such records are intended for evaluation and discussion of the project's rationale and result. While this distinction may appear fuzzy to the end user, distinction between process and documenting outputs is a more appropriate approach. A high-level guide to digitization is provided by the German research foundation [15].

2.2 Documentation of 3D Models

Documentation of Results

The documentation of 3D modelling results through metadata is well established nowadays. Numerous initiatives are advancing the development of domain-specific thesauruses for art and architectural history content – e.g., ICONCLASS[3] and the Getty Art & Architecture Thesaurus (AAT).[4] Ontologies such as Wikibase[5] or CIDOC-CRM also defining relations between data. Especially CIDOC-CRM became an overarching standard for heritage documentation [20] and is fixed as an ISO standard. Several sectoral standards like IFC for BIM [21] and GML [22] for geo and city-scale models are of

---

[2] Published in: [1]. Parts of this section were also published in [6–8].
[3] http://www.iconclass.org/rkd/61F/ and http://www.iconclass.org/rkd/47/, accessed 15.07.2021.
[4] http://vocab.getty.edu/aat/300000885, accessed 15.07.2021.
[5] https://www.wikimedia.de/projects/wikibase/, accessed 15.07.2021.

relevance. The quality of implementation in application ontologies is heterogeneous [23, 24]. Derived categories for classification can be the employed reference ontology, as well as the adopted application ontology [25]. Besides the description of results, the demand for standardization of 3D models – comprising digitization and reconstruction – is still high [26].

Process Documentation

In contrast to result documentation strategies, current approaches to documentation of the creation process are still theoretical [27] or highly prototypic [19]. For 3D digitization processes and workflows differ greatly by application scenario (cf. [28]). For 3D reconstruction it is evident that in a majority of projects process documentation occurs by personal notes, communication artifacts, or versioning of states [6]. While these artifacts "document" a workflow and communication history, another question concerns the employed software, algorithms, and documentation of computational processing. For 3D reconstruction from historical sources, guidelines are provided by the Charters of London [29] and Seville [30], but these do not present a clearly applicable methodology and therefore are rarely applied in practice [8], so they are a long way from providing a transparent workflow. Despite much research [c.f. 31] and numerous methods/tools [25, 32–36] (e.g., reverse design to validate reconstructions according to their fit to historical images or acquired data [e.g. 37, 38]; documentation methods to justify modelling steps and decisions taken during the 3D reconstruction [35, 39, 40]; assessment of possible scenarios by numerically calculating an index of reliability [27, 41, 42]) there is still no consensus about methodology to document the creation process of 3D reconstructions in a transparent way.

2.3 3D Data

A wide range of 3D file types is currently available. A main distinction is between proprietary 3D model formats (C4D for Maxon Cinema 4D or MAX for Autodesk 3D Studio Max), which are specific to the software in which they were created, and overarching formats like OBJ, DAE, STL, FBX, X3D, and glTF, which can be opened and created by many software tools [43]. Surface representations as in the formats mentioned above are distinct from volume information as in DICOM. Several approaches are using specific standards integrating both 3D and metadata, such as IFC for BIM [44] or Shapefiles for GIS [45]. Since formats such as OBJ and PLY are proprietary structured, DAE and X3D follow an XML-based data organization. Formats like X3D and glTF are specifically designed for browser-based viewing [46]. Another issue is storing 3D information. Generative approaches do not rely on storing resultant 3D geometries, but on parameters, and generate a 3D object in real time [47, 48]. In contrast, discrete approaches store all 3D information: (A) point clouds as a set of points in a defined coordinate system; (B) wireframe/polygon models as vertices connected with edges and polygons; and (C) voxels as volume pixels. While geometric data can largely be sorted to one of these archetypes, there is a heterogeneous scope of formats for radiometric or dynamic information.

2.4 Scientificity

Scientificity is characterised by scientific principles, which are commonly understood to include attributes as e.g. objectivity, reliability, validity and honesty (e.g. [49]). Another important approach in science is the distinction between data and methods, which allows the discussion and reproduction of results and the assessment of possible shortcomings, but also mechanisms to formally compare and criticise results obtained by different methods.

3 Documentation and Scientificity of Automated 3D Modelling

The application of AI in 3D for CH has gained significant attention in the research community to enhance the analysis, interpretation, and preservation of CH in 3D environments [4]. How could AI applications contribute to the documentation of 3D reconstruction models? In the following section I want to highlight the use of AI technologies for 3D building generation used by our group [50].

3.1 Automated 3D Model Generation

Photographs and plans are an essential source for historical research [51–53]. Numerous digital image archives, containing vast numbers of photographs, have been set up in the context of digitization projects. Within the Jena4D research group we are investigating and developing methods and technologies for transferring historical media and their contextual information into a 4D – 3D spatial and temporal scaled - model to support research and education on urban history. Content is made accessible as a location-dependent virtual reality 4D browser application for mobile devices and a 4D desktop browser application. Within former articles we highlighted the prospected research agenda [54] as well as technological venues [55, 56] but also conceptual challenges to automatically reconstruct the past [28, 57]. The main purpose of this contribution is to (1) highlight current conceptual and technological challenges, (2) examine a state of the art and (3) our approach towards data collection, 4D modelling and visualization at world scale, as well as present (4) results from demo cases in Dresden, Jena and Amsterdam and at world-scale.

Virtual reconstruction of past architectures are still a very complex and research and labour intense approach [28]. In our work we assess to which extent virtual reconstructions could be created according to principles of the critical digital 3D model [58] via technical pipelines and generative AI tools.

3.2 Proposer and Validator Architectures to Generate Virtual Reconstructions

In our work with mainly include historical photographs and building footprints gained from historical plans and maps (Fig. 1). To create time-variate 3D meshes, we use multi-step pipelines [3, 50]:

Image Spatialization Is done via an SfM reconstruction using SOTA and -content based image retrieval (EigenPlaces) and neural matching algorithms (DISK features [59] with LightGlue [60]).

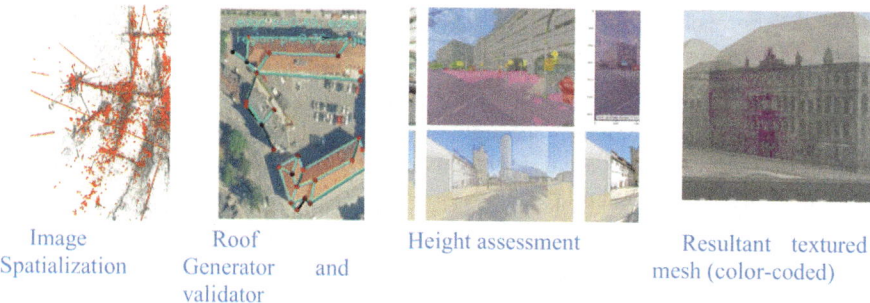

| Image Spatialization | Roof Generator and validator | Height assessment | Resultant textured mesh (color-coded) |

Fig. 1. Steps of automated virtual reconstructions (Images: Komorowicz, Rajan, Maiwald)

Roof Generator: This includes parametric roof generators as proposers and extracted roof structure features from satellite and aerial imagery for validation. The proposer uses Straight Skeleton/Parametric modeler and the validator a HEAT pipeline from satellite imagery [50]. Current limitations include the applicability only for still extant geometries – therefore SAM [61] segmented terrestrial imagery will be also used in a next step.

Height Assessment: A height calculation of features is done via SIHE [62] and then used as height information for the parametric building generation. A cross validation is currently prepared for the Dresden set by using a AI based estimator [63].

Result of this pipeline are building geometries with simplified roof shape features and projected textures. As an overall finding the pipeline is shifting human intervention from object specific tasks towards data selection and processing tasks – e.g. by building datasets and optimizing processing quality. Another methodical issue is the question for ground-truth – already validated data, which enable to assess processing results.

3.3 GenAI Approaches for Virtual Reconstructions

| Façade texture generated via Stable Diffusion 3.5 Large Turbo | Model generated from 4 coordinate points | Single view reconstruction via Threestudio/Zero123 |

Fig. 2. Steps of automated virtual reconstructions (Images: Muenster, Rajan)

Various approaches enable the creation of architectural representations from sparse sources (Fig. 2).

Façade Image Generation: In a current experimental setup, we generate facade textures using text2img generators - currently using Stable Diffusion 2 and 3.5 Turbo. In a second step, these images are described using VLMs (Llava, Mistral 7b) to inquire about suitability, quality and proportions.

Mesh Prediction: Our current approach starts from point data and utilizes a parametric wall and roof feature proposer as well as projected textures from the previous step [50].

3D Mesh Generation from Single Imagery: Recent approaches as multimodal transformer architectures are proposed to generate 3D meshes from single images or even textual prompts. In our work we used Threestudio/Zero123 [64] to which extent these approaches work from single historical images. Although results are not convincing yet these approaches already show some potential but also raise fundamental questions.

3.4 A Leap Forward Towards Scientific 3D Reconstructions?

From a formal point of view, the reproducibility and objectivity of virtual reconstructions created by pipelines can be closer to scientific principles than ever before. They can be fully documented and uncertainty can be quantified in terms of probabilities and deviations between validator and proposer. However, the issues raised are of a different nature and include, for example, biased training data, parameter sets and numbers, and explainability [4].

A key issue is the truth of the content generated by the generative AI. As the proposer and validator architectures are still very similar to the process of traditional virtual reconstructions - as reconstructing and validating a 3D hypothesis [65] - generative AI raises questions about the nature of scientific 3D reconstructions: While there is no doubt that the results are hypothetical and lack object specificity, the extent to which the results (such as inferring patterns from large examples to propose a single case) are a valid intellectual deduction and thus a scientific result is questionable [66].

4 Conclusion

Despite many attempts to increase the amount of high-quality online data, e.g., through massive digitization campaigns, art historians still have limited access to digital resources containing primary material and good-quality open access visual information, which is digitized and presented according to their preferences and needs. Against this background the provision of widely accepted workflows and standards for data, metadata and paradata is important to overcome the current issue of insufficient documentation.

A recent approach includes the AI processing of data to reconstruct objects but also enrich data post factum and on demand. A connecting question is if 3D reconstructions could become merely a view on multimodal data – created from data, on demand and according to specific purposes. This is closely coupled to current trends in

AI development such as Explainable AI [67], or recent developments regarding LLMs and transformer-based approaches.

Nevertheless, this is closely linked to quality and different concepts. While the level of uncertainty in hypothetical reconstructions, as well as the basis of reconstruction results, can be quantified or codified, a general limitation of AI-generated content stems from the lack of explainability of AI processes. When viewed through the lens of AI-generated 3D models as scientific results, this poses the challenge of a lack of process transparency. Quality assurance and evaluation procedures for 3D reconstruction models currently mainly target technical quality, e.g. completeness and model contingency, while standardised procedures for content evaluation are widely lacking. Conversely, GenAI procedures enable results to be reproduced and therefore seem promising with regard to the current lack of reliability of human-made reconstructions. This allows the division between data (historical sources) and modelling processes (modelling pipelines) that is already very common in other domains. From a documentation perspective, creating 3D models via GenAI potentially provides more comprehensive documentation and reproduction of procedures. Conversely, challenges such as explainability and quality assessment procedures, as well as suitability for very specific scenarios such as low-detail architectural objects, are currently – and perhaps fundamentally – hurdles.

Acknowledgements. The research which this paper is based on was carried out in the EU projects INDUX-R (Grant No. 101135556), 5DCulture (Grant No. 101100778) and 3DBigDataSpace (Grant No. 101173385). Special thanks to the Jena4D group and particularly Jonas Bruschke, Clemens Beck, Rebecca Pressler, Vaibhav Rajan, Dominik Ukolov and David Komorowicz for their work on the 4D pipeline.

References

1. Muenster, S.: Digital 3D technologies for humanities research and education: an overview. Appl. Sci. **12**(5), 2426 (2022)
2. Münster, S.: Advancements in 3D heritage data aggregation and enrichment in Europe: implications for designing the Jena experimental repository for the DFG 3D viewer. Appl. Sci. **13**(17), 9781 (2023)
3. Münster, S., Maiwald, F., Bruschke, J., Kröber, C., Sun, Y., Dworak, D., et al.: A digital 4D information system on the world scale: research challenges, approaches, and preliminary results. Appl. Sci. **14**(5), 1992 (2024)
4. Münster, S., Maiwald, F., Lenardo, I.d., Henriksson, J., Isaac, A., Graf, M., et al.: Artificial intelligence for digital heritage innovation. Setting up a R&D roadmap for Europe. MDPI Herit. **7**, 794–816 (2024)
5. Daniela Pscheida, C. M., Herbst, S., Albrecht, S., Köhler, T.: Use of social media and online-based tools in academia. Results of the science 2.0-survey 2014, Dresden (2014)
6. Münster, S., Prechtel, N.: Beyond software. design implications for virtual libraries and platforms for cultural heritage from practical findings. In: Ioannides, M., Magnenat-Thalmann, N., Fink, E., Žarnić, R., Yen, A.Y., Quak, E. (eds.) EuroMed 2014. LNCS, vol. 8740, pp. 131–145. Springer, Cham (2014). https://doi.org/10.1007/978-3-319-13695-0_13
7. Münster, S., Hegel, W., Kröber, C.: A model classification for digital 3D reconstruction in the context of humanities research. In: Münster, S., Pfarr-Harfst, M., Kuroczyński, P., Ioannides, M. (eds.) 3D Research Challenges in Cultural Heritage II. LNCS, vol. 10025, pp. 3–31. Springer, Cham (2016). https://doi.org/10.1007/978-3-319-47647-6_1

8. Münster, S.: Digital cultural heritage as scholarly field – topics, researchers and perspectives from a bibliometric point of view. J. Comput. Cult. Herit. **12**(3), 22–49 (2019). https://doi.org/10.1145/3310012
9. Stock, W., Stock, M.: Handbook of Information Science. De Gruyter Saur, Berlin/Boston (2015)
10. Graziano, E.E.: On a theory of documentation. Am. Doc. **19**(1), 85–000 (1968). https://doi.org/10.1002/asi.5090190115
11. Gorichanaz, T.: A first-person theory of documentation. J. Doc. **75**(1), 190–212 (2019). https://doi.org/10.1108/Jd-07-2018-0110
12. Bowker, G.C., Star, S.L.: Sorting Things Out. Classification and Its Consequences. The MIT Press, Cambridge (1999)
13. Huvila, I., Douglas, J., Gorichanaz, T., Koh, K., Suorsa, A.: Conceptualizing and studying information creation: from production and processes to makers and making. Proc. Assoc. Inf. Sci. Technol. **57**(1), e226 (2020). https://doi.org/10.1002/pra2.226
14. Wilson, T.D.: Models in information behaviour research. J. Doc. **55**(3), 249–270 (1999). https://doi.org/10.1108/Eum0000000007145
15. DFG: DFG-Praxisregeln "Digitalisierung" (2016)
16. Deutsche Forschungsgemeinschaft: Grundlagen guter wissenschaftlicher Praxis. WILEY-VCH, Weinheim (2013)
17. Greenberg, J.: Metadata and the world wide web. Encycl. Libr. Inf. Sci. **3**, 1876–1888 (2003)
18. Flanagan, H.: Request for Comments: 8700: Fifty Years of RFCs (2019)
19. Pfarr-Harfst, M.: Documentation system for digital reconstructions. Reference to the Mausoleum of the Tang-Dynastie at Zhaoling, in Shaanxi Province, China. In: 16th International Conference on "Cultural Heritage and New Technologies" Vienna, 2011, Wien, pp. 648–658 (2011)
20. Doerr, M.: The CIDOC CRM – an ontological approach to semantic interoperability of metadata. AI Mag. **24**(3) (2003)
21. ISO: BIM – The present EN ISO 19650 standards provide the construction industry with an approach to manage and exchange information on projects (2022). https://group.thinkproject.com/de/ressourcen/bim-standards-und-praktiken/. Accessed 2 Feb 2022
22. OGC: OGC City Geography Markup Language (CityGML) Encoding Standard, Version 2.0.0 (2012). In G. Gröger, T. Kolbe, C. Nagel, & K.-H. Häfele (eds.)
23. Ronzino, P., Amico, N., Niccolucci, F.: Assessment and comparison of metadata schemas for architectural heritage. In: XXIII CIPA Symposium - Proceedings (2011)
24. Felicetti, A., Lorenzini, M.: Metadata and tools for integration and preservation of cultural heritage 3D information. In: XXIII CIPA Symposium - Proceedings, 2011 (2011)
25. Kuroczyński, P., Hauck, O., Dworak, D.: 3D Models on triple paths - new pathways for documenting and visualizing virtual reconstructions. In: Münster, S., Pfarr-Harfst, M., Kuroczyński, P., Ioannides, M. (eds.) 3D Research Challenges in Cultural Heritage II. LNCS, vol. 10025, pp. 149–172. Springer, Cham (2016). https://doi.org/10.1007/978-3-319-47647-6_8
26. Time Machine FET-FLAGSHIP-CSA: Time Machine: Big Data of the Past for the Future of Europe. A proposal to the European Commission for a Large-Scale Research Initiative, Brussels (2020)
27. Hermon, S., Nikodem, J., Perlingieri, C.: Deconstructing the VR - data transparency, quantified uncertainty and reliability of 3D models. In: Arnold, D., Ioannides, M., Niccolucci, F., Mania, K. (eds.) 7th International Symposium on Virtual Reality, Archaeology and Cultural Heritage (VAST 2006), pp. 123–129. Eurographics Association, Nicosia (2006)
28. Münster, S., Apollonio, F., Blümel, I., Fallavollita, F., Foschi, R., Grellert, M., et al.: Handbook of Digital 3D Reconstruction of Historical Architecture. Springer, Heidelberg (2024). https://doi.org/10.1007/978-3-031-43363-4

29. Beacham, R., Denard, H., Niccolucci, F.: An introduction to the London charter. In: Ioannides, M., Arnold, D., Niccolucci, F., Mania, K. (eds.) Papers from the Joint Event CIPA/VAST/EG/EuroMed Event, pp. 263–269 (2006)
30. Bendicho, Lopez-Menchero, V.M.: The principles of the Seville Charter. In: XXIII CIPA Symposium - Prague, Czech Republic – 12–16 September 2011 - Proceedings, 2011 (2011)
31. Bentkowska-Kafel, A., Denard, H., Baker, D.: Paradata and Transparency in Virtual Heritage. Ashgate, Burlington (2012)
32. Münster, S., Kuroczyński, P., Pfarr-Harfst, M., Grellert, M., Lengyel, D.: Future research challenges for a computer-based interpretative 3D reconstruction of cultural heritage – a German community's view. ISPRS Ann. Photogramm. Remote Sens. Spat. Inf. Sci. **II-5-W3**, 207–213 (2015). XXV International CIPA Symposium
33. Niccolucci, F.: Setting standards for 3D visualization of cultural heritage in Europe and beyond. In: Bentkowska-Kafel, A., Denard, H., Baker, D. (eds.) Paradata and Transparency in Virtual Heritage, pp. 23–36. Ashgate, Burlington (2012)
34. Grellert, M., Pfarr-Harfst, M.: Die Rekonstruktion – Argument – Methode: Vorschlag für einen minimalen Dokumentationsstandard im Kontext digitaler Rekonstruktionen. In: Kuroczyński, P., Pfarr-Harfst, M., Münster, S. (eds.) Der Modelle Tugend 2.0: Digitale 3D-Rekonstruktion als virtueller Raum der architekturhistorischen Forschung, Heidelberg (2019)
35. Bruschke, J., Wacker, M.: Simplifying documentation of digital reconstruction processes. In: Münster, S., Pfarr-Harfst, M., Kuroczyński, P., Ioannides, M. (eds.) 3D Research Challenges in Cultural Heritage II. LNCS, vol. 10025, pp. 256–271. Springer, Cham (2016). https://doi.org/10.1007/978-3-319-47647-6_12
36. Kuroczyński, P., Bajena, I., Große, P., Jara, K., Wnęk, K.: Digital reconstruction of the new synagogue in Breslau: new approaches to object-oriented research. In: Niebling, F., Münster, S., Messemer, H. (eds.) UHDL 2019. CCIS, vol. 1501, pp. 25–45. Springer, Cham (2021). https://doi.org/10.1007/978-3-030-93186-5_2
37. Verdiani, G.: Reading the project and "reverse design": an architectural approach to digital reconstruction. In: Proceedings of the 20th International Conference on Cultural Heritage and New Technologies, Vienna, Austria, 2–4 November 2015 (2015)
38. Pöchtrager, M., Styhler-Aydın, G., Hochreiner, G., Özkan, T., Döring-Williams, M., Pfeifer, N.: Bridging the gap. Digital models of historic roof structures for enhanced interdisciplinary research. SCIRES-IT **10** (2020)
39. Pfarr-Harfst, M., Grellert, M.: The reconstruction – argumentation method. In: Ioannides, M., et al. (eds.) EuroMed 2016. LNCS, vol. 10058, pp. 39–49. Springer, Cham (2016). https://doi.org/10.1007/978-3-319-48496-9_4
40. Kuroczyński, P.: Digital reconstruction and virtual research environments – a question of documentation standards. In: Access and Understanding – Networking in the Digital Era, Proceedings of the annual conference of CIDOC, Dresden, 06.09.–11.09.2014 (2014)
41. Niccolucci, F., Hermon, S.: A fuzzy logic approach to reliability in archaeological virtual reconstruction. In: Niccolucci, F., Hermon, S. (eds.) Beyond the Artifact. Digital Interpretation of the Past, Budapest (2006)
42. Hermon, S.: Reasoning in 3D. A critical appraisal of the role of 3D modelling and virtual reconstructions in archaeology. In: Frischer, B. (ed.) Beyond Illustration: 2D and 3D Digital Technologies as Tools for Discovery in Archaeology, Oxford, vol. 1805, pp. 36–45. Tempus Reparatum (2008)
43. Fernie, K., Blümel, I., Corns, A., Giulio, R.d., Ioannides, M., Niccolucci, F., et al.: 3D content in Europeana task force. Europeana Network Association, The Hague, The Netherlands (2020)
44. ISO: ISO 16739:2013: Industry Foundation Classes (IFC) for data sharing in the construction and facility management industries (2013)
45. Special Interest Group 3D (Ed.). CityGML Specification (2007)

46. Cieslik, E.: 3D Digitization in Cultural Heritage Institutions Guidebook. University of Maryland, Baltimore (2020)
47. Havemann, S., Fellner, D.W.: Generative parametric design of gothic window tracery. In: VAST 2004: The 5th International Symposium on Virtual Reality, Archaeology and Cultural Heritage, Brussels and Oudenaarde, Belgium, pp. 193–201. Eurographics Association (2004)
48. Garagnani, S., Manferdini, A.M.: Parametric accuracy: building information modeling process applied to the cultural heritage preservation. In: 3DARCH 2013 (2013)
49. Meinsen, S.: Konstruktivistisches Wissensmanagement, Weinheim (2003)
50. Münster, S., Bruschke, J., Dworak, D., Komorowicz, D., Rajan, V., Ukolov, D.: 4D geo modelling from different sources at large scale. In: ACM Multimedia Melbourne (2024)
51. Burke, P.: Augenzeugenschaft. Bilder als historische Quellen (Wagenbachs Taschenbuch 631), Berlin (2003)
52. Paul, G.: Von der Historischen Bildkunde zur visual history. In: Visual History. Ein Studienbuch, Göttingen, pp. 7–36 (2006)
53. Pérez-Gómez, A., Pelletier, L.: Architectural Representation and the Perspective Hinge. University Press, Cambridge (1997)
54. Münster, S., Maiwald, F., Lehmann, C., Lazariv, T., Hofmann, M., Niebling, F.: An automated pipeline for a browser-based, city-scale mobile 4D VR application based on historical images. Paper Presented at the Proceedings of the 2nd Workshop on Structuring and Understanding of Multimedia Heritage Contents, Seattle, WA, USA (2020)
55. Muenster, S., Bruschke, J., Maiwald, F., Kleiner, C.: Software and content design of a browser-based mobile 4D VR application to explore historical city architecture. Paper Presented at the Proceedings of the 3rd Workshop on Structuring and Understanding of Multimedia Heritage Contents, Virtual Event, China (2021)
56. Münster, S., Lehmann, C., Lazariv, T., Maiwald, F., Karsten, S.: Toward an automated pipeline for a browser-based, city-scale mobile 4D VR application based on historical images. In: Niebling, F., Münster, S., Messemer, H. (eds.) UHDL 2019. CCIS, vol. 1501, pp. 106–128. Springer, Cham (2021). https://doi.org/10.1007/978-3-030-93186-5_5
57. Münster, S., Bruschke, J., Hoppe, S., Maiwald, F., Niebling, F., Pattee, A., et al.: Multimodal AI support of source criticism in the humanities. In: ADHO DH 2022 (2022)
58. Apollonio, F.I., Fallavollita, F., Foschi, R.: The critical digital model for the study of unbuilt architecture. In: Niebling, F., Münster, S., Messemer, H. (eds.) UHDL 2019. CCIS, vol. 1501, pp. 3–24. Springer, Cham (2021). https://doi.org/10.1007/978-3-030-93186-5_1
59. Tyszkiewicz, M., Fua, P., Trulls, E.: DISK: learning local features with policy gradient. In: Advances in Neural Information Processing Systems, vol. 33 (2020)
60. Lindenberger, P., Sarlin, P.-E., Pollefeys, M.: LightGlue: local feature matching at light speed. In: ICCV (2023)
61. Kirillov, A., Mintun, E., Ravi, N., Mao, H., Rolland, C., Gustafson, L., et al.: Segment anything (2023)
62. Yan, Y., Huang, B.: Estimation of building height using a single street view image via deep neural networks. ISPRS J. Photogramm. Remote Sens. **192**, 83–98 (2022). https://doi.org/10.1016/j.isprsjprs.2022.08.006
63. Farella, E.M., Rigon, S., Remondino, F., Stan, A., Ioannidis, G., Münster, S., et al.: Methods, data and tools for facilitating a 3D cultural heritage space. Int. Arch. Photogramm. Remote Sens. Spatial Inf. Sci., **XLVIII-2/W4-2024**, 197–204 (2024). https://doi.org/10.5194/isprs-archives-XLVIII-2-W4-2024-197-2024
64. Guo, Y.-C., Liu, Y.-T., Shao, R., Laforte, C., Voleti, V., Luo, G., et al.: Threestudio: a unified framework for 3D content generation (2023)

65. Pfarr-Harfst, M.: Typical workflows, documentation approaches and principles of 3D digital reconstruction of cultural heritage. In: Münster, S., Pfarr-Harfst, M., Kuroczyński, P., Ioannides, M. (eds.) 3D Research Challenges in Cultural Heritage II. LNCS, vol. 10025, pp. 32–46. Springer, Cham (2016). https://doi.org/10.1007/978-3-319-47647-6_2
66. Mirzadeh, I., Alizadeh, K., Shahrokhi, H., Tuzel, O., Bengio, S., Farajtabar, M.: GSM-symbolic: understanding the limitations of mathematical reasoning in large language models. arXiv, 2410.05229 (2024)
67. Xu, F., Uszkoreit, H., Du, Y., Fan, W., Zhao, D., Zhu, J.: Explainable AI: a brief survey on history, research areas, approaches and challenges. In: Tang, J., Kan, M.Y., Zhao, D., Li, S., Zan, H. (eds.) NLPCC 2019, Part II. LNCS, vol. 11839, pp. 563–574. Springer, Cham (2019). https://doi.org/10.1007/978-3-030-32236-6_51

Representation and Preservation of Traditional Crafting Techniques

Xenophon Zabulis[1](✉), Partarakis Nikolaos[1], Vasiliki Manikaki[1], David Arnaud[2], Noël Crescenzo[2], Arnaud Dubois[3], Ines Moreno[4], Juan José Ortega Gras[5], José Francisco Puche Forte[5], Valentina Bartalesi[6], Nicolò Pratelli[6], Carlo Meghini[6], Sotiris Manitsaris[7], and Gavriela Senteri[7]

[1] Institute of Computer Science, Foundation for Research and Technology Hellas, Heraklion, Greece
{zabulis,partarak,vmanikaki}@ics.forth.gr
[2] Centre Européen de Recherches et de Formation Aux Arts Verriers, Vannes-le-Châtel, France
{david.arnaud,noel.crescenzo}@cerfav.com
[3] French National Center for Scientific Research, Paris, France
arnaud.dubois@mnhn.fr
[4] Conservatoire National des Arts et Métiers, Paris, France
ines.moreno@lecnam.net
[5] Technology Centre of Furniture and Wood of the Region of Murcia, CETEM, Yecla, Spain
{jj.ortega,jf.puche}@cetem.es
[6] Institute of Information Science and Technologies, National Research Council of Italy, Pisa, Italy
{valentina.bartalesi,nicolo.pratelli,carlo.meghini}@isti.cnr.it
[7] Centre for Robotics, MINES ParisTech, PSL Université, Paris, France
{sotiris.manitsaris,gavriela.senteri}@minesparis.psl.eu

Abstract. This paper presents a comprehensive methodology for documenting and analysing traditional craft practices through ethnographic observation, enhanced by digital technologies. The process begins with thorough preparation, including workshop setup, glossary development, and action forecasting. Data collection integrates the digitisation of tools and workspaces alongside multimodal recordings—audio, video, and motion capture—to document practitioner actions in detail. The recorded data is then systematically parsed to identify objects and actions, with expert practitioner input guiding segmentation and interpretation. These actions are subsequently modelled through simulations, linking them to archetypal behaviours for analysis and visualisation. This framework establishes a structured, semantically rich knowledge base for craft actions, offering new insights into the mechanics and meaning of traditional practices.

Keywords: traditional crafts · digital ethnography · semantic representation · craft simulation

1 Introduction

The photographic and 3D documentation of CH objects has been studied for over three decades, leading to the proliferation and employment of a breadth of approaches to capture and share their geometry and appearance [5,6,9,28]. The digitisation of CH activities focused on recording kinetic or vocal activities in dance and theatre [11,12,16,27]. Human motion has been investigated more particularly in crafts [29] [?]. Video dictionaries of crafting gestures were proposed in [33].

Despite advancements in digital ethnography, current methodologies often lack a structured framework for interpreting and simulating the causal physical dynamics of craft practices. This paper introduces a novel approach that integrates semantic representations and physics-based simulations to bridge this gap.

Ethnography [1,15,21] is used in craft documentation, with examples in carpentry [31], glasswork [2], and textile manufacturing [19]. Digital recordings were proposed for craft practice documentation in [34] and are used systematically to acquire verbal and visual content in the workshop [31].

The CIDOC-CRM [7] is a widely-adopted standard for the representation of CH. It is used in [35] to represent crafting objects, actors, and processes and endowed by an online platform in [25] to streamline the authoring of craft representations. The CRM has been used to represent contextual knowledge about crafts in the form of narratives [24]. This work employs and extends the platform above.

To enhance the understanding of craft processes, we integrate finite element method (FEM) simulations, approximating real-world material behaviours under crafting actions. This simulation layer enables both verification of observed processes and extrapolation to different material and tool configurations. Crafting processes are analysed into actions transforming materials in [37] and classified into subtractive, formative, interlocking, and additive. These classes are accompanied by "simulation models" that can be refined with object geometries and material parameters to instantiate specific craft actions. These models are employed in this work.

2 Ethnography

A digitally-aided ethnographic session is proposed. Following [38], a preparation workshop is held between ethnographers and practitioners on the crafting actions to study. The practitioner is then recorded in the workshop. In a follow-up session, the practitioner and ethnographer review the recording.

2.1 Preparation

In the workshop, a glossary of terms that describe the actions to be recorded is prepared, with each entry semantically annotated, illustrated, and exemplified as in [36]. The definitions are multilingual and include idioms and emic names. An illustrated storyboard and diagram are developed for the actions to be recorded. Diagrams decompose a scene into actions and help identify steps in the crafting process. The storyboard is forecasts the process, illustrating input materials, intermediate products, and outcomes, as well as directing requirements visually transcribed (e.g., viewing angles).

During or after the workshop, the LCT method of inquiry is employed in one or more interviews with each practitioner. Focus is placed on training paths, knowledge transmission, and professional stages. This analysis enables us to understand the overlaps between their technical and social dimensions. The professional life of the practitioner is represented as a chronological narrative using the method and online system in [24]. Life Course Theory (LCT) [13] is a sociological framework for analysing career trajectories and professional biographies within a life course context. It conceptualises an individual's life as a sequence of social events and roles [8,23], shaped by historical, social, and personal factors [10].

2.2 Recording

In the recording, the practitioner(s) demonstrate the process tasks described in the storyboard. If discrepancies arise, the ethnographer and practitioner make necessary adjustments to ensure an accurate representation of the crafting workflow.

We first digitise the 3D geometry and appearance of the tools, workpieces, and workspaces. Workpieces are digitised multiple times at the intermediate stages of their processing and their final state. The digitisation of objects and workspaces follows [35]. Objects are annotated with material properties describing their composition and mechanical behaviour. They are measured from the 3D model and weighted, to estimate their momentum when needed. Material properties relevant to object appearance are encoded using Bidirectional Scattering Distribution Functions [3]. The 3D models are converted from surface to volumetric meshes of hexahedra [26]. Mechanical, thermal, and appearance material properties are retrieved from authoritative academic databases. Workspace illumination is captured using a 360° camera or downloaded from online libraries.

Action recordings use audio, video, and motion capture (MoCap). Key photographs are extracted from video or individually acquired to serve in visual summaries and illustrated instructions. Conventional [4] and ego-centric audio/video [14] documents the action. Ego-centric video from worn cameras shows the practitioner's hands and approximates the practitioner's viewpoint. While ego-centric video approximates the practitioner's viewpoint, it is unstable for viewing purposes. Static overviews are more practical in constrained workspaces, such as a workbench. We record from two viewpoints, a static and an egocentric, to cover the scene. When inertial MoCap is impractical, markerless human motion estimation from video provides reliable results in unobstructed scenes [30]. During the recording, the ethnographer keeps written and audio notes. If possible, the practitioner explains the task at hand. The camera is operated automatically or by a third person.

2.3 Representation

The data and knowledge collected in this session are entered into the knowledge base using the conventional online interface. The acquired digital assets are encoded as media objects in the knowledge base, as detailed in [35,38]. The encoding of digital assets, metadata, and semantic annotations follows the CIDOC-CRM.

Formalising physical entities enables us to streamline their representation as organised knowledge. We automate the formation of basic knowledge elements representing objects, locations, persons, and motions. Spatiotemporal and technical metadata are automatically created for the asset. These knowledge elements are managed by registering the ethnographic recording event in the knowledge base and linking the recordings to it. All digital assets are viewed online and available to the ethnographer and practitioner.

3 Analysis

The analysis of ethnographies targets the analytic identification and representation of crafting actions and their elements. Similarly to [34], we analyse the recording as soon as possible with the practitioner. We use event logs to temporally parse the recording and review each with the practitioner to document it. We obtain an action-centric representation of the crafting process, where actions are semantically and physically represented as events.

3.1 Parsing

Parsing involves identifying meaningful components in a scene, such as objects, actions, spatial relationships, and contextual cues. Practitioner input is integrated at each stage of data interpretation, particularly during segmentation, ensuring that the contextual meaning behind each action is accurately captured and reflected in the simulation.

First, we identify the physical objects in the scene. Next, we segment the activity into actions based on the principle that 'action is the unit activity identified by the practitioner' [17]. This segmentation is performed with the practitioner. Complex activities are hierarchically analysed. The practitioner is invited to describe the gesture and intentionality of each action through relations between them. During parsing, the ethnographer's notes help determine action boundaries and are cross-referenced with video segments to refine segmentation and interpretation.

This segmentation triggers the partitioning of the recorded data channels based on action timestamps. The outcome is a set of time stamps delimiting actions in the video. The resultant segments are converted to individual media objects and associated with the specific segment. An action event is instantiated in the knowledge base and these media objects are linked to it, as recordings of this event. The knowledge elements representing the objects involved in the action are also linked to this event.

The practitioner and ethnographer review the recording to identify the physical entities involved in craft practice. This self-confrontation interview method [32] prompts detailed discussion because participants relive the activity while watching and thinking about themselves working. The imagery reimmerses the practitioners in their activity, confronting them with the recorded gesture [20], and triggering comments on intentions, goals, and decision-making processes. We collect verbal descriptions of the recorded technical acts. The practitioner's comments are compiled into text and associated with the time segment. As causes of each crafting action, we identify the physical entities that bring the changes induced by that action. These entities can be events, constraints, or potentials. Typically, causing entities are forces (incl. gravity), heat, moisture, or chemical agents. Per action, the physical entities involved are identified and semantically annotated.

3.2 Recognition

Objects are represented through 3D models and material properties, retrieved from the knowledge base. Unlike previous methods that only named objects, we now semantically structure them within an ontology, linking their roles (e.g., tool, material, product) to actions and physical transformations, as in [38]. Also, following [35] and [37], actions are classified as additive, joining, subtractive, or forming. In this work, we identify and model the causes of actions as forces, motions, friction, heat, moisture, ventilation, chemical agents, or others. While these capture physical interactions, certain tacit knowledge aspects of craftsmanship (e.g., sensory judgment, corrective intuition) may require additional qualitative analysis. Some causal entities, such as micro-scale friction or muscle forces, may require indirect estimation or approximation through tool motion instead of direct measurement.

In our online implementation, online forms facilitate defining causing entities when representing actions. In Fig. 1, shown is the 3D model of an object (left), its entry form as a tool (middle), and the definition of an action event where it is used (right).

Fig. 1. Representation of a 3D model (left) as a tool (middle) and documentation of its use in a crafting action (right).

In the example, the movement of a tool and gravity are registered as causing entities, showing the combination of heterogeneous physical entities; i.e., forces and tool motion. Although identifying causing entities is straightforward, their quantification can be challenging. In the example, muscle forces exerted by the practitioner are difficult to measure. Instead, modelling tool motion as the causing entity serves is simpler because it can be measured more easily from the video. These causal relationships were validated by analysing video recordings alongside motion capture data, allowing for the identification of key physical variables such as applied force, friction coefficients, and material deformation.

Intuitively, the action description template models the physical entities that govern the action. Representing physical entities as knowledge elements associates the functional and semantic action counterparts. The result is a structured, ontology-based instantiation of an action schema. Completing the online template for this schema triggers the instantiation of the corresponding knowledge elements. In the ontology, causing entities are represented as events that affect the object (physical entities) in the simulated scene.

3.3 Representation

In [37], actions are mapped to "archetypa" FEM-based simulations abstracting elementary crafting actions. The schema translates these archetypes into executable simulations with specific objects, shapes, gestures, and materials. These elements are enriched with attributes that represent physical material properties. Technically, the simulation is dynamically prescribed in a simulation file for the Simulia Abaqus 6.23-1 FEM implementation.

The toolbox in [39] is used to realistically render the simulated actions, using light-transport models and Mitsuba 3 as the rendering engine. The simulation results are interfaced with the toolbox to render crafting action results across conventional and challenging materials, such as metals and glass. The toolbox hides the programming complexity and interfaces with the simulator, approximating the original action. We found two useful ways to visualise the simulation result. The first is to employ a 360° image map to immerse in a specific workspace. The second is abstracting the scene to its essential elements to reduce cognitive load and enhance comprehension. The virtual camera pose is arbitrarily defined and can be used to create first-person or panoramic views.

The simulation approximates recorded actions and supports variations in materials and tool configurations for broader analysis. However, complex material transformations, such as phase changes or fine-scale plastic deformation, may require additional material models or empirical validation for high accuracy. An online platform documents these knowledge entities as objects, events, and relations between them. The semantic annotation of the knowledge elements provides linguistic references and thesauric organisation of the represented knowledge.

4 Experiments

4.1 Plaster Throwing

This experiment explores plaster-throwing for creating moulds. The objective is to analyse the practitioner's movements, encode the crafting actions semantically, and simulate material behaviour in a virtual environment for analytical and training purposes.

Initially, we digitised in 3D the plaster-throwing tools used in the process and represented them in the knowledge base. Then we recorded the process using an egocentric camera, capturing the practitioner's perspective and hand movements, and a scene overview, providing a stable external reference for workspace interactions. Using the recordings we reconstructed the practitioner's motion as a 3D avatar. Using event logs from the video data, we semi-automatically segmented the crafting process into elementary plaster-throwing actions. The extracted movements were semantically structured, linking each action to a functional role. The recording was registered as an event in the knowledge base and the digital assets from the session were linked to it and made available online through Web browser access for review. This includes the 3D models and the synchronised audio-visual recordings. In Fig. 2, shown is the registration of the recording event in the knowledge base (left), the list of recorded actions (middle), and the collection of video segments (right).

Fig. 2. Event registration (left), action collection (middle), and recordings preview (right).

Following the workshop findings, our study focused on tools and body posture during the actions. The motion-extracted 3D avatar effectively captured the hand and body movements aligning with real-world observations. Including 3D-scanned tools enhanced the accuracy of tool-material interactions, enabling a more faithful simulation of practitioner techniques. Deviations are observed in fine-scale, due to the complexity of modelling material behaviour. The simulation provided a meaningful approximation but would benefit from more advanced material calibration and experimental validation through high-speed imaging. An interactive physics-based application of the plaster-throwing provides an introduction to the craft and workshop. The tools models and the motion data guide the virtual throwing dynamics, allowing for real-time exploration of tool-material interactions. Key components of the application include (a) 3D-integrated plaster throwing tools, (b) gravity, inertia, and real-world dynamics constraints, and (c) real-time interaction to practice with throwing speed and tool angles. In Fig. 3, shown are two views from the overview and worn camera (left column, top and bottom, respectively). The rest of the columns show the reconstruction of body posture (top) and tool manipulation (bottom) in simulation.

Fig. 3. Ethnographic videos of plaster throwing (left) and virtual reenactment (middle, right).

A formative comparison analysis was conducted between the real-world plaster-throwing process and the simulated environment, focusing on the accuracy of material deposition compared to real-world footage, the effect of the practitioner's wrist angle on the final body formation, and differences between recorded and simulated tool-material interactions. This identified discrepancies and areas for refinement. The use case demonstrates the decomposition of the throwing process into action sequences and causal interactions, a computational model linking motion to material behaviour, supporting analysis and learning, and an interactive training tool, where users can adjust physical parameters and explore different throwing strategies.

4.2 Carving

We investigated the suitability of the approach in comparing mechanical and semantic similarities of carving in wood and marble crafts as similar subtractive processes. The commonalities analysed are tool use and carving mechanics. We demonstrate that while materials differ in mechanical properties, the consistency of fundamental principles of carving is reflected in the obtained representation.

The experiment involved two practitioners, one working with wood and the other with marble. The carving strokes were documented through egocentric and overview video recordings, capturing hand movements, tool-material interactions, and material removal dynamics. These recordings were processed to digitise gestures and workpieces, enabling a structured analysis of technique commonalities and differences.

The collected digital assets were integrated into the knowledge base, where both processes were classified as members of the same class of subtractive processes. The ontology semantically linked the carving tools, tool-material interactions, and action sequences, allowing for comparative reasoning between the two craft traditions. Additionally, 3D scans of the workpieces before and after carving were recorded, along with the digitised tools, making the dataset accessible for review and analysis.

The digital assets were registered into the knowledge base. The ontology links tools to their edge geometries, and interaction forces within the context of the action, capturing how the tool's shape affords material removal. The ontology stores the digitised workpieces before and after carving, recording material transformation across strokes. This enables the comparison of tool force and angle variations. The semantic structuring of mechanics enables the reuse of mechanical principles across materials. In Fig. 4, this process is illustrated by showing the ethnographic record of the action (left), its FEM simulation (middle), and its photorealistic rendering (right).

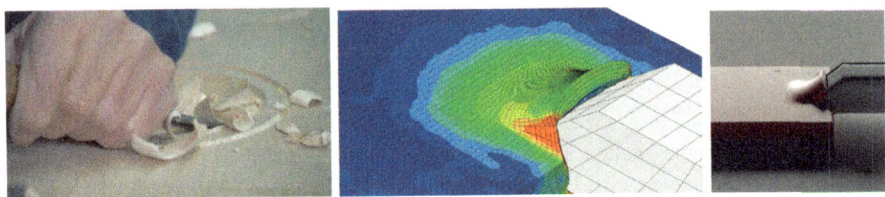

Fig. 4. Observation (left), simulation (middle), and rendering (right) of a woodcarving action.

In the simulation experiments, we compared the properties of tools and actions, accounting for (a) tool shape and composition, (b) stroke duration, momentum, and incidence angle, and (c) material damage. The simulations highlight that, despite the differences in how materials react to carving, the fundamental structure of the action sequence remains consistent. This type of study supports generalisation to other materials with similar properties and the prediction of the results of new tools or different strokes. In Fig. 5, shown is the retrieval of knowledge entities on tools, recordings, and simulations for the carving technique in marble (top) and wood (bottom).

5 Discussion

With this work, we validate a foundation for supporting ethnographic and craft documentation, through structured semantic modelling and physics-based simulation. The association of semantic representation, recording, and physics-based simulation provides a framework for systematically expanding knowledge, potentially even from existing recordings. The structured, semantically enriched representations of craft actions, contribute to the long-term preservation of intangible cultural heritage, offering future researchers a detailed framework for understanding and analysing traditional practices.

Our outlook is a refinable, semantically annotated vocabulary of simulators. This would contribute to formal schemas for crafting processes that allow for knowledge transfer and structured comparisons of techniques. By bridging real and virtual actions, we can create physically consistent training datasets, for

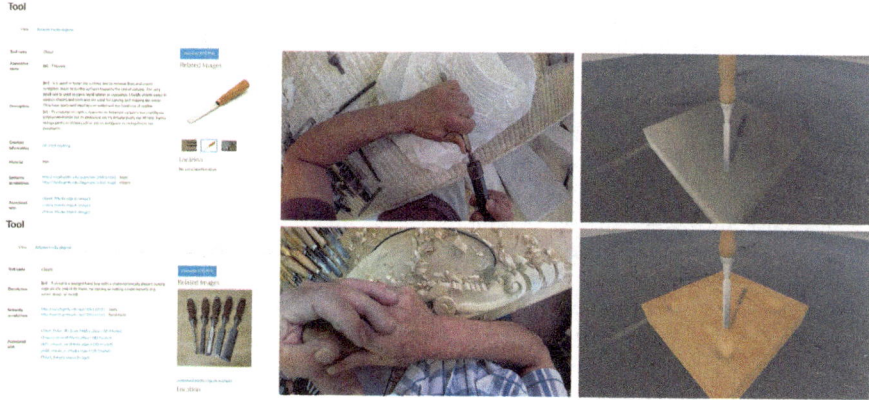

Fig. 5. Comparative study of carving actions on marble (top) and wood (bottom).

machine-learning within real-world constraints. By modifying material properties, tool geometries, and causal entities, we can predict artefact appearance and generate realistic renderings for several Given recent progress in Neural Radiance Fields [22] and Gaussian Splatting [18] in the generation of dynamic content the possibility of reproducing and predicting interactions between tools and materials is envisaged.

Funding Information. This work was implemented under the project Craeft, which received funding from the European Union's Horizon Europe research and innovation program under grant agreement No. 101094349.

References

1. Atkinson, P.: The Ethnographic Imagination: Textual Constructions of Reality. Routledge, London (1990). https://doi.org/10.4324/9781315852065
2. Atkinson, P.: Blowing hot: the ethnography of craft and the craft of ethnography. Qual. Inq. **19**(5), 397–404 (2013). https://doi.org/10.1177/1077800413479567
3. Bartell, F., Dereniak, E., Wolfe, W.: The theory and measurement of bidirectional reflectance distribution function and bidirectional transmittance distribution function. In: Radiation Scattering in Optical Systems. SPIE (1981). https://doi.org/10.1117/12.959611
4. Bates, C. (ed.): Video Methods: Social Science Research in Motion. Routledge, New York (2015). https://doi.org/10.4324/9781315832739
5. Corns, A.: 3D-icons: guidelines and case studies (2013). https://doi.org/10.5281/zenodo.1311796
6. Daneshmand, M., et al.: 3D scanning: a comprehensive survey (2018). https://doi.org/10.48550/ARXIV.1801.08863
7. Doerr, M.: The CIDOC conceptual reference module: an ontological approach to semantic interoperability of metadata. AI Mag. **24**(3), 75–92 (2003). https://doi.org/10.1609/aimag.v24i3.1720

8. Elder, G.: The life course as developmental theory. Child Dev. **69**(1), 1 (1998). https://doi.org/10.2307/1132065
9. Commission, E.: Study on quality in 3D digitisation of tangible cultural heritage. Publications Office of the European Union (2022). https://doi.org/10.2759/581678
10. Garfinkel, H.: Studies in Ethnomethodology. Prentice-Hall, Englewood Cliffs (1967)
11. Georgiev, G., Hristov, G., Zahariev, P., Kinaneva, D.: Innovative conservation of intangible cultural heritage through motion capture and 3D scanning methods. In: International Conference on Communications, Information, Electronic and Energy Systems, pp. 1–5. IEEE (2024). https://doi.org/10.1109/ciees62939.2024.10811258
12. Hou, Y., Kenderdine, S., Picca, D., Egloff, M., Adamou, A.: Digitizing intangible cultural heritage embodied: state of the art. J. Comput. Cult. Heritage **15**(3), 1–20 (2022). https://doi.org/10.1145/3494837
13. Hutchison, E.: Life Course Theory, pp. 1–10. Springer (2017). https://doi.org/10.1007/978-3-319-32132-5_13-2
14. Jeong, E., Yu, J.: Ego-centric recording framework for Korean traditional crafts motion. In: Ioannides, M., et al. (eds.) EuroMed 2018. LNCS, vol. 11197, pp. 118–125. Springer, Cham (2018). https://doi.org/10.1007/978-3-030-01765-1_14
15. Jones, J., Watt, S. (eds.): Ethnography in Social Science Practice. Routledge, London (2010)
16. Joshi, M., Chakrabarty, S.: An extensive review of computational dance automation techniques and applications. Proc. Roy. Soc. A **477**(2251), 20210071 (2021). https://doi.org/10.1098/rspa.2021.0071
17. Keller, C., Keller, J.: Cognition and Tool Use: The Blacksmith at Work. Cambridge University Press, Cambridge (1996)
18. Kerbl, B., Kopanas, G., Leimkuehler, T., Drettakis, G.: 3D gaussian splatting for real-time radiance field rendering. Trans. Graph. **42**(4), 1–14 (2023). https://doi.org/10.1145/3592433
19. Konstantinou, K., Anagnostopoulos, A.: Interweaving contemporary art and "traditional" crafts in ethnographic research. Art/Res. Int.: Transdisc. J. **4**(1), 58–82 (2019). https://doi.org/10.18432/ari29420
20. Bellu, S., Blanc, B.: How to characterize professional gestures to operate tacit know-how transfer? Electron. J. Knowl. Manage. **10**(2), 142–153 (2012)
21. McGranahan, C.: What is ethnography? Teaching ethnographic sensibilities without fieldwork. Journal **4** (2015). https://doi.org/10.22582/ta.v4i1.421
22. Mildenhall, B., Srinivasan, P., Tancik, M., Barron, J., Ramamoorthi, R., Ng, R.: NeRF: representing scenes as neural radiance fields for view synthesis. Commun. ACM **65**(1), 99–106 (2021). https://doi.org/10.1145/3503250
23. Moen, P., Sweet, S.: From 'work-family' to 'flexible careers': a life course reframing. Commun. Work Fam. **7**(2), 209–226 (2004). https://doi.org/10.1080/1366880042000245489
24. Partarakis, N., et al.: Representation of socio-historical context to support the authoring and presentation of multimodal narratives: the Mingei online platform. J. Comput. Cult. Herit. **15**(1), 1–26 (2021). https://doi.org/10.1145/3465556
25. Partarakis, N., et al.: A web-based platform for traditional craft documentation. Multimodal Technol. Interact. **6**(5), 37 (2022). https://doi.org/10.3390/mti6050037
26. Pietroni, N., et al.: Hex-mesh generation and processing: a survey. ACM Trans. Graph. **42**(2), 1–44 (2022). https://doi.org/10.1145/3554920
27. Sporleder, C.: Natural language processing for cultural heritage domains. Lang. Linguist. Compass **4**(9), 750–768 (2010). https://doi.org/10.1111/j.1749-818x.2010.00230.x

28. Storeide, M., George, S., Sole, A., Hardeberg, J.: Standardization of digitized heritage: a review of implementations of 3D in cultural heritage. Herit. Sci. **11**(1) (2023). https://doi.org/10.1186/s40494-023-01079-z
29. Strand, E.A., Lindgren, S., Larsson, C.: Capturing our cultural intangible textile heritage, MoCap and craft technology. In: Ioannides, M., et al. (eds.) EuroMed 2016. LNCS, vol. 10059, pp. 10–15. Springer, Cham (2016). https://doi.org/10.1007/978-3-319-48974-2_2
30. Sun, Y., Liu, W., Bao, Q., Fu, Y., Mei, T., Black, M.: Putting people in their place: monocular regression of 3D people in depth. In: IEEE/CVF Conference on Computer Vision and Pattern Recognition, pp. 13233–13242. IEEE (2022). https://doi.org/10.1109/cvpr52688.2022.01289
31. Vannini, P., Vannini, A.: Artisanal ethnography: notes on the making of ethnographic craft. Qual. Inq. **26**(7), 865–874 (2019). https://doi.org/10.1177/1077800419863456
32. Cranach, M.: Goal-Directed Action. Academic Press, London (1982)
33. Wang, K.-A., Liao, Y.-C., Chu, W.-W., Chiang, J.Y.-W., Chen, Y.-F., Chan, P.-C.: Digitization and value-add application of bamboo weaving artifacts. In: Xing, C., Crestani, F., Rauber, A. (eds.) ICADL 2011. LNCS, vol. 7008, pp. 16–25. Springer, Heidelberg (2011). https://doi.org/10.1007/978-3-642-24826-9_6
34. Wood, N.: Transmitting craft knowledge: designing interactive media to support tacit skills learning. Ph.D. thesis, Sheffield Hallam University, Sheffield, UK (2006)
35. Zabulis, X., et al.: Digitisation of traditional craft processes. J. Comput. Cult. Herit. **15**(3), 1–24 (2022). https://doi.org/10.1145/3494675
36. Zabulis, X., et al.: Multimodal dictionaries for traditional craft education. Multimodal Technol. Interact. **8**(7), 63 (2024). https://doi.org/10.3390/mti8070063
37. Zabulis, X., et al.: Modelling and simulation of traditional craft actions. Appl. Sci. **14**(17), 7750 (2024). https://doi.org/10.3390/app14177750
38. Zabulis, X., et al.: A representation protocol for traditional crafts. Heritage **5**(2), 716–741 (2022). https://doi.org/10.3390/heritage5020040
39. Zabulis, X., et al.: Simulation and visualisation of traditional craft actions. Heritage **7**(12), 7083–7114 (2024). https://doi.org/10.3390/heritage7120328

3D and Annotations: The Memory Viewer as a Hub in the Semantic Web for Cultural Heritage

Øyvind Eide[1,2]

[1] Department for Digital Humanities, University of Cologne, Cologne, Germany
oeide@uni-koeln.de
[2] Center for Data and Simulation Science, University of Cologne, Cologne, Germany

Abstract. Annotations were traditionally a way to add comments and extensions to manuscripts, which developed into the footnote as a formalised system for second layers in texts. With the development for 3D modelling as a means to digitise physical objects, as well as to make born digital models, annotation was also extended to such objects. Based on this wider view on annotations, a truly integrated semantic web for cultural heritage can be developed, based on contextual modelling of memory twins. This paper describes this development and discuss where it might go from here, seeing annotations as mechanisms for the integration of complex objects across media borders.

Keywords: 3D Models · Annotation · Modelling · Semantic Web · Memory Twins · Memory Viewer

1 The Arrigo Showcase: A Semantic Web for Cultural Heritage

The EPOCH network of excellence was a significant collection of cultural heritage institutions in Europe, with around 100 partners involved.[1] Its goals included the integrating of cultural heritage resources and the improvement of production pipelines for digital resources. Towards the end of the project, a need for better integrating 3D resources to textual sources was identified, and an ontological approach was tried out for the concrete connection between resources.

The results of this experiment was published in [6]. As a case study, the burial monument of Arrigo VII was chosen, as many of the building blocks already existed for this artefact. The original 3D model of the Arrigo VII monument included textual annotation, but within a closed system—even the texts were bitmaps. The new system opened up the 3D model, converting it into the COLLADA file format.[2] The texts were retrieved from the original Word files

---

[1] http://epoch-net.org.
[2] https://en.wikipedia.org/wiki/COLLADA.

and converted to TEI-XML,[3] which was then converted to HTML in the web system. Between the text and the 3D models, a CIDOC-CRM[4] compatible model was created and linearised in RDF. It was visualised through the MAD Semantic Web Viewer developed in the EPOCH network of excellence and worked as a connector between annotations on the 3D models and specific textual descriptions, for instance, offering information about the head of the statue.

The system as a whole was an example of a small experimental multi-modal semantic web system for cultural heritage. As shown in Fig. 1, the intermodal connections between the 3D model annotations, the CIDOC-CRM knowledge base, and the TEI documents were hypothetically complemented with further intermodal connections between the 3D model and other spatial objects, between the knowledge base and other ontological objects, and between the TEI-XML document and other online texts.

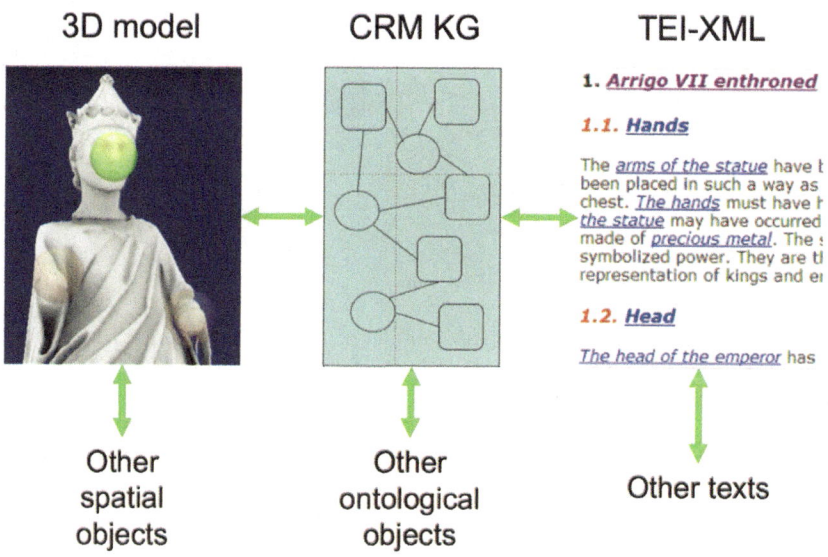

Fig. 1. A semantic web for cultural heriatage.

2 Oseberg

In 1903, a ninth century viking ship burial was found close to the farm Oseberg in Norway. The site was excavated in 1904–5, based on state of the art archaeological documentation methods, including professional drawers making figures of the objects and their context. One example can be found in Fig. 2. The advantages over photo documentation in certain use cases, for instance, if the purpose

---

[3] https://www.tei-c.org.
[4] https://cidoc-crm.org.

is to understand the context and layout of the burial, is clearly visible if one compare to Fig. 3, cf. [4].

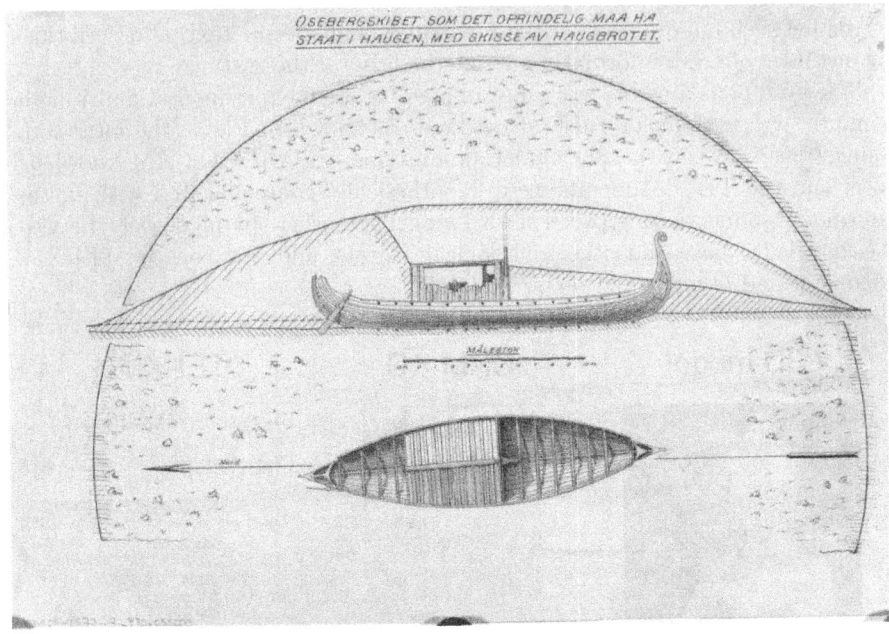

Fig. 2. A drawing representing a spatial model of the Oseberg Viking Ship. Museum of Cultural History, University of Oslo, Saksnr 05_8823_2_835_C55000.

Whether these drawings are twins of their motive will not be addressed in this paper, but a number of digital twins have later been created, of the viking ship as well as of specific artefacts found during the excavation. One example is a laser scan of the ship which also documents central aspects of the construction of it. This 3D model was among the sources for a stress model used to assess the future stability of the ship, as part of discussions about possibly moving the ship to a new location in the early 2000s [7]. These two models represent different aspects of the ship and are developed for different purposes [2], cf. [3]. As digital twins, they both have the nature of "twinness," but it is stronger connected to some aspects than to other for both twins. Seen as models, they focus on different aspects in the modelling process, affording different uses of the models.

If we look at the available documentation system for the Oseberg ship, a significant amount of material has been made available by The Museums for Cultural Heritage at the University of Oslo,[5] which is the institution responsible for the collections. This includes images, 3D models, textual object descriptions,

---

[5] http://khm.uio.no/.

Fig. 3. Photography from the excavation of the Oseberg ship in 1904. Museum of Cultural History, University of Oslo/Olaf Væring.

and also text introducing the ship and its pre-historical and historical context. These stories are memory stories, but not twins in the meaning intended here.[6]

3 Lehre in 3D

Annotations were traditionally a way to add comments and extensions to manuscripts, which developed into footnotes as a formalised system for a second level of sequential communication in texts [5].[7] It was also used to add information to images and grew into text encoding as part of digitisation of paper based resources—mainly texts, but later also documents as spatial objects, also with images being annotated.

Another tradition is the use of objects in teaching. This has always been fundamental to practical learning. Learning how it build a musical instrument or a boat will always involve studying existing instruments and boats as well as working intensively with the materials used, such as wood. This tradition was taken up in the performative turn in theatre studies in the twentieth century, as represented by Carl Niesen at the Theatre Collection at the University of Cologne (TWS) [9].

---

[6] On the concepts of 'Memory Twin,' see [8].

[7] It does not always stop at two levels, footnotes on footnotes are possible, as are parallel systems of footnotes with different numbering systems.

Teaching with objects in the context of museums and other collections is by nature difficult, given the focus on the preservation of historical objects in such collections. Indeed, at TWS, using the more and more fragile objects for teaching became increasing difficult. A solution to this conundrum was to create digital replica of the objects to be used in teaching, adding the key information communicated in teaching to specific points of the 3D replica of the object as annotations, and chaining these annotations together to stories. This was the basis for the project "Lehre in 3D",[8] in which the Kompakkt tool was born as a 3D annotation tool and story telling device.

4 Kompakkt

With the development of 3D modelling as a means to digitise physical objects, as well as to create born digital models, annotation was also extended beyond 2 dimensional documents.[9] The Kompakkt annotation tool[10] does not only enable annotations of different digital objects including 3D models, but also the annotations themselves are extended multimodal objects, and they can be linked together for storytelling. In the Artest project,[11] a digital lab was being developed as a Wordpress system where storytelling in text and image includes 3D annotated models using embedded Kompakkt windows as part of the narrative structure.

This integrates the three main use cases from Kompakkt. From the beginning in 2017 it was planned and implemented as a tool for *extended artefact based learning*. It is also a *research project* in which a deeper understanding of what annotations are and can be, and how they connect to other systems for information integration and contextualisation, is established. It is part of the extension of annotations beyond *an-notation*, that is, notational systems in a strict symbolic sense, seeing annotation more as meaningful links between complex multimodal objects. And third, it is an *infrastructure* for the storage and publication of digital 3D objects, enabling annotation based storytelling. This has a significant potential for the democratisation of the establishment of metadata and paradata connected to objects which are often contested and have a complex provenience.

It is crucial to the success of Kompakkt, in past and well as presently and for the future, that these three aspects are playing together to enable a multi-perspective development of research software as not only software for research, but also for research based teaching and project work. Software development is an integrated part of research and teaching, integrating theory and praxis in a cycle of modelling.

---

[8] http://tinyurl.com/UoC3D.
[9] Kompakkt can also be used to annotate 2D documents.
[10] http://www.kompakkt.de/.
[11] https://www.artest-project.eu/.

5 Cultural Heritage Storytelling and the Memory Viewer

This takes us back to the semantic web for cultural heritage mentioned in the beginning of the paper. A knowledge graph represents aspects of cultural heritage, including objects, parts of objects, destructive and non-destructive analysis of objects such as sample taking and analysis and multispectral light analysis, respectively. Each node in these knowledge graphs which represents information about a part of an object, whether visible or not, can in principle be connected to a point, line, or area of the 3D object through a formal annotation representing an object which belongs to a class in an ontology. This will, again in principle, integrate any aspect of relevance of a 3D object, being it a replica or a born digital object, to a semantic web for cultural heritage.

Such a system is currently under development by the Kompakkt consortium,[12] continuing the focus on Kompakkt as a research and education project, in addition to its usefulness as a cultural heritage documentation platform. A proof of concept will be developed as a materialisation of the concept of 3D models as memory twins: the Kompakkt tool for annotation and storytelling will be developed into a Memory Viewer connecting textual, visual, non-visual analysis, and in principle information objects of any other mediality to a formal ontology based backbone, pushing the integration of storytelling with objects towards a formal representation of relationships in cultural heritage. Still, even if the system includes a formal representation, the tradition of text based annotation is still kept, enabling the inclusion of information which cannot be formalised into a formal ontology.

6 Conclusion

This article discuss some aspects of the development of a multimodal semantic web for cultural heritage. It is shown that the development and publication of replica in the form of digital twins is not enough. It is also necessary to model the objects as meaningful entities embedded in deep cultural meaning, developing a contextualised set of memory twins. By integrating knowledge graphs based on well defined formal ontologies, textual information encoded in TEI-XML, and other media types, the 3D objects can be accessed in what we here call a memory viewer. This opens up for a change in the representation and expression of knowledge which is comparable to what happened in spatial humanities when GIS systems were extended with Deep Maps [1].

This enables a deep meaningful integration of different aspects of cultural heritage. For 3D objects, it supports the development from object via modelling and annotation to learning in a wide sense. The Memory Viewer develops the computer based work with 3D models from 3D viewing to tools for 3D storytelling, in which annotations function as complex meaningful multimodal links, enabling a deeper integration between 3D annotation points and human knowledge through formal knowledge graphs.

---

[12] https://kompakkt.de/about.

References

1. Bodenhamer, D.J.: Deep Maps and Spatial Narratives. The Spatial Humanities Series. Indiana University Press, Bloomington (2015)
2. Ciula, A., Eide, Ø., Marras, C., Sahle, P.: Modelling Between Digital and Humanities: Thinking in Practice. Open Book Publishers (2023)
3. Ciula, A., Marras, C.: Circling around texts and language: towards "pragmatic modelling". Digit. Humanit. Q. **10**(3) (2016)
4. Eide, Ø.: Visual representations as models of the past. Informacionnye tehnologii v gumanitarnyh naukah. Sbornik dokladov Mezhdunarodnoj nauchno-prakticheskoj konferencii. Krasnojarsk, 18–22 sentjabrja 2017, pp: 15–26. SFU, Krasnojarsk (2018)
5. Grafton, A.: The Footnote: A Curious History. Faber and Faber, London (1997)
6. Havemann, S., Settgast, V., Berndt, R., Eide, Ø., Fellner, D.W.: The Arrigo showcase reloaded - towards a sustainable link between 3D and semantics. ACM J. Comput. Cult. Heritage **2**(1) (2009)
7. Hørte, T., Sund, O., Ronold, K., Rove, H.: Strength analysis of the Oseberg ship. Det Norske Veritas, Oslo (2006)
8. Ioannides, M., Karittevli, E., Panayiotou, P., Baker, D.: Integrating paradata, metadata, and data for an effective memory twin in the field of digital cultural heritage. In: Ioannides, M., Baker, D., Agapiou, A., Siegkas, P. (eds.) 3D Research Challenges in Cultural Heritage V: Paradata, Metadata and Data in Digitisation, pp. 24–35. Springer, Cham (2025)
9. Probst, N.: Objekte, die die Welt bedeuten: Carl Niessen und der Denkraum der Theaterwissenschaft. Vol. 4. Szene & Horizont. Theaterwissenschaftliche Studien. J.B. Metzler, Stuttgart (2023)

The eArchiving Initiative and Long-Term Digital Preservation (LTDP) of 3D Models

Janet Anderson[1,2(✉)], Stephen Mackey[3], and Sven Schlarb[4]

[1] Highbury R&D, County Cork, Ireland
janet.anderson@highbury.ie
[2] ELTE, Institute of History, Department of Digital Humanities, Budapest, Hungary
[3] Penwern Limited, Brighton, United Kingdom
[4] Austrian Institute of Technology, Giefinggasse 4, 1210 Vienna, Austria

Abstract. The eArchiving Initiative is a European Commission programme that provides specificity and guidance for implementing conformant and interoperable Open Archival Information Systems (OAIS, ISO 14721) via core package specifications, software, a reference architecture, training and a Conformance Seal. Content Information Type Specifications (CITS) further extend this core to support data types such as relational databases, geospatial data, and record management systems in domains such as eHealth, Engineering and Cultural Heritage.

In the last two years, the Initiative has produced a new specification for 3D Product Model data that supports the domain of engineering product models (such as Computer Aided Design) and builds on the existing standards LOTAR (Long Term Archiving and Retrieval, EN/NAS 9300) and STEP (Standard for the Exchange of Product Model Data, ISO 10303). This CITS was recently published by the DILCIS Board (https://dilcis.eu/).

eArchiving is now working with domain experts, including Marinos Ioannides (Cyprus University of Technology) and Franco Niccolucci (Prisma) to develop a new CITS for 3D models in Cultural Heritage.

This paper will introduce the eArchiving Initiative and its core and 3D specifications. The roles of paradata, metadata, technical metadata and authentication of models are highlighted for the Cultural Heritage CITS and there is a framework for archiving complete product designs, construction projects or heritage memory twins via collections of archival packages (AIPs) linked via the new International Council on Archives (ICA) Records in Contexts ontology (RiC).

Archiving the Lambousa boat 3D model using the E-ARK 3D CITS and the eArchiving earkweb tool is demonstrated. (250 words).

Keywords: eArchiving · Digital Preservation · DCH 3D models

1 Introduction

1.1 Rationale

The eArchiving Initiative is a procurement of the European Commission[1], funded under DIGITAL[2], and it builds upon the eArchiving Building Block[3] and the original E-ARK Project[4]. The Initiative is run by the E-ARK Consortium[5], led by the Group Leader AIT Austrian Institute of Technology GmbH, with Group Members Highbury R&D Ltd (Ireland), DLM Forum MTÜ (Estonia), Gabinete Umbus SL (Spain), and KEEP Solutions LDA (Portugal). Six subcontractors participate via AIT, and fifteen organisations join directly via the DLM Forum[6]. The primary objective of this initiative is to promote sustainable eArchiving across Europe and provide access to E-ARK's open-source standards, specifications, tools, validation procedures, training resources, and outreach services. Also, as part of this overall remit, eArchiving has a key task to collaborate with experts from within the DCH domain to develop specifications and guidance for the LTDP of 3D models in that domain. For this purpose, the Italian company Prisma, participating via DLM Forum, occupies a crucial role in the E-ARK Consortium: in the first instance Prisma's Franco Niccolucci has a key role to liaise with the 4CH project (https://www.4ch-project.eu/, now ended) for which he was the Technical Director.

This paper is the write-up of the Euromed 24 presentation "eArchiving and Long-Term Preservation of 3D models: My 3D model is wonderful now, but will it last?" and it springs directly from the work of the eArchiving 3D network of experts. Prisma continues to provide expertise and guidance in the 3D domain, and the material in this section relies heavily on their comprehensive and detailed report into 3D preservation by Amico and Felicetti [1], hereafter referred to as the Prisma report.

The Prisma report stresses the need for **Digital continuity** within the DCH community: the ability to use and keep using digital information over time, despite the technological obsolescence that ravages the domain with its frequently shifting file formats and software offerings. In order not to be caught out by these technological sinking sands, **it is crucial to create a Data Management Plan [2] at the beginning of any project/undertaking, not as an afterthought at the end**. Here the **FAIR** principles [3] come to our aid, because we need our digital objects to be Findable, Accessible, Interoperable and Reusable for the short, medium and longer terms, and for this, we

---

[1] https://digital-strategy.ec.europa.eu/en/news/earchiving-enters-new-phase-under-digital-europe-programme.

[2] Contract number LC-01905904.

[3] The Connecting Europe Facility (CEF) eArchiving Building Block was operated via two grants: E-ARK4ALL, Grant Agreement number: LC-00921441 CEF-TC-2018–15 eArchiving (2018–2019), and E-ARK3, Grant Agreement No. LC-01390244 CEF-TC-2019–3 E-ARK3, (2019–2021).

[4] The E-ARK project (2014–2017) was funded by the European Commission under the ICT Policy Support Programme (PSP) within Call 7 of the Competitiveness and Innovation Framework Programme, Grant number 620998.

[5] https://digital-strategy.ec.europa.eu/en/news/earchiving-enters-new-phase-under-digital-europe-programme.

[6] https://www.e-ark-foundation.eu/consortium-members/.

need to record metadata and paradata together with our data, which is much better done as we go along, and not left as a massive and overwhelming task at the end. But you may say, surely, we can just put all our data in a repository at the end of the process, and they will sort out everything? Unfortunately, it does not work quite like that, as you need to do a lot more than just passively store your data.

First, you need to choose a repository that can cope with open protocols and standards; persistent identifiers; and complex metadata, and also actively preserves the data – e.g. migrating the data when file formats become obsolescent. Certified **Trustworthy repositories** fulfil these requirements, e.g. the Digital Repository of Ireland (https://www.ria.ie/research-programmes/digital-repository-of-ireland/), as do eArchiving-conformant digital archives.

The eArchiving Initiative mission is to provide **non-hosted** archival services (specifications, S/W tools, reference architecture, etc.) to **preserve** digital material based on current best practices. The services address the three main endeavours of an archive: acquiring, preserving and enabling re-use of information (FAIR). Archival processes at a pan-European level are harmonised to promote interoperability across borders and institutions, supported by guidelines and recommended practices that cater for a range of data from different types of source including geospatial data, databases, 3D data etc. How the eArchiving specifications are implemented now follows.

2 eArchiving Specifications and Standards – E-ARK

The E-ARK specifications are a family of specifications that provide a common set of requirements for packaging digital information. Based on common, international standards for transmitting, describing and preserving digital data, the specifications have been produced to help data creators, software developers and digital archives tackle the challenge of short, medium and long-term data management and reuse.

The foundation for these specifications is the Reference Model for an Open Archival Information System, (OAIS[7]) which has Information Packages at its core. Namely: Submission Information Packages (SIPs), Archival Information Packages (AIPs) and Dissemination Information Packages (DIPs). Thus, the eArchiving specifications are structured as shown in Fig. 1 with the common specification as a foundation and package, metadata and content information specifications providing extensions to it.

2.1 Organisational Support

Governance for the specifications is provided by the Digital Information LifeCycle Interoperability Standards Board (DILCIS Board[8]). The DILCIS Board was created to enhance and maintain the draft specifications developed in the E-ARK project which are available in GitHub[9] and on the DILCIS Board website[10].

---

[7] http://www.oais.info/
[8] http://dilcis.eu/.
[9] https://github.com/dilcisboard.
[10] https://dilcis.eu/specifications.

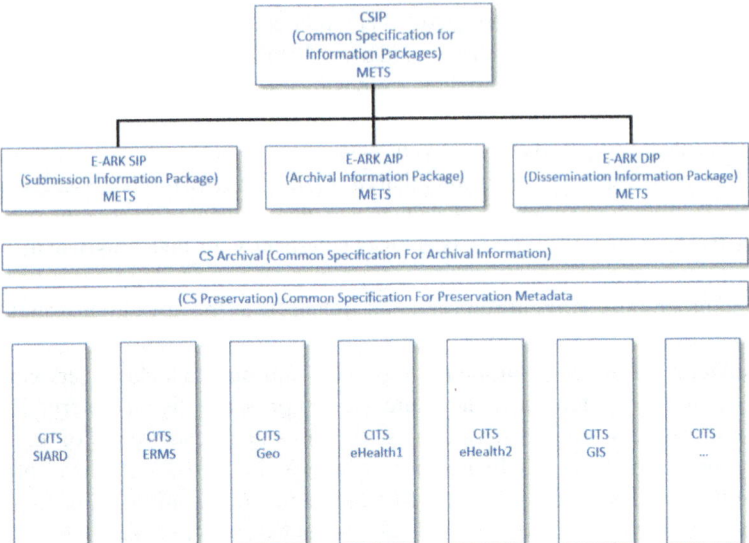

Fig. 1. E-ARK Specification Dependency Hierarchy

2.2 The Common Specification for Information Packages (CSIP)

The three main purposes of the CSIP are to:

- Establish a common understanding of the requirements that need to be met in order to achieve interoperability of Information Packages.
- Establish a common base for the development of more specific Information Package definitions and tools within the digital preservation community.
- Propose the details of an XML-based implementation of the requirements using to the largest possible extent standards which are widely used in international digital preservation.

Ultimately the goal of the Common Specification is to reach a level of interoperability between all Information Packages so that tools implementing the specification can be adopted by institutions without the need for further modifications or adaptations.

2.3 Principles for Interoperable Information Packages

At the heart of any standardisation activity is a clear understanding of the needs and aims which are to be addressed and as such each E-ARK specification document presents a series of high-level principles to guide the technical details that follow. Most of the principles are driven by the aim of interoperability, specifically that Information Packages shall be easy to exchange, identify, validate and (re)use with a wide variety of software tools and systems. Practical technical interoperability is only possible when a certain set of technologies have been agreed upon and implemented. Any technology will become outdated sooner or later and previously agreed-upon approaches will have to be updated to accommodate new, better and more efficient ones. Because of this, the developers of this Common Specification have reused wherever possible existing powerful, standardised and well-established best practices in order to achieve long-term sustainability of the specifications.

> **CSIP Principle 1.1**
>
> It MUST be possible to include any data or metadata in an Information Package regardless of its type or format. This is one of the most crucial principles of the CSIP. To be truly "common", technical implementations of the CSIP MUST NOT introduce limitations or restrictions which are only applicable to certain data or metadata types. If an Information Package implementation fails to meet this principle, it is not possible to use it across different sectors and tools, thereby limiting practical interoperability.

2.4 Metadata

The primary consideration for metadata within the specifications is interoperability and specifically the capability for Information Packages to be prepared, transferred and received, regardless of the institutions or tools involved.

Tasks can include:

- Uniquely identifying an Information Package and its components,
- Validating an Information Package and its contents,
- Establishing the authenticity of the Information Package,
- Accessing the contents of an Information Package.

In technical terms, the CSIP proposes metadata needed by tools or users to:

- navigate data and metadata components within the package (i.e. packaging metadata);
- validate that no component has been damaged during transfer or preservation (i.e. fixity information);
- understand the processes used when creating and managing the package (i.e. provenance and preservation metadata); and
- understand how the data within the package can be accessed (i.e. representation information).

Prescription of specific descriptive metadata and technical metadata is outside the scope of the CSIP and as such, it does not provide for complete semantic interoperability between different systems. The Content Information Type Specifications, however, are intended to achieve interoperability at a more detailed level.

The core metadata requirements of an E-ARK package are described using the Metadata Encoding & Transmission Standard[11] (METS), the main requirement being for METS files in an Information Package to follow the official METS Schema[12] and

---

[11] https://www.loc.gov/standards/mets/.
[12] http://www.loc.gov/standards/mets/mets-schemadocs.html).

the CSIP extension schema[13]. As new versions of METS Schema become available the DILCIS Board will evaluate these and if necessary, update the CSIP and other specifications.

In addition to the use of METS CSIP recommends the inclusion of PREMIS metadata (PREservation Metadata Implementation Strategies[14]) a standard for recording preservation and technical metadata about digital objects. The use of PREMIS is further described in the "E-ARK Common Specification for Preservation Metadata using PREMIS" (CS PREMIS[15]).

2.5 Package Structure

The CSIP describes a logical model for Information Packages for which the preferred implementation is a strict physical (folder) structure that precisely follows this logical structure as shown in Fig. 2. While the specification does not prohibit alternative implementations of the logical model, the practice is not recommended. The main reason for this implementation recommendation is that a fixed and documented folder structure makes the package layout clear to both human users and automated tools so that many archival tasks (e.g. file format risk analysis), can be executed directly on the appropriate portion of the package structure as opposed to first processing potentially large amounts of metadata to discover file locations. This allows for more efficient processing, which is valuable in the case of large collections and bulk operations.

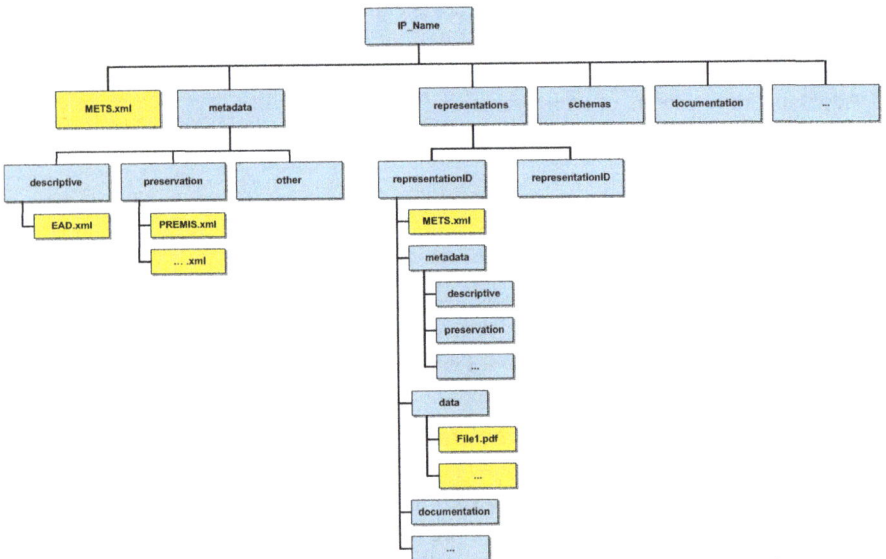

Fig. 2. CSIP Package Structure

---

[13] https://DILCIS.eu/XML/METS/CSIPExtensionMETS.
[14] http://www.loc.gov/standards/premis/.
[15] https://citspremis.dilcis.eu/specification/.

A fixed folder structure provides efficiency and scalability. Many archiving and digital preservation solutions however, do not explicitly support folder structures but use other means for structuring and storing data and metadata. The purpose of the specification is to facilitate and support Information Package interoperability so when solutions do not support the implementation of Archival Information Package (AIP) structures, it is still possible to implement the physical structure for say SIPs and DIPs, allowing interoperability between tools, easy transfer of IPs to new repository systems and the establishment of consolidated archives.

2.6 Content Information Type Specifications

As interoperability standards it must be possible to use the E-ARK specifications regardless of the type and format of the content users need to handle. Each individual content type, domain and use case may have specific characteristics which need to be taken into account for purposes of validation, preservation and curation and E-ARK introduces the concept of Content Information Type Specifications (CITS) to facilitate in-depth control over requirements and recommendations for specific content types and use cases. A Content Information Type Specification can include detailed requirements as to how data, metadata, and documentation for specific content types (for example relational databases, geospatial data or patient medical records) should be handled within an Information Package.

As such, the scope of a CITS can include any of the following:

- Relevant use cases,
- General principles (in addition to those of the CSIP),
- Package structure extensions,
- Contextual documentation requirements,
- Minimum data and data structure requirements,
- Related standards conformance,
- Minimum and additional metadata requirements, profiles and schemas.

3 3D Content Information Type Specifications

3.1 3D Product Model CITS (3DPM)

The first in a family of specifications for 3D data, the CITS for 3D Product models such as Computer Aided Design (CAD) was published by the DILCIS board in December 2024. The specification is designed to be used for the transfer of 3D Product Data to archives as well as for records exchange between different 3D Product Model systems and archive consolidation (such as could be seen through mergers and acquisitions). The objectives for a 3D Product Model archive can be seen as business related - such as keeping knowledge for the future but also legal – such as providing proof via technical documentation for actions in law.

The 3DPM specification builds on LOTAR (Long Term Archiving of digital technical product information), published as EN/NAS 9300 which in turn references OAIS and STEP (Standard for exchange of product model data, ISO 10303). The CITS 3DPM in particular introduces the concept of 'Authentication', the processes of determining the authenticity of a data set through Verification (the quality of data within tolerances), Validation (the consistency of data between representations) and Digital Signature (the attestation by an individual of the content's veracity on submission to the archive). CITS 3DPM recommends the use of PREMIS for recording events related to Authentication and the inclusion of both rules data and authentication output reports in specified documentation locations. The CITS 3DPM is available at the DILCIS Board website[16] and on Github[17].

3.2 3D Cultural Heritage CITS (3DHM)

The planned second 3D content specification is to be for 3D Cultural Heritage models, or CITS 3DHM. Development work on the specification is being assisted by the working group of domain experts as described above, with the specification at an early draft stage aiming to be available for public review later in 2025.

The scope of the CITS is for 3D models for cultural heritage in any format, created by any capture or creation method, for example:

- Point Cloud models (for example by: photogrammetry, laser scanning, structured light),
- CAD based models (including building information models, BIM and heritage building information models, HBIM),
- Volumetric models (computer tomography),
- GIS models, and
- Procedural models (reconstructions).

The use of 3D in Heritage is being driven by needs of conservation, academic research, public access demonstrated by projects such as the European Commission 'TwinIt'[18] which states "Making cultural heritage available for future generations to enjoy and be inspired by is a major public policy goal in the EU. 3D technologies offer unprecedented opportunities to advance this objective, widening access to culture, supporting digital preservation and fostering the reuse of Europe's cultural assets."

Academic work such as by Niccolucci and in the Parthenos report[19] "Digital 3D Objects in Arts and Humanities: challenges of creation, interoperability and preservation" [4] aim to continue work to establish best practice and standards for the creation and long-term preservation of 3D models started by the seminal "London Charter" in 2006[20].

The use cases for the creation of 3D Heritage Models then are wide ranging, but the use cases for the archiving of 3D Heritage Models remains fairly straightforward while serving a wide community:

---

[16] https://dilcis.eu/content-types/cits-3d-product-model-data.
[17] https://github.com/DILCISBoard/CITS-3DPM.
[18] https://pro.europeana.eu/page/twin-it-3d-for-europe-S-culture.
[19] https://www.parthenos-project.eu/about-the-project-2.
[20] https://londoncharter.org/.

1. To enable long-term archiving of 3D Heritage Model data whilst preserving the usability, authenticity and accessibility of the data over time,
2. To enable inter-organisational exchange of 3D Heritage Model data whilst facilitating the understanding of the provenance, context and means to render,
3. To enable acceptance of 3D Heritage Model data submission packages (SIPs) at a central repository.

A particular feature of the new CITS is the recognition of the need for preserving contextual documentation regarding the creation or transformations of models, so called Paradata and so makes a recommendation for inclusion of such documentation or metadata in specified directory locations. It also adopts the optional accommodation for authentication metadata and documentation from the sister 3DPM specification.

3.3 Descriptive Metadata and Paradata

According to the CSIP: "packages should contain general Descriptive Metadata about the digitised object and may contain specific Descriptive Metadata about the individual representations". According to the Common Specification for Archival Description "Descriptive metadata can be expressed according to many current standards (e.g., EAD[21], MARC[22], MODS[23], Dublin Core[24]) or a locally produced XML schema".

For 3D content types, users however may find that the archival metadata standards above do not provide sufficient elements to adequately describe 3D models and their creation. This is particularly true for structured Paradata. This issue, however, can be overcome through the use, in addition to the use of standards above of specialised cultural heritage metadata schemas (e.g. CARARE[25], LIDO[26]) or creation of locally produced, well-formed schema as described in the CS Archival Information. The use of standards is encouraged, and greater extensibility can be achieved through use of for example the CIDOC-CRM[27] (Conceptual Reference Model) ontology, its extensions or the International Council on Archive's (ICA's) new standard, Records in Context (RiC)[28]. Serialisation methods for metadata are not prescribed in the CSIP but use of XML for the encoding of METS and PREMIS is mandatory, and hence encoding of additional, descriptive metadata in XML is also preferable and wherever possible linked data ontologies such as CIDOC-CRM or RiC should be encoded in XML when used in an E-ARK package.

3.4 Digital and Memory Twins

The paper by Niccolucci *et al.* entitled: "The Heritage Digital Twin: a bicycle made for two. The integration of digital methodologies into cultural heritage research" [5]

---

[21] https://www.loc.gov/ead/index.html.
[22] https://www.loc.gov/marc/.
[23] https://www.loc.gov/standards/mods/.
[24] https://www.dublincore.org/.
[25] https://www.carare.eu/en/services/carare-aggregation-services/carare-metadata-schema/.
[26] https://cidoc.mini.icom.museum/working-groups/lido/lido-overview/about-lido/what-is-lido/.
[27] https://cidoc-crm.org/.
[28] https://www.ica.org/resource/records-in-contexts-conceptual-model/.

describes the concept of a digital twin, "the digital replica of a real-world object. It contains all the necessary information and is able to simulate – in a digital environment – the characteristics and the behaviour of its real counterpart". This is further extended to that of a so called 'memory Twin' by Ioannides, Karittevli, Panayiotou and Baker in the paper "Integrating Paradata, Metadata and Data for an Effective memory Twin in the Field of Cultural Heritage" [6] which explains that the memory twin "also considers factors such as contextuality, temporality and experience of archaeological sites and cultures. The main intention behind this technique is not only to replicate the material characteristics of cultural artefacts but also consider their use and historical settings".

Such extensive information sets, which may contain both local and linked external information, are challenging to accommodate in a simple or even subdivided Information Package architecture as described in the E-ARK AIP specification. There is a need then for extended Information Package sets, which may be arranged as hierarchies or as networked topologies where the relationships must be described within both 'master' IPs and within the archival packages themselves. The use of linked data ontologies such as CIDOC-CRM or RiC may hold the answer to this conundrum which is a possibility which will have to be investigated further for this and other content types (e.g. product structures in CITS 3DPM). Existing ontologies are not intended specifically for this purpose, but commonality in standards bases plus the possibility to add extensions means that these and other ontologies can co-exist and can potentially be used for encoding complex 3D metadata and the relationships between data objects in complex structures.

4 3D Model Using the eArchiving Reference Implementation

The eArchiving Reference Implementation "*earkweb*"[29] is a web-based application designed to support digital archiving processes and is used to demonstrate the use of E-ARK specifications.[30]

One of the key features of *earkweb* is its ability to handle the ingest and validation of Submission Information Packages (SIPs), ensuring that digital records conform to E-ARK specifications. It also provides metadata management and uses the widely recognized standards such as METS, EAD, and PREMIS to maintain archival information in line with E-ARK recommendations. Designed with conformance to the specifications in mind, it adheres to the E-ARK Common Specification for Information Packages (CSIP), making it compatible with other archival systems which implement the E-ARK specifications.

A practical application of *earkweb* is demonstrated through the digital preservation of the Lambousa fishing trawler, a historic vessel part of Cyprus' maritime heritage. It was built in 1955, was used in the Mediterranean Sea for several decades, and today represents an object of cultural heritage interest and the region's fishing traditions.[31]

To ensure the long-term preservation of this cultural artifact, a comprehensive 3D model of the Lambousa was created using advanced digitization techniques. This model serves not only as a digital replica but also as a rich source of historical, environmental,

---

[29] https://earkweb.sydarkivera.se.
[30] https://dilcis.eu/specifications.
[31] https://erachair-dch.eu/portfolio/fishing-boat-lambousa-in-progress/.

and societal information. Creating the 3D model is the first step in preserving a memory for future generations. As technology, software, and specifications continue to evolve, it is crucial to ensure the model remains accessible. This may require updates to archival information, such as migrating the model to a different format to maintain compatibility.

Utilizing *earkweb*, the 3D model and its associated metadata were packaged into an E-ARK Submission Information Package (SIP).[32] Two distinct representations of the Lambousa fishing trawler 3D model have been created to ensure flexibility in access and long-term usability.

The first representation is stored in the GLB (GL Transmission Format Binary) format which is a widely used binary file format optimized for efficient storage and transmission of 3D models.

The second representation is stored using the MTL (Material Template Library) format, which is used alongside the OBJ (Object) file format, a widely accepted standard for describing 3D models. While the OBJ file defines the structural geometry of the model—such as vertices, faces, and texture coordinates—the MTL file provides detailed material properties that dictate how the object should appear when rendered. This includes settings for colour, texture mapping, transparency, and reflectivity, ensuring that the 3D model is accurately visualized with realistic material properties.

By storing the 3D model in both GLB and MTL formats, this approach ensures compatibility with various 3D rendering and visualization platforms. Additionally, maintaining these two representations separately simplifies future migrations, as preservation actions can be applied selectively to the format best suited for generating a new representation. Using PREMIS events, all preservation actions are documented, capturing not only the reasons behind each action but also the tools used to execute them. Archiving the information packages in the E-ARK AIP format[33] ensures that the complete history of the package is retained, providing future custodians with a comprehensive record of past preservation measures.

The Lambousa Fishing Boat E-ARK Information Package is accessible through the instance of the eArchiving Reference Implementation "earkweb"[34], maintained by the eArchiving Initiative.[35] Users can inspect the package structure and metadata, and if assistance is needed, the eArchiving Initiative's support desk is available to provide help or onboarding guidance.[36]

5 Summary

This paper has set out the practical steps needed to actually preserve 3D model data, and as such is the first of its kind we believe. Key points to take away are for creators of 3D models to: familiarise themselves with the effects of technological obsolescence and plan for digital continuity by setting up a Data Management Plan (DMP); understand the

---

[32] https://earksip.dilcis.eu/.
[33] https://dilcis.eu/specifications/aip.
[34] https://earkweb.sydarkivera.se/earkweb/access/urn:uuid:ccea586d-c5b5-4651-b378-4319224bcb35/.
[35] https://digital-strategy.ec.europa.eu/en/activities/earchiving.
[36] https://digital-strategy.ec.europa.eu/en/activities/support-provision-and-onboarding-services.

need to adhere to the FAIR principles and create the metadata to achieve this; and choose a Trustworthy Repository or create an eArchiving certified digital archive. The need to capture and record the relevant metadata (descriptive, preservation and technical) and paradata from the outset of any work is paramount and should be included in the DMP. There are many sources of information that can help here – we have drawn on the Prisma report, but there are others from the 4CH project as well as the recent volume on Paradata [see 6]. The eArchiving Initiative does not provide any hosted services, but can help with every other aspect of digital archiving: by providing Open Source specifications; S/W tools; training; guidelines; certification; support; use cases; success stories; etc. As well as providing a practical and user-friendly implementation of the OAIS standard for Information Packages, eArchiving also produces specialist specifications for different data types, CITS, and the 3D CITS family has been outlined here, together with a detailed examination of the basic Information Package – the Common Specification for Information Packages. Lastly, the CITS 3D PM for Product Models was put into practice to preserve two different representations of the Lambousa boat 3D model using the earkweb Reference Implementation, and the files produced can be accessed and explored (reuse). Next steps will include looking at using earkweb for other 3D models and also looking at opportunities for using enterprise-scale software as shown in the use case of the European Union's Publication Office[37].

Acknowledgments. This study was funded by the European Commission no. LC-01905904.

References

1. Amico, N., Felicetti, A.: 3D data long-term preservation in cultural heritage, Published on 17 December 2024 by the eArchiving Initiative. https://digital-strategy.ec.europa.eu/en/library/report-long-term-preservation-3d-data-cultural-heritage. Accessed 17 Feb 2025
2. Verburg, M., Braukmann, R., Mahabier, W.: Making qualitative data reusable - a short guide-book for researchers and data stewards working with qualitative data. Zenodo (2023). https://doi.org/10.5281/zenodo.8160880.
3. Wilkinson, M.D., et al.: The FAIR guiding principles for scientific data management and stewardship. Sci. Data **3**(1), 160018 (2016). https://doi.org/10.1038/sdata.2016.18
4. Laroche, F., et al.: Digital 3D objects in art and humanities: challenges of creation, interoperability and preservation. White Paper, Parthenos Project (2017). https://www.academia.edu/120516742/Digital_3D_Objects_in_Art_and_Humanities_challenges_of_creation_interoperability_and_preservation_White_paper. Accessed 17 Feb 2025
5. Niccolucci, F., et al.: The heritage digital twin: a bicycle made for two. The integration of digital methodologies into cultural heritage research. Open Research Europe (2023). https://doi.org/10.12688/openreseurope.15496.1
6. Ioannides, M., Karittevli, E., Panayiotou, P., Baker, D.: Integrating paradata, metadata, and data for an effective memory twin in the field of digital cultural heritage. In: Ioannides, M., Baker, D., Agapiou, A., Siegkas, P. (eds.) 3D Research Challenges in Cultural Heritage V. Lecture Notes in Computer Science, vol. 15190, pp. 24–35. Springer, Cham (2025). https://doi.org/10.1007/978-3-031-78590-0_3

---

[37] https://digital-strategy.ec.europa.eu/en/library/nine-years-earchiving-publications-office-eu-reason-celebrate.

Introducing Scientific Reference Model and Critical Digital Model – Methodological Approach in Hypothetical Source-Based 3D Reconstruction of Built Cultural Heritage

Piotr Kuroczyński[1]([✉]) [iD] and Fabrizio Ivan Apollonio[2] [iD]

[1] Hochschule Mainz – University of Applied Sciences, Holzstraße 36, 55116 Mainz, Germany
pzaborowski@ogc.org
[2] Alma Mater Studiorum - University of Bologna, V.le Risorgimento 2, 40136 Bologna, Italy

Abstract. In 3D digital documentation for Digital Cultural Heritage (DCH), integrating Scientific Reference Models (SRM) and Critical Digital Models (CDM) presents a structured method for managing metadata, paradata, and geometrical data—key components for ensuring high-quality, transparent, and reusable 3D heritage assets. These models directly tackle significant challenges in the DCH community: establishing rigorous documentation standards, promoting scholarly transparency, and aligning with international charters and EU quality standards for 3D digitization. SRM sets up a foundational framework that emphasizes web-based publication, metadata and paradata, and technical reliability based on standardized data exchange formats. It stresses interoperability and FAIR principles (Findable, Accessible, Interoperable, Reusable), enabling the creation of models that serve as foundational references for ongoing digital heritage research and reusability. CDM explores the interpretive aspect of documentary sources, tracking hypothetical and conjectural decisions while representing uncertainty levels that inform digital heritage models. By integrating documentation and classification standards, CDM guarantees methodological transparency and scholarly credibility in 3D reconstructions. Together, SRM and CDM form a cohesive methodology that improves structure, interoperability, reliability, and interpretive clarity in digital heritage documentation. This methodological framework, rooted in research and educational practices, provides a viable scientific standard for sustainable digital heritage preservation.

Keywords: Digital Cultural Heritage · 3D Reconstruction · Hypothetical Modeling · Scientific Reference Model · Critical Digital Model · Open Science

1 Introduction

1.1 State-of-the-Art in Virtual Reconstruction

In the realm of 3D virtual reconstruction, historical artifacts and unrealized architectural projects stand out as unique case studies. These projects, conceived but never built, offer intriguing insights and specific challenges, often documented only through technical drawings or texts. Recent advances in computing have introduced new theoretical issues in virtual reconstruction, particularly in interpreting metadata and construction methods, reflected in 3D digital datasets.

Since the advent of computer-aided 3D visualization and virtual reconstruction [1], the academic community has increasingly relied on digital models to reconstruct lost or unrealized architectural heritage and archaeological remains. However, the lack of standardized methodologies has impeded scientific rigor, transparency, and sustainability in such reconstructions [2, 3]. Despite the widely recognized relevance of the London Charter [4] and Sevilla Principles [5], the findability, accessibility, interoperability, and reusability [6] of 3D models remain a major challenge.

Creating scientific 3D models, related to lost or unrealized cultural artifacts, involves subjective analysis and interpretation of evidence and documentation, requiring an interdisciplinary methodology [7]. Ensuring transparency and long-term accessibility of the information used in virtual reconstruction is crucial. The foundation of scientific 3D reconstruction lies in conceptual modeling and the cognitive process accompanying the creation of 3D models. Conceptual modeling helps to explore and communicate artefacts, considering operator subjectivity and addressing vagueness.

The source-based (hypothetical) 3D reconstruction process is based on the use, analysis and study of documentary sources - characterized by variable uncertainty - in order to define the forms of the case study, create a structured and semantically enriched 3D digital model. Decisions based on interpreted data sets guide the process, but subjectivity can compromise validity if not managed correctly. The London and Sevilla Charters provide principles for the use of computer-based visualization in cultural heritage, emphasizing intellectual integrity and reliability. Principle 4 of the London Charter highlights the need for a methodology that clarifies the relationship between research sources and visual outputs, as well as the semantic structure of the 3D model.

To address these challenges, two complementary methodological frameworks have emerged:

- **The Scientific Reference Model** (SRM) [8], which structures object-based 3D documentation, ensuring data credibility, interoperability and reusability.
- **The Critical Digital Model** (CDM) [3], which emphasizes documentation, interpretive decision-making, and uncertainty representation in hypothetical reconstructions.

1.2 History of the Scientific Reference Model (SRM)

The beginnings of the SRM can be traced to authors experience in research projects concerned with the 3D reconstruction and the visualization of architecture at the Technische Universität Darmstadt and the confrontation with the potentials and challenges of documentation and publication of the findings represented by the 3D models in the first decade of the new millennium [9].

According to the recognized lacking in transparency and accessibility of the generated research data the project *Virtual reconstructions in transnational research environments – the web portal: Palaces and Parks in former East Prussia* was started [10]. The project explores virtual reconstruction of lost architecture and interior decoration. It focuses on the reconstruction of the ruins of two Baroque palaces. Key aspects include source indexing, documentation, semantic modeling, and WebGL-based visualization.

The project also develops a Cultural Heritage Markup Language (CHML) for semantic annotation of 3D data. Beyond reconstruction, it aims to advance knowledge integration across architecture, art history, history, and IT, while establishing web-based standards for documentation and presentation of destroyed landmarks.

Based on the project findings from the former East Prussian Baroque palaces the project *Breslau New Synagogue in the Context of Three Religious Communities* [11] explores the historical significance of the 19th-century synagogue in Breslau, reflecting Jewish emancipation. It employs a semantically enriched 3D information model using Building Information Modeling (BIM) standards to digitally reconstruct the synagogue while addressing architectural and art historical questions. The project also ensures sustainable documentation of the reconstruction process through CIDOC CRM referenced Linked Data within a WissKI-based research environment. The outcome is a detailed 3D reconstruction facilitating contextual analysis.

The above-mentioned projects set up a groundwork for introduction of the SRM, addressing an applicable low threshold workflow for hypothetical 3D reconstruction of architecture. Giving practical guidelines and answers to questions, like how to document and publish the object-based research in the Web. The implementation of the SRM methodology was introduced and successfully tested in the infrastructure project *DFG 3D Viewer – Infrastructure for Digital 3D Reconstructions* [12]. The project aims to establish an infrastructure for publishing and preserving 3D models in Digital Cultural Heritage (DCH). Funded by the German Research Foundation (DFG), it extends the existing *DFG Viewer*, an open-source multimedia viewer for libraries and archives in Germany. Using METS and MODS as data exchange formats, the project integrates a web-based 3D viewer, a metadata documentation scheme, and a dataset transfer container. The beta version of the further developed *WissKI 3D Repository* is in use for documenting and preserving virtual reconstructions in academic settings.

1.3 History of the Critical Digital Model (CDM)

The definition of the CDM [3] arises from a long series of studies on the reconstructions of design hypotheses and interpretations of architectural drawings that utilize digital three-dimensional modeling techniques. This methodology was already well-established by the early nineties, to the extent that it produced various representations with excellent results, including the famous example of Cluny III Abbey presented in 1992 [13]. The progressive advancement of technologies, along with the development of interpretative and cognitive systems based on three-dimensional semantics [14], has enabled models derived from hypothetical reconstruction to be used not as ends in themselves, but as tools capable of providing self-representation and defined on a scientific methodological basis [7].

The experiments conducted, in the context of the source-based (hypothetical) reconstruction of buildings never built and/or no longer existing, allowed (a) to underline the use of a semantic construction of the digital model, not only as a means of modeling a building but as a cognitive system [15], (b) to show conceptual similarity between architectural treatises and information systems [16], (c) to propose robust methodologies capable of allowing the verification of the hypotheses formulated during the reconstruction pipeline [17], (d) to make use of classification schemes, aimed at developing a knowledge acquisition process capable of annotating and making understandable the analysis of the preliminary data and the interpretative criteria used. Validating the entire process gives the ability to visually evaluate the correct level of knowledge relating to the reconstruction process and to carry out comparative operations on the set of data and information possessed [18, 19].

2 Methodological Foundations

2.1 The Scientific Reference Model (SRM)

The SRM method provides a rigorous and standardized approach to 3D reconstruction in architectural research (Fig. 1) [8]. It can be summarized by the following topics:

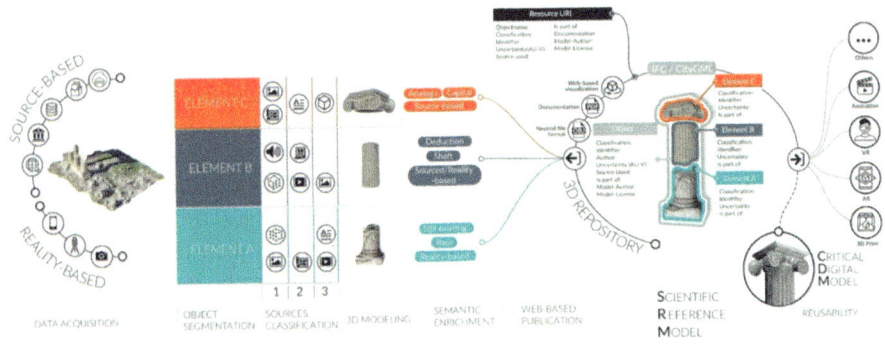

Fig. 1. Data-driven SRM and its derivatives (Kuroczyński P. and Bajena I.P., 2023, CC BY-NC-SA).

1. **Object Identification & Source Collection**. The process begins with identifying the historical object and defining its context. Primary and secondary sources, such as architectural plans, historical texts, and images, are collected and evaluated for credibility and completeness. Once gathered, the data is processed and structured into metadata and paradata categories.
2. **3D Model Development & Standardization**. A hierarchical segmentation approach is then applied to organize the model, while structural classifications are implemented using controlled vocabularies like the Getty Art & Architecture Thesaurus (AAT). The initial 3D model, or SRM prototype, is developed with a focus on information enriched geometric representation, ensuring interoperability through standardized 3D data exchange formats [2], like IFC and CityGML
3. **Semantic Annotation & Validation**. Elements are categorized based on certainty levels, from highly reliable to speculative, and are annotated with justification and traceability logs to maintain academic integrity. Semantic enrichment is ensured through metadata and paradata integration in the 3D data exchange formats.

4. **Publication & Reusability**. Finally, the completed SRM model is published in FAIR-compliant repositories, allowing for further scholarly analysis, modification, and reuse. Documentation standards are maintained to ensure long-term research integrity, enabling future studies to build upon the reconstruction with transparency and scientific rigor.

2.2 The Critical Digital Model (CDM)

While SRM ensures structured data collection, data processing, and technical rigor, CDM focuses on several key aspects: the **geometric accuracy** and **qualification of 3D models**; **traceability**, including the use of sources and documentation; the quality of historical (re-)construction; and **visualization**, which encompasses graphic outputs that communicate scientific content via 3D models. This includes diplomatic representations and the depiction of uncertainty in the historical (re-)construction of the model. CDM introduces a critical analysis, comprehensive documentation, and visualization layer, ensuring (Fig. 2).

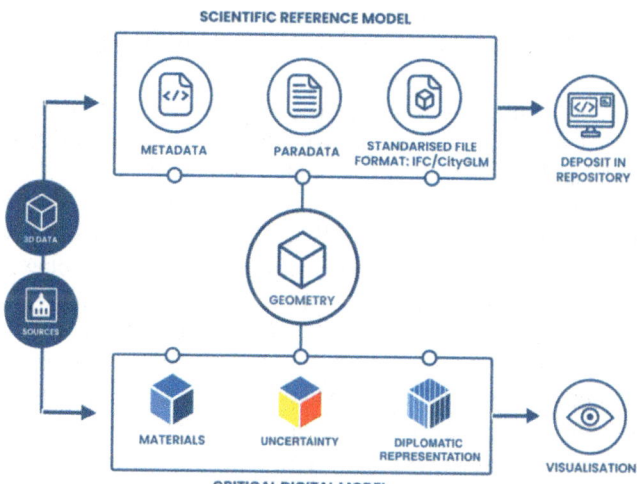

Fig. 2. CDM approach within the process chain of SRM (Apollonio F.I. and Bajena I.P., 2025, CC BY-NC-SA).

1. Transparent decision-making in hypothetical reconstructions.
2. Justification of interpretive choices, clarifying how uncertain elements were inferred.
3. Scholarly evaluation criteria, allowing assessment of historical fidelity.
4. Color-coded uncertainty visualization, aiding non-expert interpretation.

CDM builds upon SRM by addressing the epistemological and interpretive challenges inherent in source-based 3D reconstructions. Together, they ensure scientific validation and methodological transparency in digital heritage documentation in the range of a minimal (low threshold) up to a comprehensive standard for documentation, publication, and visualization.

2.3 Comparison of the Concepts

The SRM and the CDM are two different approaches used in 3D reconstructions of historical objects that no longer exist. While they share some similarities, their purposes and focus set them apart.

The SRM is designed to be a **findable referential result** of scholarly research. It serves as a structured and standardized way to document a material object that has disappeared. The emphasis is on creating an accessible 3D model that can be used as a reference in future studies. The SRM is more focused on context rather than the final (visual) product. Instead of simply providing a visually accurate reconstruction, it organizes a set of data, information, and instructions that serve as a foundation for further research and reconstructions.

Both methods document the decisions, choices, and hypotheses made throughout the reconstruction process. They include metadata, which provides descriptive information about the object's creation, physical characteristics, historical background, and provenance, as well as paradata, which records details about the digital modeling process itself. Another common feature is their approach to uncertainty. Both acknowledge that some reconstructed elements are more certain than others and use false colors to indicate different levels of certainty. They also assess the reliability of sources and analyze how uncertainty impacts the reconstruction.

Despite these similarities, the two approaches differ in key ways. SRM emphasizes the use of standardized 3D formats, ensuring that models are stored in a way that makes them widely accessible and useful for future research. It promotes the availability of models in multiple file formats, including both native files and exchange formats, something that CDM does not explicitly implement. When it comes to visualization, SRM does not enforce specific methods of rendering or texturing. Instead, it allows for material identification through graphic symbols, making it possible for further refinements to be made after the initial model is published. CDM, however, takes a different approach by analyzing the effects of different shading techniques and explaining the impact of realistic versus unrealistic visualizations in hypothetical reconstructions.

In summary, SRM is best suited for creating standardized 3D models that can serve as reliable references for further research. It ensures accessibility and documentation in structured formats. CDM, meanwhile, is more about understanding and analyzing the historical sources, providing a deeper look into the reasoning (and uncertainty) behind each decision rather than just delivering an initial referencing model. CDM focuses on the visual representation (e.g., shading) of the model, its appearance and materiality as a result of texturing and exposure, being a **visually accurate model** as final product. Both approaches contribute significantly to the field of digital heritage, preserving and reconstructing lost historical objects in meaningful ways (Table 1).

3 Implementation in Higher Education

3.1 The Theoretical Foundation and Practical Applications

The theoretical foundation and practical applications of SRM and CDM have been carried out in higher education activities, particularly within the context of research projects focused (i.e. Erasmus + project CoVHer [20]) on systematizing and rationalizing issues

Table 1. Comparative analysis between CDM and SRM.

SRM Focus	CDM Focus
Practical workflow requirements as groundwork for supporting the scholarly 3D reconstruction represented by human- and machine-readable documentation and web-based publication. Delivery of applicable guidelines, specifying the web-based documentation and publication of 3D data set. Initial referential model as final product	Source-based 3D reconstruction used for scientific dissemination and as a three-dimensional reference document for architectural heritage scholars, limiting personal contribution to the interpretation of sources, documenting the criteria followed for the reconstruction and representation of the 3D model in a clear and transmittable way. Visually enriched model as final product
SRM Potential	**CDM Potential**
Accessible and referenceable 3D models under clarified licenses. Reusable for further development and derivatives	A transmissible methodology for constructing, viewing and evaluating 3D models (critical visual representation)
SRM Foundation	**CDM Foundation**
Structured and comprehensible methodology postulating the documentation of decision-making and the web-based publication of interoperable 3D data formats (in addition to the native formats)	Visualization and communication of the procedures adopted and the different qualities of the historical reconstruction
SRM Use	**SRM Use**
Initial referential 3D model for further research and applications of architectural heritage	Visual 3D reference document for scholars of architectural heritage
SRM Visualization of Uncertainty	**CDM Visualization of Uncertainty**
Not focusing on specific methods of visualization. Documentation of the uncertainty in the properties of the building elements (e.g. IFC Property Sets)	Focusing on the visualization method. Photorealistic solution (only if reliable documental sources support it) For all the other cases: Non-PhotoRealistic/Abstract graphical styles (e.g.: Diplomatic Representation)

related to digital 3D reconstruction within the academic/scientific community, with the key objective to define shared good practices as standards [21].

The Erasmus + CoVHer project fosters international collaboration to support digital capabilities in higher education and promote innovative teaching practices. CoVHer aims to define standards and methods for 3D hypothetical reconstruction, create a repository of 3D models of cultural heritage (CH), disseminate these outcomes, develop dedicated university teaching modules, and raise awareness about scientifically reconstructing the past [22].

Both SRM and CDM have been integrated into academic curricula, particularly within the EU-funded Erasmus + CoVHer project, enhancing students' ability to engage in scholarly approved 3D modeling.

3.2 Experience at the Hochschule Mainz

Since the academic year 2023, the SRM has been successfully integrated in the course *Computer Aided Design – 3D Modeling* in first year of the first-degree architecture studies at the Hochschule Mainz.

As part of their training, students engage in 3D modeling based on the virtual reconstruction of wooden synagogues from Eastern Europe [23]. This process not only enhances their technical skills but also familiarizes them with scientific documentation and the publication of knowledge gained through the interpretation of historical sources. A key aspect of their training involves semantically enriched 3D modeling, ensuring a structured and research-oriented approach. The documentation process follows the standards set by the IDOVIR project [24], while the publication is facilitated through the DFG 3D Viewer prototype repository [12] and its further development in the customized CoVHer 3D repository [25].

In result since the introduction of the course 54 synagogues were reconstructed, documented, and published according the SRM methodological framework. The supervised student work ranges from medium to excellent quality and serves as a reference point for further research and educational work to be done. The further professional development of five selected synagogues for the web-based presentation on the DEHIO OME portal [26] can serve as current example of the findability and re-usability of the SRM.

The principles of **documentation and publication**, which form the core of the SRM, are extensively explored and analyzed in the doctoral thesis of Igor Piotr Bajena [27], developed in the framework of above-mentioned research projects at the Hochschule Mainz.

3.3 Experience at the University of Bologna

For several years, the *Architectural Drawing lab course* (second year of the five-year Architecture Degree at the University of Bologna) has served as a testing ground for defining an effective and clear methodology to be shared, afterward, at an international level [28]. From a pedagogical standpoint, the integration of this experiential methodology aims to cultivate advanced competencies in the following areas:

– Proficient application of advanced 3D modeling techniques for architectural representation.
– Sophisticated digital representation and visualization of architectural design and analysis.

Furthermore, concerning the consolidation of previously acquired skills, this didactic experience is designed to strengthen:

– The student's capacity to conduct scientifically rigorous and transparent documentary research and analysis.

- The student's ability to develop a comprehensive architectural 3D reconstruction project from inception to completion.
- Emphasis on the visualization of uncertainty and the application of interpretive modeling.
- Integration within the domain of cultural heritage research, exemplified by studies in Renaissance and Utopian architecture.
- The development of interactive educational tools predicated on CDM-based reconstructions.

These implementations highlight SRM's role in structuring data and CDM's role in scholarly analysis, making virtual reconstructions more reliable and accessible.

Over the last academic year, approximately 100 students participated, resulting in 41 models produced and uploaded to the CoVHer platform, with some of them complying the requirements and characteristics of CDM and SRM.

4 Conclusion and Future Perspectives

The Scientific Reference Models (SRM) and Critical Digital Models (CDM) represent a complementary and robust methodological framework that furnishes a solid intellectual foundation for scholarly 3D modeling within the realm of Digital Cultural Heritage. Their synergistic application offers a demonstrably scientifically sound, broadly accessible, and critically sustainable approach to the complex endeavor of hypothetical virtual reconstructions of cultural heritage assets.

The strength of this combined methodology lies in its dual focus. SRM provides the essential bedrock of scientific rigor by emphasizing standardized data formats, meticulous metadata and paradata capture, and a commitment to web-based dissemination adhering to FAIR principles. This ensures that the resulting 3D models are not merely visual representations but also constitute verifiable and reusable datasets, transparently documented and readily available for scrutiny and further research by the wider scholarly community. This foundational layer addresses the critical need for accountability and reproducibility in digital scholarship, moving beyond purely aesthetic renderings towards verifiable digital artifacts.

Complementing this, CDM addresses the inherently interpretive nature of historical reconstruction. By explicitly documenting conjectural decisions, tracking the lineage of interpretive choices, and critically representing levels of uncertainty, CDM injects a crucial layer of scholarly transparency into the modeling process. This acknowledges that hypothetical reconstructions are not definitive representations of the past but rather informed interpretations based on available evidence. By making these interpretive layers explicit and auditable, CDM fosters critical engagement with the models and encourages a nuanced understanding of the inherent limitations and possibilities of virtual reconstruction as a scholarly tool.

The convergence of SRM's emphasis on scientific validity and accessibility with CDM's focus on interpretive transparency and scholarly rigor creates a powerful synergy. This integrated approach not only enhances the credibility and reusability of 3D heritage models but also promotes a more critical and informed engagement with the past. By providing a clear framework for both the technical creation and the intellectual interpretation of virtual reconstructions, SRM and CDM pave the way for a more robust and trustworthy form of digital scholarship in cultural heritage.

However, the full potential of this methodological framework is yet to be realized, and significant future developments must be addressed to further its impact and integration within the broader cultural heritage landscape. These future challenges necessitate a focused effort on the following key areas:

Integrating SRM/CDM into international cultural heritage policies, ensuring widespread adoption of high-quality, interoperable digital heritage, by developing aligned guidelines and best practices to establish a global standard for academic 3D modeling, providing essential institutional support and ensuring the long-term value of virtual reconstructions.

Expanding technical infrastructures of metadata-rich 3D repositories for effective SRM/CDM implementation. Robust and scalable infrastructures for managing extensive metadata and paradata will enable advanced search, version control and documentation linkage capabilities, crucial for the long-term preservation, accessibility and reusability of these digital resources in the scientific field.

Improving AI-based automation for uncertainty assessment (e.g., analyzing conflicting sources) and assist in academic validation by cross-referencing models with existing data, thereby increasing the efficiency and rigor of the SRM/CDM methodology and enabling scholars to focus on higher-level analyses.

Addressing these future developments is paramount for fully harnessing the transformative potential of SRM and CDM in advancing scholarly understanding and engagement with cultural heritage through the power of scientifically sound, accessible, and critically informed 3D virtual reconstructions.

Acknowledgments. The findings of this study are based on project *DFG Viewer 3D - Infrastructure for digital 3D reconstructions*, funded by the German Research Foundation, DFG-LIS, MU 4040/5-1, and *Computer-based Visualization of Architectural Cultural Heritage*, funded by the European Commission, Erasmus+, KA2 – Capacity building in the Field of Higher Education, 2021-1-IT02-KA220-HED-000031190. The successful integration and evaluation of the SRM methodological framework in the course *Computer Aided Design – 3D Modeling* was conducted by Jan Lutteroth, to whom special thanks are due.

Disclosure of Interests. The authors have no competing interests to declare that are relevant to the content of this article.

References

1. Reilly, P.: Towards a virtual archaeology. In: Rahtz, S., Lockyear, K. (eds.), CAA90. Computer Applications and Quantitative Methods in Archaeology 1990 (BAR International Series), vol. 565, pp. 132–139. Tempus Reparatum, Oxford (1991)
2. Kuroczyński, P., Apollonio, F.I., Bajena, I.P., Cazzaro, I.: Scientific reference model -defining standards, methodology and implementation of serious 3D models in archaeology, art and architectural history. In: ISPRS International Archive on Photogrammetry Remote Sensing Spatial Information Science, XLVIII-M-2-2023, pp. 895–902 (2023)

3. Apollonio, F.I., Fallavollita, F., Foschi, R.: The critical digital model for the study of unbuilt architecture. In: Niebling, F., Münster, S., Messemer, H. (eds.) Research and Education in Urban History in the Age of Digital Libraries, CCIS 1501, pp. 3–24. Springer International Publishing, Cham (2021)
4. Denard, H.: The London Charter. For the Computer-Based Visualisation of Cultural Heritage, Version 2.1. King's College, London (2009). https://www.londoncharter.org. Accessed 5 Mar 2025
5. Apollonio, F.I., Fallavollita, F., Foschi, R.: The critical digital model and two case studies: the churches of Santa Margherita and Santo Spirito in Bologna. Nexus Netw. J. **25**(Suppl 1), 215–222 (2023). https://doi.org/10.1007/s00004-023-00707-2. Accessed 5 Mar 2025
6. Wilkinson, M.D., Dumontier, M., Aalbersberg, I.J., et al.: The FAIR guiding principles for scientific data management and stewardship. Sci. Data **3**(1), 160018 (2016)
7. Apollonio, F.I.: The three-dimensional model as a 'scientific fact': the scientific methodology in hypothetical reconstruction. Heritage **7**(10), 5413–5427 (2024)
8. Kuroczyński, P., Bajena, I.P., Cazzaro, I.: The scientific reference model - a methodological approach in the hypothetical 3D reconstruction of art and architecture. Heritage **7**(10), 5446–5461 (2024)
9. Pfarr-Harfst, M.: Virtual scientific models. Presented at the Electronic Visualisation and the Arts (EVA 2013) (2013). https://doi.org/10.14236/ewic/EVA2013.33
10. Kuroczyński, P., Hauck, O., Dworak, D.: 3D models on triple paths - new pathways for documenting and visualizing virtual reconstructions. In: Münster, S., Pfarr-Harfst, M., Kuroczyński, P., Ioannides, M. (eds.) 3D Research Challenges in Cultural Heritage II. Lecture Notes in Computer Science, vol. 10025, pp. 149–172. Springer, Cham (2016). https://doi.org/10.1007/978-3-319-47647-6_8
11. Kuroczyński, P., Bajena, I., Große, P., Jara, K., Wnęk, K.: Digital reconstruction of the new synagogue in breslau: new approaches to object-oriented research. In: Niebling, F., Münster, S., Messemer, H. (eds.) Research and Education in Urban History in the Age of Digital Libraries. UHDL 2019. Communications in Computer and Information Science, vol. 1501, pp. 25–45. Springer, Cham (2021). https://doi.org/10.1007/978-3-030-93186-5_2
12. Bajena, I.P., Kuroczyński, P.: Development of the methodology and infrastructure for digital 3D reconstruction. In: (IN)TANGIBLE HERITAGE(S): Design, Culture and Technology – Past, Present, and Future, pp. 72–83. AMPS, Canterbury (2022)
13. Koob, M.: Die dreidimensionale Rekonstruktion und Simulation von Cluny III. In: Cramer, H., Koob, M. (eds.) Cluny: Architektur als Vision, pp. 58–85. Edition Braus, Heidelberg, Germany (1993)
14. Stefani, C., De Luca, L., Véron, P., Florenzano, M.: Modeling building historical evolutions. In: Proceedings of Focus K3D Conference on Semantic 3D Media and Content. INRIA, Sophia Antipolis (2010)
15. Stefani, C.: A web platform for the consultation of spatialized and semantically enriched iconographic sources on cultural heritage buildings. J. Comput. Cult. Heritage (JOCCH) **6**(3), 1–17 (2013). Article No. 13
16. Baldissini, S., Gaiani, M.: Interacting with the Andrea Palladio works: the history of palladian information system interfaces. J. Comput. Cult. Heritage (JOCCH), **7**(2), 1–26 (2014). Article No. 11
17. Apollonio, F.I., Fallavollita, F., Foschi, R.: The critical digital model and two case studies: the churches of Santa Margherita and Santo Spirito in Bologna. Nexus Netw. J. **25**, 215–222 (2023)
18. Strothotte, T., Masuch, M., Isenberg, T.: Visualizing knowledge about virtual reconstructions of ancient architecture. In: Proceedings of the Computer Graphics International, Canmore, AB, Canada, 7–11 June 1999, pp. 36–43 (1999)

19. Münster, S., Kröber, C., Weller, H., Prechtel, N.: Researching knowledge issues on virtual historical architecture. In: Ioannides, M., Fink, E., Moropoulou, A., Hage-dorn-Saupe, M., Fresa, A., Liestøl, G., Rajcic, V., Grussenmeyer, P. (eds.) Digital Heritage - Progress in Cultural Heritage: Documentation, Preservation, and Protection. Proceedings of the 6th International Conference, EuroMed 2016, Nicosia, Cyprus, 31 October–5 November 2016. LNCS, Part I, pp. 362–374. Springer, Cham (2016). https://doi.org/10.1007/978-3-319-48496-9_29
20. CoVHer Project Website. https://covher.eu/. Accessed 20 Mar 2025
21. Münster, S., et al.: Handbook of Digital 3D Reconstruction of Historical Architecture. Synthesis Lectures on Engineers, Technology, & Society (SLETS), vol. 28. Springer, Cham (2024)
22. Bajena, I.P. et al.: Documentation and publication of hypothetical virtual 3D reconstructions in the CoVHer project. In: Ioannides, M., Baker, D., Agapiou, A., Siegkas, P. (eds.) 3D Research Challenges in Cultural Heritage V. LNCS, vol. 15190. Springer, Cham (2025). https://doi.org/10.1007/978-3-031-78590-0_10
23. Lutteroth, J., Kuroczyński, P., Bajena, I.P.: Digital 3D reconstructions of synagogues for an innovative approach on Jewish architectural heritage in East Central Europe. Virtual Archaeol. Rev. **16**, 144–160 (2025)
24. Grellert, M., Wacker, M., Bruschke, J., Beck, D., Stille, W.: IDOVIR – a new infrastructure for documenting paradata and metadata of virtual reconstructions. In: Ioannides, M., Baker, D., Agapiou, A., Siegkas, P. (eds.) 3D Research Challenges in Cultural Heritage V. pp. 103–114. Springer Nature, Cham (2025). https://doi.org/10.1007/978-3-031-78590-0_9
25. CoVHer 3D Repository. https://repository.covher.eu/. Accessed 21 Mar 2025
26. DEHIO OME Portal. https://ome.dehio.org/de/start. Accessed 21 Mar 2025
27. Bajena, I.P.: Digital 3D Reconstruction as a Research Environment in Art and Architecture History. Infrastructure for Documentation and Publication. Alma Mater Studiorum Università di Bologna, Bologna (2025)
28. Apollonio, F.I., Fallavollita, F., Foschi, R.: An experimental methodology for the 3D virtual reconstruction of never built or lost architecture. In: Münster, S., Pattee, A., Kröber, C., Niebling, F. (eds.) Research and Education in Urban History in the Age of Digital Libraries, Proceedings of Third International Workshop, UHDL 2023, Munich, Germany, 27–28 March 2023. CCIS, vol. 1853, pp. 3–18. Springer, Cham (2023). https://doi.org/10.1007/978-3-031-38871-2_1

Developing the Core Data Model for 3D – Exploring Metadata and Paradata Throughout Current 3D Infrastructure Projects

Igor Piotr Bajena(✉)

Institute of Architecture, Hochschule Mainz - University of Applied Sciences,
Lucy-Hillebrand-Straße 2, 55128 Mainz, Germany
`igor.bajena@hs-mainz.de`

Abstract. The rapid digitization of cultural heritage during the COVID-19 pandemic led to a surge in the creation of 3D models. However, the absence of standardized metadata and documentation practices has hindered their interoperability, discoverability, and reuse. This article presents the development of the 3D Core Data Model (3D-CDM), initiated within the DFG 3D-Viewer project, as a proposed solution for improving metadata harmonization. Drawing from comparative analysis across several German infrastructure projects and aligning with established standards, the study identifies a flexible core of documentation fields for 3D cultural heritage in the context of data aggregation. The paper proposes a tiered model of metadata necessity and highlights the importance of transparency in modeling methods, authenticity, and provenance. Recommendations are designed to support both aggregation and domain-specific needs, promoting better access and sustainability of 3D cultural heritage data across institutional repositories and research environments.

Keywords: 3D models · virtual 3D reconstruction · cultural heritage · metadata · paradata · 3D documentation schema · core data model · 3D-CDM

1 Introduction

The digital transformation of the cultural heritage sector accelerated during the COVID-19 pandemic. Museums, galleries, and heritage sites rapidly digitized their collections, producing an enormous amount of 3D models [1]. However, despite this growth, the lack of clear documentation standards makes reusing and preserving these resources highly challenging. Researchers are struggling to find their way around various approaches and documentation guidelines. There is still no universal vocabulary or terminology common to the entire 3D modeling community, leading to misunderstandings between researchers from different backgrounds [2]. Although 3D models have become recognized as valuable knowledge resources worthy of preservation and dissemination [3], their descriptions and documentation remain fragmented [4]. The lofty slogans about ensuring the interoperability of 3D models and the possibility of reusing them in practice still seem far from being realized [5].

The community frequently highlights the lack of standardization in 3D models, particularly concerning documentation, publication, and data transfer [6]. The challenges associated with 3D models can be categorized into several areas. Firstly, there is a need for the appropriate format for sharing a 3D model, and secondly, the method of describing 3D resources using metadata and paradata. Additionally, there is the persistent issue of terminology and vocabulary, which, despite ongoing efforts [7, 8], has not been uniformly standardized. Regarding file formats, there is an established standard for sharing 3D models on the web. It is the Graphics Library Transmission Format (glTF), developed and maintained by the Khronos Group and formalized as ISO/IEC 12113:2022. This format is supported by most of the available 3D viewers and was widely applied by the heritage community [9].

Requirements for metadata and paradata for 3D models remain challenging [10]. Although the research community focusing on 3D models of cultural heritage has compiled general guidelines, their adaptation has dispersed into smaller disciplinary or thematic communities, leading to more application-oriented than standardized solutions. To address this issue, the DFG 3D-Viewer project [11] has initiated the development of a 3D Core Data Model (3D-CDM), aiming to serve as a 3D data exchange standard for German libraries and establish a unified approach to documenting 3D cultural heritage assets, facilitating better interoperability and accessibility within the sector.

2 Common Ground Between 3D Infrastructure Projects

The initial step was taken during the first project phase (April 2021-June 2023). It aimed to develop a documentation scheme for digital reconstructions, serving as a base for the prototype repository for 3D models of cultural heritage [12]. The first scheme was designed to be simplified and cover topics related to the hypothetical 3D reconstruction of lost architectural heritage. It differentiates between mandatory and optional fields covering metadata and paradata associated with the 3D resource [13]. The mandatory fields were intended to form the foundation for a subsequent 3D-CDM, as presented in Table 1.

The proposed documentation scheme underwent testing by four project partners: research institutions specializing in archaeology, art history, and architecture and a museum with a digitized technology collection. During this phase, project partners expressed the need for additional fields tailored to their disciplines, such as the dating of archaeological artifacts or details about photogrammetry equipment. On the other hand, some fields in the documentation scheme were criticized for not matching the requirements of their field. The issue occurred with the requirement to provide information about the *"location of the object,"* which is overly aligned with architectural heritage. While relevant for buildings, this concept was less applicable to archaeological artifacts, where "location" could refer to either the discovery site, the current holder of a physical object, or the repository with a digital deposit. Another point of confusion was the *"reconstructed timespan"* field. While crucial for multi-phase architectural reconstructions, archaeologists and museum professionals used it to indicate the object's dating. Semantically, this was incorrect, as 3D models of digitized objects depict their present state. As a result, the *"reconstructed phase"* proved overly domain-specific—not in terms of discipline but in the specification of digital intervention made on the object, as it applies primarily to hypothetical reconstructions.

Table 1. Overview of essential metadata elements forming the foundation of the schema in the prototype repository for 3D cultural heritage objects developed during the initial phase of the DFG 3D-Viewer project.

Mandatory information	Description
Title	The official name or designation of the 3D model
Copyrights	Details specifying the license and author, ensuring proper attribution and legal clarity
Object	Identification of the object represented in the model and its geographical location
Reconstructed Phase	The specific historical period or timespan represented by the 3D model
Specification	A simplified overview of the technical aspects of the model, such as file format, file size, and software used

	TYPE OF 3D CONTENT	REPOSITORY FOCUS	DATA MODEL
DFG 3D-viewer	Mostly hand-made models	Web-based publication and reusability of 3D models	Application ontology OntSciDoc3D based on CIDOC-CRM
IDOVIR	Mostly hand-made models	Documentation of projects about digital 3D reconstruction	CIDOC CRM (considered)
(boundles.online)	Scans, Pointclouds, SfM-Model, BIM	Documentation and Provision of Research Data concernig architecture	RADAR (DataCite)
heidICON	3D Scans, Hand-made models	Archiving of Cultural Heritage object with Multidisciplinary approach	Object-oriented and event-based, similar to the XML schema LIDO.
B.A.U. digital	BIM models, Hand-made models, 3D scans, point clouds	Web publication of research data	For 3D architectural models: DURAARK-Modell for Arch. Data (buildm, e57m, ifcm)
COMPA<<T	Hand-made models, 3D scans, point clouds	Description of cultural objects, their media representations and annotations	Generic Wikibase Model for Cultural Data

Fig. 1. Overview of selected German infrastructure projects for documenting and publishing 3D models of cultural heritage that took part in metadata mapping workshops.

The feedback received showed that isolating a core metadata schema for 3D models without an interdisciplinary approach may be unfeasible. Therefore, we organized a metadata mapping workshop to align schemas across various infrastructures documenting 3D cultural heritage models [14]. It brought together representatives from six German infrastructure projects with distinct purposes and types of 3D models (see Fig. 1).

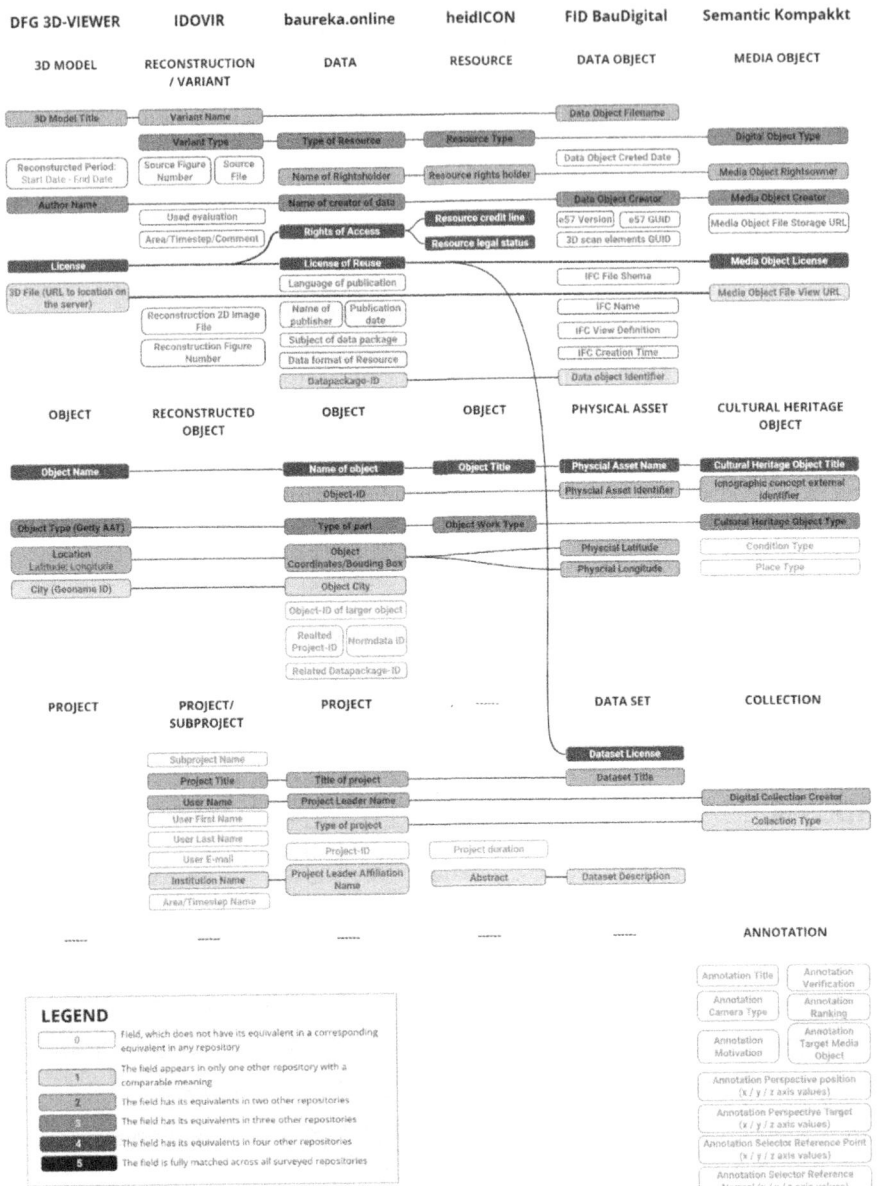

Fig. 2. Mapping of mandatory fields across the surveyed repositories. The darker the color, the more repositories contain a field (or a set of fields) intended to store the same type of information. This image illustrates the development of repositories from December 2022.

Isolating and mapping mandatory fields across various infrastructures proved particularly beneficial. Initially, these fields were organized into thematic groups: information about the *physical object*, its *digital representation* (referred to as a *3D model, media object, data, reconstruction,* or *resource*), the *project* (also referred to as a *dataset* or *collection*), and *annotations*. Despite differing terminologies among infrastructures, fields within these groups often served similar purposes. This mapping process clarified shared fields across documentation schemes, irrespective of discipline, establishing a foundation for a core metadata schema (see Fig. 2). The study identified two essential elements in all repositories: *title* (or *name*) and *copyrights*. The '*name*' attribute varies based on the infrastructure's focus, potentially referring to the *digital resource, cultural heritage object, dataset,* or *project*.

Equally important is *copyright* information, which appears in various forms, including *license, creator attribution, rights holder* identification, or a *credit line*. Nearly half of the analyzed infrastructures also emphasize *categorizing* digital resources and cultural heritage objects and assigning or utilizing existing *identifiers* for their identification. Some repositories further stress *linking* assets to their respective *projects* or *digital collections*. Repositories oriented on architectural heritage also highlight specifying the object's *geographical location*.

Limiting 3D-CDM metadata to fields consistently present among mandatory fields in the surveyed repositories suggests that the common denominator for all 3D models of cultural heritage includes the *name, copyright information, type of digital resource*, and the *identification* and *typology of the cultural heritage object*. In contrast, elements such as *project* or *collection* and *geographical location* are too domain-specific to be included in the core schema. However, merely identifying information groups for 3D-CDM does not fully resolve the issue, as *typology, name/title,* and *copyrights* can be declared in various ways and with differing levels of granularity.

3 Metadata Recommendations for Aggregation of 3D Heritage

The resulting metadata documentation closely aligns with the documentation scheme used by Sketchfab [15], a platform hosting one of the largest collections of 3D cultural heritage models worldwide [16]. Sketchfab prioritizes the visual presentation of 3D models, limiting user input to four fields: title, description, category, and tags. The title and description primarily serve human readers, while the category and tags facilitate content organization and improve findability through filtering. The category is based on a controlled vocabulary defined by the platform, allowing users to select the most appropriate classification for their content. In contrast, tags provide an open-ended system where users can freely assign keywords or phrases that characterize a given model. When users choose to make their 3D models downloadable on Sketchfab, they must specify the license under which their work is shared. Sketchfab offers various licensing options, including Creative Commons licenses. Once a model is published, an extensive section of technical metadata—automatically extracted from the uploaded file—becomes available. This feature enables users to assess whether the content meets their technical requirements for reuse.

The core metadata schema should follow this approach and identify required documentation fields that meet the main objective behind the schema. However, achieving a universal standard for all cultural heritage objects at the first publication level is virtually impossible[1], considering diverse requirements across disciplines. Therefore, 3D-CDM implementation should occur during the aggregation of digital resources via a central access point capable of processing data into a unified documentation framework, facilitating efficient content filtering. That phase of the digital asset lifecycle already has some established metadata solutions, such as Dublin Core [17] or the Europeana Data Model (EDM) [18]. These schemas define the elements available for describing a transmitted resource but do not specify the minimum required information. Recent studies also indicate that the elements listed in these data models may not be sufficient to describe 3D resources [19, 20]. This led us to develop a new proposal for the list of the documentation units required for 3D model transfers:

1. **Descriptive Information**: Provides human-readable content detailing the 3D model, including titles, descriptions, and contextual narratives.
2. **Classification**: This involves categorizing the 3D model and its content based on predefined taxonomies or controlled vocabularies, facilitating organized retrieval and analysis.
3. **Specification**: Details the technical attributes of the 3D model, such as file format, size, and dimensional accuracy, ensuring compatibility and usability across platforms.
4. **Copyrights**: This section addresses the intellectual property rights associated with the 3D model, specifying licensing terms, usage permissions, and attribution requirements.
5. **Digitization Event**: Documents the process of converting the physical object into digital data, including information on the date, location, equipment used, and personnel involved.
6. **Creation Event**: Records information about the creation of the 3D model, encompassing the creator's identity, creation date, and used software.
7. **Publication Event**: This captures information regarding the dissemination of the 3D model, such as publication date, used platform, and associated digital object identifiers (DOIs) or uniform resource identifiers (URI).
8. **Heritage Object**: Provides detailed information about the cultural heritage item represented by the 3D model, including the object's name, location or current holder, creation date, and creator, founder, or contractor. It can also include physical attributes such as dimensions, architectural or artistic style, and materials.
9. **Agent**: Identifies individuals or organizations associated with the 3D model's lifecycle, including creators, digitization specialists, curators, and rights holders.
10. **Relations**: This defines links between the 3D model and related resources, such as different versions, alternative reconstructions, associated datasets, or external references.

3.1 Minimum for Publication of 3D Model

Not all those elements are essential when describing a 3D model. If a model isn't intended for public use due to copyright restrictions, lacks connections to other datasets, and is

---

[1] Here, the first publication level refers to the initial upload of 3D data, often in domain-specific repositories tailored to particular use cases. Each domain has its own metadata requirements, conflicting with a universal approach.

not indexed in the data aggregator, providing only descriptive information and copyright details may suffice for the end user. Descriptive metadata, which includes human-readable content, offers enough context to identify the object and understand its significance. This approach aligns with core elements identified in analyses of mandatory fields within German infrastructure projects and platforms like Sketchfab. However, due to flexibility in naming and describing resources, developing future guidelines to standardize content preparation for these fields to improve clarity and consistency would be recommended. Other required information is copyright and provenance of data [21]. The scope of this information depends on the applied license. While acknowledging model authors, data-managing institutions, and contributors is advisable, such attributions are mandatory only for attribution types of licenses. Nonetheless, it is advisable to follow attribution standards widely used in the scientific community and ensure appropriate credit to funding bodies and individuals who contributed.

3.2 Requirements for 3D Cultural Heritage

As already stated, the reference to descriptive metadata and copyright information should be sufficient to present the 3D model in a web environment. However, in the context of cultural heritage, there is an abundant emphasis on the transparency of virtual representation and authenticity. The guidelines on the computer-based visualization of cultural heritage, London Charter, declares in Principle 4.4 the necessity of clear distinction between the existing state and an evidence-based restoration in 3D models of cultural heritage [22]. 3D models often strive for realistic representations, leading to misconceptions about their authenticity. Therefore, it's essential to convey information about the model's nature through metadata. While the topic of uncertainty estimation in 3D models is extensive [23, 24], for 3D-CDM, it can be simplified into three cases:

- **Actual phase**: Digitization of the object's current state, where the form of the object is entirely certain.
- **Historical phase**: Reconstruction based on analysis of historical materials, incorporating hypotheses to address gaps in knowledge.
- **Conceptual phase**: Representation of ideas that were never realized or physically manifested, including imaginative objects of the highest hypothetical value.

Models of past concepts by deceased authors are inherently hypothetical, lacking certainty regarding the author's intended realization. When design drawings are the sole medium of this heritage, there's a significant risk that some design solutions may be mutually exclusive, placing considerable interpretative responsibility on the modeler. Although hypothetical 3D models, often hand-made, clearly differ from those produced through digitization, these distinctions may not be evident to individuals outside the 3D modeling community. Therefore, information about the reconstructed heritage phase should be presented clearly and transparently. A similar issue arises in identifying the entity responsible for interpreting the input data, which can be done by humans or machines. Artificial intelligence is increasingly utilized across various scientific domains, including cultural heritage. According to the European Union's Artificial Intelligence Act, content created or assisted by AI must be explicitly labeled [25].

3.3 Tailoring for Aggregation Needs

Due to 3D-CDM's main objective, aggregation, metadata must expand the pool of required information, allowing appropriate classification and filtering of data from aggregated collections. This might include specifying the contextual discipline of the origin of 3D data or the heritage object's temporal phase, type, or condition. Clarifying the model's relevance to specific fields—such as architecture, archaeology, art history, or other disciplines—allows users to filter models pertinent to their research interests.

While no official controlled vocabularies currently exist for standardized classification of 3D models, initiatives like the Community Standards for 3D Data Preservation (CS3DP) have made significant strides in developing suitable typologies. CS3DP has proposed classifications based on creation methods (distinguishing between manually made models, automatically generated by machines and produced by application algorithms), initial input (source-based, reality-based, or imagination-based), or digital forms of representation (mesh, point cloud, voxel) [26].

The significant filtering possibility might also be assigned to the type of digital intervention made on cultural objects. Determining whether a model constitutes a hypothetical reconstruction of an unrealized concept, a digital restoration of a lost or damaged artifact, a blend of real and conceptual elements, or an accurate digitization of an existing cultural heritage object is crucial. The Seville Principles, which provide guidelines for virtual archaeology, preliminarily define processes such as virtual reconstruction, virtual restoration, virtual recreation, and virtual anastylosis [27]. However, the cultural heritage community has yet to establish standardized and universally accepted controlled vocabulary to classify possible interventions comprehensively.

3.4 Reuse of 3D Data

Although the elements mentioned above could define the scope of 3D-CDM, it is also necessary to consider the case where a 3D model or raw data is available under an open license. In this case, information related to the digitization process (equipment and technology used), modeling (software used), and the model's technical specification is desired by users who want to check whether they can use the 3D model for their purposes. Specification typically includes file size, vertex or polygon count, materials used, and texture mapping. Most of this information can be automatically extracted from the attached file, so providing it is not always necessary.

3.5 Requirements for Scientific 3D Models

The research community also recognized the need to establish relational links between 3D models and other resources. This is particularly important in source-based modeling to indicate the sources used [28] or when it is necessary to demonstrate the versioning of work or the various variants of a past form in hypothetical models [29]. This section can also be used for the connection of the 3D models with appropriate collection paradata, which can explain the scientific processes behind the model in detail [30]. Although relational links might not be mandatory, offering such connections significantly contributes to the depth and reliability of research.

3.6 Recommendations Matrix

After considering all the cases outlined above, it is clear that the core documentation required for 3D models varies depending on context and must retain a degree of flexibility. For this reason, the 3D-CDM has been structured as a set of attributes assigned to the documentation units defined earlier in the chapter. Each attribute is linked to a specified degree of necessity for its inclusion. The proposed framework organizes these levels into five distinct categories:

- *'Required'* elements are essential for every 3D model, as they provide the minimum information needed for basic identification and usability.
- *'Conditionally required'* elements become necessary only in particular contexts or under specific conditions, depending on the model's intended use or the target repository's requirements.
- *'Recommended'* elements are not mandatory but are strongly encouraged to improve completeness and ensure interoperability across different platforms.
- *'Conditionally recommended'* elements are valuable in certain situations but are not universally applicable, depending on the model's use case.
- *'Optional'* elements are not required but can enhance the overall quality of documentation when included, offering further insight into the model's characteristics.

The classification was conducted on two levels. The first level addressed ten documentation areas, identifying four as mandatory for every 3D heritage model submitted for aggregation: descriptive information, copyrights, classification, and publication event. The second level involved assigning metadata to each specific information category and a designation indicating the degree to which each piece of information is required. This process established a universal minimum core for all models based solely on metadata from the categories deemed mandatory. A summary of the 3D-CDM, outlining the data categories, associated metadata, and the necessity level assigned to each element, is presented in Fig. 3.

The current stage of 3D-CDM development does not yet define how individual metadata elements should be expressed, which field types should be used, or how many fields are necessary. The selection of this information is planned in alignment with metadata standards already implemented in the DFG Viewer environment, specifically the Metadata Encoding and Transmission Standard (METS) and the Metadata Object Description Schema (MODS) [31].

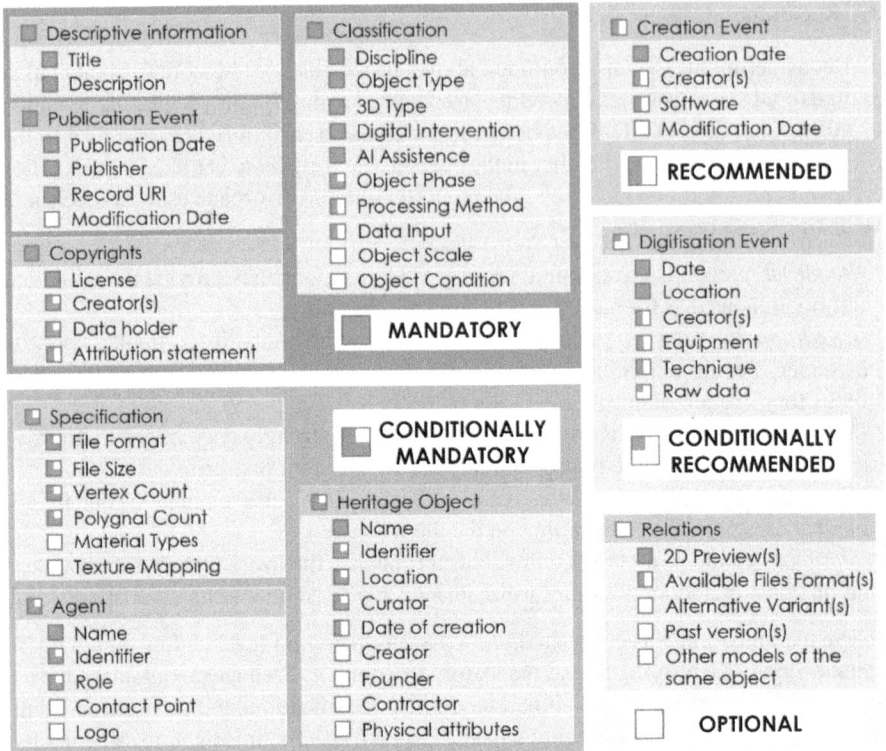

Fig. 3. 3D-CDM diagram showing the categories of 3D model documentation with metadata and the selected level of information required. The levels are illustrated by the degree of filling of the square - a full square means mandatory information, and an empty one is optional.

4 Conclusions

This study outlines a structured yet flexible approach to documenting 3D models of cultural heritage through the development of the 3D-CDM. It acknowledges the challenges posed by the fragmentation in terminology, metadata schemes, and modeling methodologies. Analyzing practices across different infrastructures and aligning with existing metadata standards has established a set of core documentation categories, including descriptive data, classification, and copyright information. The framework also introduces five levels of metadata necessity, enabling institutions to adapt documentation based on context while maintaining a baseline for aggregation and reuse. Beyond technical specification, the article emphasizes the need to communicate the nature of 3D representation, authorship, and modeling methods, especially in hypothetical reconstructions or AI-assisted processes. While the current version of 3D-CDM does not yet specify field structures, future alignment with standards like METS/MODS is anticipated. Ultimately, the 3D-CDM is a stepping stone toward a more interoperable and sustainable digital heritage infrastructure. It encourages collaboration across disciplines and supports more explicit provenance, facilitating the scientific reuse of 3D data in the digital humanities and cultural heritage sectors.

Acknowledgments. This work received funding from Deutsche Forschungsgemeinschaft (German Research Foundation) within the framework of the project "DFG-Viewer 3D—Infrastruktur für digitale 3D-Rekonstruktionen" (2024–2026), DFG-LIS, Funding number MU 4040/5-1.

Disclosure of Interests. The author has no competing interests to declare that are relevant to the content of this article.

References

1. Giannini, T., Bowen, J.P.: Museums and digital culture: from reality to digitality in the age of COVID-19. Heritage **5**, 192–214 (2022). https://doi.org/10.3390/heritage5010011
2. Cazzaro, I.: A shared terminology for hypothetical 3D digital reconstructions in the field of Cultural Heritage. In: (In)tangible Heritage(s): A Conference on Design, Culture and Technology - Past, Present and Future, AMPS Proceedings Series, vol. 29.2, pp. 204–216. University of Kent, Canterbury (2023)
3. European Commission: Basic principles and tips for 3D digitisation of cultural heritage. Shaping Europe's Digital Future (2020). https://digital-strategy.ec.europa.eu/en/library/basic-principles-and-tips-3d-digitisation-cultural-heritag. Accessed 27 Feb 2025
4. Koller, D., Frischer, B., Humphreys, G.: Research challenges for digital archives of 3D cultural heritage models. ACM J. Comput. Cult. Heritage **2**(3), 7:1–7:17 (2009). https://doi.org/10.1145/1658346.1658347
5. Storeide, M.B., George, S., Sole, A., et al.: Standardization of digitized heritage: a review of implementations of 3D in cultural heritage. Heritage Sci. **11**, 249 (2023). https://doi.org/10.1186/s40494-023-01079-z
6. Hardesty, J.L., et al.: 3D data repository features, best practices, and implications for preservation models: findings from a national forum. Coll. Res. Libr. **81**(5), 789–807 (2020). https://doi.org/10.5860/crl.81.5.789
7. Computer-based Visualization of Architectural Cultural Heritage (CoVHer) Glossary. https://covher.eu/glossary/. Accessed 27 Feb 2025
8. Community Standards for 3D Data Preservation (CS3DP) Glossary. https://cs3dp.org/dev/glossary/. Accessed 7 Mar 2025
9. Champion, E., Rahaman, H.: Survey of 3D digital heritage repositories and platforms. Virtual Archaeol. Rev. **11**, 1 (2020). https://doi.org/10.4995/var.2020.13226
10. Baker, D.: Paradata: the digital prometheus. In: Ioannides, M., Baker, D., Agapiou, A., and Siegkas, P. (eds.) 3D Research Challenges in Cultural Heritage V: Paradata, Metadata and Data in Digitisation. vol. 15190, pp. 12–23. Springer Nature Switzerland, Cham (2025). https://doi.org/10.1007/978-3-031-78590-0_1
11. DFG 3D-Viewer Project Website. https://dfg-viewer.de/en/about-dfg-3d-viewer. Accessed 7 Mar 2025
12. WissKI-based 3D Repository for Cultural Heritage. https://3d-repository.hs-mainz.de/. Accessed 10 Mar 2025
13. Bajena, I., Kuroczyński, P.: WissKI 3D Repository as a tool for the preservation and exploration of 3D models of cultural heritage. In: Stilo, F., et al. (eds.) EXploЯA UID 2024: Virtual Journeys to Discover Inaccessible Heritages, pp. 467–488. Publica, Alghero (2024)

14. Bajena, I., Kuroczyński, P.: Metadata for 3D digital heritage models. In the search of a common ground. In: Münster, S., Pattee, A., Kröber, C., and Niebling, F. (eds.) Research and Education in Urban History in the Age of Digital Libraries, vol. 1853, pp. 45–64. Springer Nature Switzerland, Cham (2023). https://doi.org/10.1007/978-3-031-38871-2_4
15. Sketchfab Homepage. https://sketchfab.com/. Accessed 18 Mar 2025
16. Flynn, T.: Over 100,000 cultural heritage 3D models on Sketchfab. In: Sketchfab Community Blog. https://sketchfab.com/blogs/community/over-100000-cultural-heritage-3d-models-on-sketchfab, last accessed 2025/03/18
17. Dublin Core Metadata Initiative: Dublin Core™ Metadata Element Set, Version 1.1. https://www.dublincore.org/specifications/dublin-core/dces/. Accessed 19 Mar 2025
18. Europeana Foundation: Europeana Data Model Documentation. https://pro.europeana.eu/page/edm-documentation. Accessed 19 Mar 2025
19. Isaac, A., et al.: Making the Europeana data model a better fit for documentation of 3D objects. In: Ioannides, M., Baker, D., Agapiou, A., and Siegkas, P. (eds.) 3D Research Challenges in Cultural Heritage V: Paradata, Metadata and Data in Digitisation vol. 15190, pp. 63–74. Springer Nature Switzerland, Cham (2025). https://doi.org/10.1007/978-3-031-78590-0_6
20. Kakali, C., et al.: Integrating Dublin Core metadata for cultural heritage collections using ontologies. In: Proceedings of the 2007 International Conference on Dublin Core and Metadata Applications: Application Profiles: Theory and Practice, pp. 128–139. Dublin Core Metadata Initiative, Singapore (2007)
21. Directive (EU) 2019/790 of the European Parliament and of the Council of 17 April 2019 on copyright and related rights in the Digital Single Market and amending Directives 96/9/EC and 2001/29/EC. Official J. Eur. Union L **130**, 92–125 (2019). http://data.europa.eu/eli/dir/2019/790/oj. Accessed 21 Mar 2025
22. London Charter (2009). https://londoncharter.org/. Accessed 20 Mar 2025
23. Cazzaro, I.: Digital 3D reconstruction as a research environment in art and architecture history: uncertainty classification and visualisation. Alma Mater Studiorum Università di Bologna. Dottorato di ricerca in Architettura e culture del progetto, 35 Ciclo (2023). https://doi.org/10.48676/unibo/amsdottorato/10817
24. Apollonio, F.I.: Classification schemes for visualization of uncertainty in digital hypothetical reconstruction. In: Münster, S., Pfarr-Harfst, M., Kuroczyński, P., Ioannides, M. (eds.) 3D Research Challenges in Cultural Heritage II. Lecture Notes in Computer Science, vol. 10025, pp. 173–197. Springer, Cham (2016). https://doi.org/10.1007/978-3-319-47647-6_9
25. Regulation (EU) 2024/1689 of the European Parliament and of the Council of 13 June 2024 laying down harmonised rules on artificial intelligence and amending Regulations (EC) No 300/2008, (EU) No 167/2013, (EU) No 168/2013, (EU) 2018/858, (EU) 2018/1139 and (EU) 2019/2144 and Directives 2014/90/EU, (EU) 2016/797 and (EU) 2020/1828 (Artificial Intelligence Act) (Text with EEA relevance). (2024). http://data.europa.eu/eli/reg/2024/1689/oj. Accessed 20 Mar 2025
26. Blundell, J., Clark, J.L., DeVet, K.E., Hardesty, J.L.: Metadata requirements for 3D data. In: 3D Data Creation to Curation: Community Standards for 3D Data Preservation, pp. 164–211. Association of College and Research Libraries, Chicago, Illinois (2022)
27. Seville Principles (2017). http://sevilleprinciples.com/. Accessed 20 Mar 2025
28. Gherardini, F., Sirocchi, S.: Systematic integration of 2D and 3D sources for the virtual reconstruction of lost heritage artefacts: the equestrian monument of Francesco III d'Este (1774–1796, Modena, Italy). Heritage Sci. **10**, 1–19 (2022). https://doi.org/10.1186/s40494-022-00711-8
29. Guillem, A., Samuel, J., Gesquière, G., De Luca, L., Abergel, V.: Versioning virtual reconstruction hypotheses: revealing counterfactual trajectories of the fallen voussoirs of Notre-Dame de Paris using reasoning and 2D/3D visualization. In: Meroño Peñuela, A., et al. The

Semantic Web: ESWC 2024 Satellite Events. ESWC 2024. Lecture Notes in Computer Science, vol. 15345, pp. 201–209. Springer, Cham (2025). https://doi.org/10.1007/978-3-031-78955-7_18
30. Huvila, I.: Imperative of paradata. In: Ioannides, M., Baker, D., Agapiou, A., Siegkas, P. (eds.) 3D Research Challenges in Cultural Heritage V. Lecture Notes in Computer Science, vol. 15190, pp. 1–11. Springer, Cham (2025). https://doi.org/10.1007/978-3-031-78590-0_1
31. Metadata formats used for DFG Viewer. https://dfg-viewer.de/en/metadata. Accessed 20 Mar 2025

Comprehensive Guide of the Benefits, Opportunities, Risks and Gaps in the Management of Cultural Heritage Digitisation. A Critical Literature Review

Maria Drabczyk[1], Marco Rendina[1(✉)], Francesca Manfredini[1], Anastasia Dimou[2], Ruben Peeters[2], Jasper de Koning[3], and Jiri Svorc[3]

[1] European Fashion Heritage Association, Florence, Italy
{m.drabczyk,m.rendina,f.manfredini}@fashionheritage.eu
[2] Katholieke Universiteit Leuven, Leuven, Belgium
{anastasia.dimou,ruben.peeters}@kuleuven.be
[3] Arthur's Legal, Amsterdam, The Netherlands
{dekoning,svorc}@arthurslegal.com

Abstract. The digitisation of cultural heritage enhances accessibility, enabling Cultural Heritage Institutions to share collections widely for research, education, and public engagement. This article reviews the literature on digitisation management in Europe, focusing on six areas: access and engagement, technology, legal and policy considerations, ethical considerations, skills and competencies, and sustainability. This critical literature review highlights benefits and risks, opportunities and challenges related to the digitisation of cultural heritage. Benefits include increased access and preservation, while challenges encompass framework gaps, copyright and ethical issues, and long-term digital preservation.

Keywords: Digitisation Management · Cultural Heritage · Access · Reuse

1 Introduction

One of the primary benefits of digitising cultural heritage (CH) is that it should enable Cultural Heritage Institutions (CHIs) to make their collections more accessible to the public. By digitising artefacts, manuscripts, and other CH assets, institutions can create digital versions that can be viewed and interacted with online. These digital collections can be shared and utilised for research, education, and entertainment. Online access enhances public engagement with cultural heritage, making it more relevant to contemporary audiences. Beyond increasing accessibility, digitisation also plays a crucial role in the preservation of cultural heritage materials. Digital copies help protect original artefacts from damage caused by handling, exposure to light, and pollution. They also aid in preserving materials at risk of decay, destruction, or anthropogenic threats such as uncontrolled tourism development, urbanisation, war, or conflict.

As a result, the cultural heritage sector is under growing pressure to digitise its collections. However, digitisation - particularly when it involves public access - presents several challenges and potential risks. A significant challenge is the absence of a comprehensive digitisation framework that provides CHIs with the methodology and tools needed to prioritise, contextualise, and manage the lifecycle of their collections effectively. Key concerns include the loss of original context, mismanagement of intellectual property rights (IPR), misuse of digitised cultural heritage objects, ownership disputes, and preservation risks. Additionally, stakeholder collaboration and organisational challenges—such as sustainability, digital sobriety, and the development of necessary skills—remain significant hurdles in managing digital cultural heritage. Further challenges include storage constraints, the risk of technological obsolescence, and ethical considerations. These factors can either facilitate or hinder the potential of digital heritage in society, affecting collaboration, innovation, creative reuse, and the promotion of democratic and inclusive approaches to prioritisation and contextualisation of CH assets.

This paper aims to evaluate the benefits, risks, and gaps in the digitisation of cultural heritage artefacts from a broad, high-level perspective. It draws on a selection of European literature, including policy documents, project reports, and scholarly articles. The objective is to identify current approaches and practices in digitisation management while exploring potential opportunities. Through a critical literature review, this study seeks to provide a comprehensive guide that summarises and prioritises key elements of the digitisation management framework.

2 Methodological Approach

The type of literature review selected for this analysis is the critical review, as defined by Grant and Booth [21]. This approach was chosen because it prioritises creativity, flexibility, and expert judgement over systematicity, enabling a thorough exploration of current research while allowing for the proposal of modifications or new directions based on the team's expertise. The strength of this methodology lies in its adaptability, which facilitates a deeper understanding of complex issues by critically appraising theory and evidence from diverse sources. Furthermore, it enables researchers to continuously refine their interpretations of the problem, drawing on their perspectives to evaluate and synthesise the literature. This approach is particularly valuable when reviewers must apply their expertise and judgement to take a reasoned stance on the information uncovered, while also fostering a more inclusive and objective outcome. The analysis goes beyond merely describing the identified literature; it incorporates a degree of critical evaluation and conceptual innovation, grounded in the research team's extensive knowledge of the heritage digitisation domain under investigation.

A total of six macro areas of analysis have been identified: access and engagement, technology, legal and policy considerations, ethical considerations, skills and competencies, and sustainability. In terms of categories of sources that act as the pool of information for the literature review, the three key sources of data collection identified are presented in Fig. 1.

Fig. 1. Key data collection methods and exemplary sources

3 Discussion of the Key Findings

This document presents an analysis from a pan-European perspective, drawing on various sources, including EU strategic policy documents, regulations, reports, guidelines from European professional networks, and EU-supported cross-national research initiatives on digitisation management.

Despite clear recommendations from the European Commission [4] urging Member States to develop or maintain a comprehensive and forward-looking digital strategy for cultural heritage to accelerate the sector's digital transformation, many Member States still lack such strategies or are in the process of developing them. This absence of strategic planning at the national or regional level is one of the key gaps identified in this study, with significant repercussions for the entire heritage sector.

In countries where digitisation strategies for cultural heritage are already in place, these are often integrated into broader digital cultural policies. State involvement is essential for financing digitisation, developing technical standards, aggregating databases, and ensuring the accessibility of digital heritage [23]. Therefore, it is crucial for Member States to establish tailored digital strategies, aligned with EU guidelines and objectives.

This document structures the key findings into six building blocks. The following sections provide an overview of the information gathered throughout the research process.

3.1 Access and Engagement

In the digital heritage sector, participatory practices have become increasingly important, as reflected by EU-funded projects such as *inDICEs - Measuring the impact of Digital Culture* [24], *RECHARGE - Resilient European Cultural Heritage As Resource for Growth and Engagement* [38] and *GLAMMONS - Resilient, sustainable and participatory practices: Towards the GLAMs of the commons* [20]. By incorporating participatory practices, museums, archives, and other heritage organisations can foster deeper connections with diverse communities, encouraging active involvement in the preservation and interpretation of cultural assets [15]. Digital platforms and social media enable broader and more inclusive participation, allowing individuals from around the world to contribute to and engage with heritage collections, thus having a greater impact on society, innovation, wellbeing, etc. [41]. This collaborative approach helps democratise heritage, incorporates multiple perspectives, and enriches cultural narratives [19, 38]. However, introducing participatory methods often necessitates organisational change, a shift in mindset, and the development of soft skills within CHIs, which have traditionally followed a curator-centric model [15].

A stakeholder-focused digitisation strategy aligns priorities with the needs of researchers, educators, communities, and the general public, increasing the relevance, usability, and impact of digital collections [14]. This ensures better resource allocation, fosters community ownership, and builds institutional trust, particularly when stakeholders contribute to decision-making [10]. Moreover, emerging digital ecosystems, big data, and online platforms place CHIs within more complex networks that demand innovative managerial approaches and partnerships with technology providers [35].

Open access and reuse of digital collections extend benefits to global audiences, facilitating remote learning, research, and interactive initiatives such as crowdsourcing [44, 46]. Yet challenges remain. Unequal internet access, limited funding, and complex intellectual property regulations restrict the potential reach of digitised collections [1, 44]. Additionally, inconsistent metadata practices undermine discoverability, while issues of privacy and security demand careful attention to data biographies and stewardship [27].

Overall, participatory practices, stakeholder engagement, and open digital collections are central to building an inclusive and dynamic heritage sector. By addressing the digital divide, clarifying copyright issues, and fostering co-creation, CHIs can enhance the accessibility, diversity, and long-term value of cultural heritage.

3.2 Technology

Europe's cultural heritage digitisation landscape revolves around a few principal platforms—Europeana [16], the Common Language Resources and Technology Infrastructure (CLARIN) [2], and the Digital Research Infrastructure for the Arts and Humanities (DARIAH) [7]—that each contributes to making artefacts discoverable and fostering research and collaboration. Europeana, established in 2008, offers access to over 55 million artefacts via links to institutional aggregators rather than storing the material itself. Since 2022, the Europeana Foundation operates the common European data space for cultural heritage [6], reflecting the EU's drive toward digital transformation. CLARIN, launched in 2012, focuses on language resources (text, audio, video) by connecting data providers through national nodes called centres, which offer technical services, metadata, and knowledge-sharing [3, 8]. DARIAH, recognised as an European Research Infrastructure Consortium (ERIC) in 2014, emphasises digitally enabled research in the arts and humanities by supplying a wide range of infrastructure, tools, and community services [22].

Although these platforms address similar tasks—prioritising collections, annotating and contextualising items, and facilitating reuse—none offers an automated mechanism to decide which artefacts to digitise first, leaving that choice to each institution's resources and interests. Metadata frameworks, such as the Europeana Data Model (EDM), Component Metadata Infrastructure (CMDI), and controlled vocabularies, guide semantic enrichment of cultural assets, yet the absence of a unified standard can create data silos. Persistent identifier policies are likewise uneven: while CLARIN and DARIAH provide specific PID services, Europeana encourages their use without making them mandatory, leading to minimal adoption in practice [18].

Additionally, each platform has distinct authentication mechanisms and licensing frameworks: Europeana aggregates under CC0 license for metadata and user-contributed content under CC-BY-SA license, whereas CLARIN relies on end-user and deposition agreements to regulate access conditions [26]. All three offer custom APIs, making interoperability challenging for developers. Although none explicitly features explainable AI, they generally promote transparency and ethical awareness.

So far, the platforms for cultural heritage focused on data accessibility and discovery, as well as tools and services sharing, but less on defining concrete data sharing strategies, robust data governance practices, and reusable standards that enhance interoperability as in the case of data spaces. The last few years the cultural heritage field has also moved in this direction, e.g., building on Europeana as the heart of the data space for cultural heritage and the development of the SSH Open Marketplace, but many aspects need to be further investigated, e.g., authentication and authorisation, licensing of data and services and IP management, as well as the establishment of policies and contracts regarding further reuse of artefacts and their enforcement and a more rigid data governance policy.

3.3 Skills and Competences

In the heritage sector, the demand for new skills is driven by the rapid pace of digitisation and the expanding opportunities for online access and reuse of collections through various technologies [17]. Professionals must now acquire advanced competencies in digital curation, data management, and interactive media. These skills are crucial for navigating digitisation challenges, such as ensuring the authenticity and integrity of digital copies, managing large and diverse data sets, and protecting sensitive information. But also, to sustain the openness of cultural heritage institutions toward relevant stakeholders and user groups as a strategic proposition to upgrade their organisational attractiveness [32].

Familiarity with emerging technologies like AI is also essential, as AI can revolutionise collection analysis, automate metadata generation, and enhance user interactions. Enhanced digital literacy allows heritage professionals to leverage online platforms, expanding audience reach, facilitating collaborative research, and fostering innovative public engagement strategies.

Investing in these skills safeguards cultural heritage in the digital age and unlocks its potential for dynamic dissemination. Professionalising teams in the sector supports digital transformation, improving cultural heritage institutions' ability to protect and promote their assets [34]. New skills should be developed within the organisational context, supported by networks, and considering the broader societal framework [17]. Digital management should become an integrated professional field within cultural heritage institutions, requiring experienced experts to set goals and standards [42].

3.4 Legal and Policy Consideration

Digitisation of cultural heritage is evolving rapidly due to technological advances and shifting legal and policy frameworks. At the European level, regulators are trying to steer this development by introducing or adapting legislation that either directly or indirectly affects the digitisation of CH. While some initiatives address how organisations digitise cultural assets, this discussion generally focuses on overarching legal and policy contexts, especially those concerning intellectual property rights (IPR) and data sharing. IPR reward creative efforts but can restrict digitisation when the creators or right holders are not the ones performing the digitisation [37]. In the EU, copyright principles stem from the Berne Convention for the Protection of Literary and Artistic Works and from multiple directives (e.g., the Database Directive, Infosoc Directive, Orphan Works Directive, Digital Single Market Directive), which help protect works in the literary, scientific, and artistic realms. The Digital Single Market (DSM) Directive [12], for instance, exempts CHIs and research organisations from the usual copyright regime for text and data mining (Article 3) and stipulates that reproductions of public-domain works cannot be subject to new copyright (Article 14). It also permits CH institutions to make preservation copies (Article 6), though other uses still require permission. Articles 8–11 introduce a regime for out-of-commerce works, allowing CHIs to digitise and share such material, though the process relies on collective management organisations or copyright exemptions that rights holders can opt out of. Another barrier arises with orphan works, in which rights holders cannot be found. The Orphan Works Directive [11] was intended to ease digitisation for CHIs, but the mechanism remains underused because of limited resources and complex administrative requirements [31].

Beyond IPR, data sharing legislation supports rather than obstructs CH digitisation, although issues of access and reuse persist. In 2020, the European Commission issued the "European Strategy for Data" [5], addressing the EU's need for an innovative, strong and progressive data economy. The document presents the Commission's efforts in reaping the benefits of the overall growth in data volumes, thus ultimately improving the health and well-being of EU citizens, and having a positive impact on the environment, transparent governance and convenient public services. One of the measures designated to achieve this ambition is the creation of a European data space. This data space is intended to present a single market for data, where the value of both personal and non-personal data can be securely and easily extracted by companies and individuals alike. In this context, the Common European Data Space for Cultural Heritage exemplifies the push to foster reuse and stimulate creativity, with Europeana playing a key role by offering standardised frameworks for sharing digital content.

Other legislative acts form the backbone of data sharing in the EU. The Open Data Directive (ODD) [13] encourages the reuse of public-sector documents and addresses the digitisation of CH, stipulating that exclusive rights for private partners should not exceed ten years, after which full rights revert to the institution. The Data Governance Act (DGA) [39] provides a secure framework for sharing data that may be protected by commercial confidentiality or personal data regulations, though it largely excludes cultural and educational establishments; however, it still outlines provisions for data intermediation services that could affect CH sharing. Meanwhile, the Data Act [40], that complements the DGA, aims to enhance EU data availability and promote interoperability among data spaces, requiring participants to describe data structures and usage restrictions in a machine-readable format. By complementing each other, these legislative measures encourage greater openness and trust in data-sharing mechanisms—factors that are essential for digitising cultural heritage at scale.

3.5 Ethical Consideration

Ethical issues arise in the process of digitising cultural heritage because the preservation, selection, and sharing of artefacts can conflict with diverse cultural values, identities, and expectations. Professional ethics historically sought to uphold trust in institutions [9], but new dilemmas emerge when the digital realm introduces questions of cultural sensitivity, authenticity, privacy, accessibility, and funding. The growth of "community" or "independent" archives demonstrates how groups—particularly indigenous or marginalised communities—seek to regain power over knowledge that has often been commercialised or interpreted through a "Western" lens [30]. This creates the possibility that GLAMs may inadvertently misrepresent certain heritages through inadequate consultation or metadata practices, especially when digitised CH was originally meant for a restricted audience or intended only for community members [43].

Another concern is the ease with which digital content can be manipulated or disseminated, raising questions of authenticity and ownership. GLAMs traditionally guarantee trustworthiness, but the risk of altered or misleading reproductions grows in the online environment [43]. Privacy issues also become more pressing, since a digitised item could reveal personal information or be harmful to people mentioned or depicted in historic materials. Moreover, digitising three-dimensional sites or artefacts can limit a viewer's interpretive freedom if the experience is restricted to a predetermined angle or path and if changes over time are not captured [28, 43].

Access to digitised content often demands both technical skills and technology that some communities, especially those originally connected to the content, may lack [30]. Conversely, highly interactive online environments may allow unmoderated commentary or manipulation, and GLAMs may not be prepared to host dialogues that balance public engagement with institutional trust. The shift to business-oriented funding models adds further ethical dimensions, because selection biases can creep in when content with high donor appeal is prioritised, and private supporters may demand exclusive access or time-limited control over digitised artefacts [30]. These challenges highlight the importance of managing digitisation projects in a way that preserves cultural integrity, respects privacy, ensures broad accessibility, and promotes transparency in both the funding and dissemination processes.

3.6 Sustainability

Sustainability in digitising cultural heritage increasingly highlights "digital sobriety," which aims to minimise environmental impact by reducing energy consumption, optimising storage, and implementing green technologies [33]. Although still lacking extensive research and formal guidelines, this approach encourages institutions to focus on the relevance rather than the sheer volume of what they digitise, potentially lowering costs and energy use [25]. Yet technical challenges remain, such as deploying efficient scanners or servers and training staff in new skills. Funding is also a persistent obstacle, as large-scale digitisation efforts can exceed the budgets of many smaller institutions [29]. Public grants and EU programmes, including Creative Europe or Horizon Europe, are often critical, but heritage organisations should devise comprehensive risk management plans to address financial uncertainties and ensure they can fulfil their public missions [14]. Diversifying income sources and developing long-term sustainability strategies further strengthen institutions' resilience [36]. Pooling resources and infrastructures at national and regional level, efficient management of digitisation projects, and introduction of long-term preservation plans, can lead to significant cost savings and reduced environmental footprint, limiting obsolescence risks, and maintaining accessibility for future generations.

4 Conclusions

The digitisation of cultural heritage offers immense potential for enhancing public access, engagement, and participation in cultural heritage, fostering new collaborations and creative reuses of digital artefacts. However, this transformation is not without its challenges. The analysis presented in this document underscores the necessity of a holistic approach to digitisation management that addresses key areas such as access and reuse, technology, legal and policy considerations, ethics, skills, and sustainability.

For Cultural Heritage Institutions, to fully leverage the opportunities fostered by digitisation, comprehensive frameworks and policies are crucial. These should provide clear methodologies for prioritising, contextualising, and managing collections throughout their lifecycle. Addressing issues related to intellectual property rights, digital preservation, and organisational sustainability is essential for ensuring the longevity, reusability and integrity of digital collections.

Moreover, as CHIs navigate the digital landscape, they must responsibly embrace new technologies and adopt inclusive practices that amplify previously neglected voices, promoting equity and democratic values. The development of new skills and mindsets among CHI professionals is imperative to adapt to these changes and fully harness the potential of digital heritage.

While significant challenges remain, including legal complexities, ethical considerations, and the need for sustainable practices, the path forward lies in a collaborative, innovative, and inclusive approach to digitisation. By addressing these challenges head-on, CHIs can unlock the transformative power of digital heritage, enriching European society and fostering a more engaged and informed public.

Acknowledgments. This article has been written as part of the REEVALUATE project which has received funding from the European Union Horizon Research and Innovation programme under grant agreement No 101132389.

Disclosure of Interests. The authors have no competing interests to declare that are relevant to the content of this article.

References

1. Charles, E., Willans, R., Frank, E., Luz, A.: Social and cultural consequences of the digital divide (2024)

2. CLARIN homepage. https://www.clarin.eu/. Accessed 20 Jan 2025
3. CLARIN: The Infrastructure for Language Resources. (2022). De Gruyter. https://doi.org/10.1515/9783110767377
4. Commission Recommendation of 10.11.2021 on a common European data space for cultural heritage, Brussels, 10.11.2021, C(2021) 7953 final
5. Communication from the Commission to the European Parliament, the Council, the European Economic and Social Committee and the Committee of the Regions, A European strategy for data (COM/2020/66 final) (2020)
6. Common European Data Space for Cultural Heritage homepage. https://www.dataspace-culturalheritage.eu/en. Accessed 20 Jan 2025
7. DARIAH homepage, https://www.dariah.eu/. Accessed 20 Jan 2025
8. De Smedt, K., de Jong, F., Maegaard, B., Fiser, D., Van Uytvanck, D.: Towards an open science infrastructure for the digital humanities: the case of CLARIN. DHN, pp. 139–151 (2018). https://ceur-ws.org/Vol-2084/paper11.pdf
9. De Stexhe, G., Verstraeten, J., et al.: Matter of breath: foundations for professional ethics. Peeters, Leuven (2000)
10. Dindler, C.: Designing infrastructures for creative engagement. Dig. Creat. **25**(3), 212–223 (2014). https://doi.org/10.1080/14626268.2014.904368
11. Directive 2012/28/EU of the European Parliament and of the Council of 25 October 2012 on certain permitted uses of orphan works
12. Directive (EU) 2019/790 of the European Parliament and of the Council of 17 April 2019 on copyright and related rights in the Digital Single Market and amending Directives 96/9/EC and 2001/29/EC
13. Directive (EU) 2019/1024 of the European Parliament and of the Council of 20 June 2019 on open data and the re-use of public sector information
14. Drabczyk, M., Janus, A., Strycharz, J., Tarkowski, A.: Deliverable 3.1 - policy analysis of value chains for CHIs in the digital single market - summary. Zenodo (2023). https://doi.org/10.5281/zenodo.7500819
15. Drabczyk, M., Janus, A., Tarkowski, A., Ciesielska, Z., Gliściński, K.:Deliverable 3.6: Policy Brief: Towards community-focused cultural heritage institutions in the digital realm. Zenodo (2023). https://doi.org/10.5281/zenodo.7500839
16. Europeana homepage. https://www.europeana.eu/. Accessed 20 Jan 2025
17. Finnis, J., Kendrick, A.: The digital transformation agenda and GLAMs. A Quick Scan Report for Europeana (2020)
18. Freire, N., Manguinhas, H., Isaac, A., Charles, V.: Persistent identifier usage by cultural heritage institutions: a study on the europeana.eu dataset. In: Linking Theory and Practice of Digital Libraries, pp. 341–348. Springer Nature Switzerland (2023)
19. Giaccardi, E. (ed.): Heritage and social media: understanding heritage in a participatory culture. Routledge, London (2012)
20. GLAMMONS project homepage. https://glammons.eu/. Accessed 20 Jan 2025
21. Grant, M.J., Booth, A.: A typology of reviews: an analysis of 14 review types and associated methodologies. Health Info. Libr. J. **26**(2), 91–108 (2009)
22. Henrich, A., Gradl, T.: DARIAH(-DE): digital research infrastructure for the arts and humanities — concepts and perspectives. Int. J. Hum. Arts Comput. **7**(supplement), 47–58 (2013). https://doi.org/10.3366/ijhac.2013.0059
23. Hylland, O.M., Primorac, J.: Rapids and backwaters: comparing digital cultural policies (2024). In: Hylland, O.M., Primorac, J. (ed.) Digital Transformation and Cultural Policies in Europe, pp. 181–208 (2024)
24. inDICEs project homepage. https://indices-culture.eu/. Accessed 20 Jan 2025
25. Julie's Bicycle. Environmental Sustainability in the Digital Age of Culture. Opportunities, impacts and emerging practices. Arts Council England (2024)

26. Kelli, A., Vider, K., Lindén, K.: The Regulatory and Contractual Framework as an Integral Part of the CLARIN Infrastructure (2015)
27. Krause, H.: An introduction to the data biography (2019). https://weallcount.com/2019/01/21/an-introduction-to-the-data-biography/
28. Kuester, F., et al.: Digital archaeological landscapes & replicated artifacts: questions of analytical & phenomenological authenticity & ethical policies in CyberArchaeology. In: Digital Heritage Int'l Congress (2013)
29. Lekakis, S., Dagouni, M.: Pandemic-driven shifts of GLAMs finances and participatory practices: digital policy and management trends in Europe. GLAMMONS project (2024)
30. Manzuch, Z.: Ethical Issues in digitization of cultural heritage. J. Contemp. Arch. Stud. **4** (2017)
31. Matas, A.: The out-of-commerce works system: a promise to unlock our heritage digitally. CeLISR (2024)
32. Maye, L., Bouchard, D., Avram, G., Ciolfi, L.: Supporting cultural heritage professionals adopting and shaping interactive technologies in museums. In: DIS 2017: Proceedings of the 2017 ACM Conference on Designing Interactive Systems, pp. 221–232. ACM (2017)
33. NEMO Working Group Sustainability and Climate Action. Climate protection in museums. Guidelines (2023)
34. Palumbo, R., Ciasullo, M.V., Pellegrini, M.M., Caputo, A., Turco, M.: Locally focused and digitally oriented: examining eco-museums' digitization in a service quality management perspective. TQM J. **34**(3), 398–417 (2022). https://doi.org/10.1108/TQM-02-2021-0046
35. Pesce, D., Neirott, P., Paolucci, E.: When culture meets digital platforms: value creation and stakeholders' alignment in big data use. Curr. Issue Tour. **22**(15), 1883–1903 (2019). https://doi.org/10.1080/13683500.2019.1591354
36. Pelissier, M.: Cultural commons in the digital ecosystem. Wiley (2021)
37. Polcak, R.: Digitisation, cultural institutions and intellectual property. Masaryk Univ. J. Law Technol. **9**(2) (2015)
38. RECHARGE project homepage. https://recharge-culture.eu. Accessed 20 Jan 2025
39. Regulation (EU) 2022/868 of the European Parliament and of the Council of 30 May 2022 on European data governance and amending Regulation (EU) 2018/1724
40. Regulation (EU) 2023/2854 of the European Parliament and of the Council of 13 December 2023 on harmonised rules on fair access to and use of data and amending Regulation (EU) 2017/2394 and Directive (EU) 2020/1828
41. Sacco, P.: Culture 3.0: A new perspective for the EU 2014-2020 structural funds programming, European Expert Network on Culture (2011)
42. Sanderhoff, M.: This belongs to you. In: Sanderhoff, M. (ed.) Sharing is Caring. Openness and sharing in contemporary museum culture. Statens Museum for Kunst, Copenhagen, pp. 20–131 (2014)
43. Thompson, E.L: Legal and ethical considerations for digital recreations of cultural heritage. Chapman Law Rev. **20**(1) (2017)
44. Wallace, A.: Accessibility. Open GLAM (2021). https://openglam.pubpub.org/pub/accessibility
45. Van Dijk, D.: Exploring heritage in participatory culture: the MuseumApp. In: Trant, J., Bearman, D. (eds.) Museums and the Web 2011: Proceedings. Archives & Museum Informatics, Toronto (2011)
46. Vézina, B., Benedict, C.: Don't be a Dinosaur; or, The Benefits of Open Culture. Creative Commons (2024)

Reviving Europe's Architectural Heritage: The CoVHer Project's Standards for 3D Digital Reconstructions

Fabrizio Ivan Apollonio, Federico Fallavollita(✉), and Riccardo Foschi

Alma Mater Studiorum University of Bologna, Viale del Risorgimento 2, 40136 Bologna, Italy
{fabrizio.apollonio,federico.fallavollita, riccardo.foschi}@unibo.it

Abstract. The CoVHer project aimed to enhance digital documentation and study of lost or unbuilt European Architectural Cultural Heritage (CH) by establishing standards for scientifically accurate 3D reconstructions. Addressing the lack of clear guidelines, CoVHer distinguished credible reconstructions from amateur models, improving quality, transparency, and accessibility in Computer-based Visualisation of Cultural Heritage (CVCH).

Bringing together five universities, two companies, museums, and municipalities, the project developed a collaborative framework aligned with international standards, including the UNESCO Charter on Digital Heritage and FAIR principles. Key objectives included setting model construction standards, ensuring source traceability, promoting accessibility, and advancing scientifically grounded visualisation techniques.

A significant outcome was the creation of an Open Access platform, a dedicated repository for vanished or unbuilt European architectural heritage. This platform enabled scholars to share and critically assess 3D models with complete source documentation while also offering the public valuable insights into historical sites.

CoVHer also had an educational impact, launching a Massive Open Online Course (MOOC) to train students and the public in virtual reconstruction methodologies. This MOOC addressed digital skills gaps in higher education, providing accessible training in 3D modelling best practices, quality evaluation, and historical visualisation.

By fostering collaboration, education, and accessibility, CoVHer strengthened cultural identity through innovative digital learning, ensuring that Europe's lost architectural heritage remains part of collective knowledge.

Keywords: Digital Reconstruction · Cultural Heritage · MOOC · 3D Repository

1 Introduction

1.1 Digital Reconstruction of Lost and Unbuilt European Architectural Heritage: Challenges and Opportunities

The European Architectural and Cultural Heritage is vast and multifaceted, yet a significant portion of it remains invisible. Many historical structures (churches, synagogues, mosques) have been destroyed [1] or were never realised. The advent of digital technologies now enables their virtual reconstruction, offering new opportunities for study, dissemination, and engagement through scientifically grounded 3D models.

In recent years, virtual 3D reconstruction has gained increasing relevance both in academic research and in digital media, such as film and video game production. These reconstructions, based on textual and figurative sources, provide a means to represent lost or unbuilt heritage. Scholars from disciplines including architecture, art history, archaeology, and restoration increasingly employ these digital tools, fostering a growing international debate on the scientific rigour of such models [2]. The London Charter [3] and the Principles of Seville [4] have established foundational guidelines for the Computer-based Visualisation of Cultural Heritage (CVCH). However, despite significant research in related fields, a shared methodological framework and universally accepted standards for the digital reconstruction of vanished or never-built architecture are still lacking.

Existing European research initiatives, such as Horizon 2020, e.g. Inception [5], Time Machine [6], CrossCult [7], Dariah [8], V4Design [9] have addressed digital heritage, but none have specifically focused on the hypothetical reconstruction of lost or unbuilt architectural projects. The absence of clear reference standards complicates the recognition of scientifically validated 3D models from amateur visualisations [9]. This project aims to address this gap by establishing practical guidelines and methodological protocols for the creation, evaluation, publishing and access of CVCH models, in line with the UNESCO Charter on the Preservation of Digital Heritage [11] and the FAIR data principles [12].

A scientifically rigorous CVCH model must be accompanied by thorough documentation of sources, methods, and references. This information should be systematically stored and made accessible to ensure transparency and reproducibility [13]. To achieve this goal, international collaboration is essential. This initiative brings together five universities and two companies from different countries, including the Institute of Architecture at Hochschule Mainz, an active member of the Time Machine project. Moreover, some members of the CoVHer consortium collaborated on the DFG Research Network project *Digital 3D Reconstructions as Tools of Architectural Historical Research* (2018–2022) [14], which addressed similar topics by bringing together various disciplinary fields [15].

Beyond academic circles, the project seeks to engage museums, municipalities, and the wider public. The growing use of 3D hypothetical reconstructions in the gaming and film industries significantly shapes collective perceptions of history, underscoring the need to foster public awareness of the scientific credibility of such representations. Providing reliable tools for assessing historical reconstructions will contribute to a more accurate and widespread understanding of European architectural heritage.

2 The CoVHer Project

2.1 Advancing Digital Capabilities in Higher Education and Virtual Heritage Studies

The CoVHer project has positively strengthened digital capabilities in higher education while fostering innovative learning and teaching practices, at least for the seven institutions involved: five European universities and two private companies specialising in Digital Cultural Heritage. Through this initiative, we have achieved the following key objectives:

- Established standardised documentation, methodologies [16], and a shared vocabulary [17] for the construction and evaluation of 3D models in Computer-based Visualisation of Architectural Cultural Heritage (CVCH).
- Developed a dedicated 3D model repository for Cultural Heritage (CH), providing an infrastructure to apply these standards and methodologies.
- Disseminated CoVHer's findings within academic and public domains, promoting awareness and engagement with virtual heritage studies.

2.2 Methodological Framework and Innovations

The project has defined practical guidelines and operational methodologies for studying, developing, visualising, and critically evaluating 3D models hypothetically reconstructed from lost or unbuilt architectural artifacts. These methodologies, aligned with the UNESCO Charter on the Preservation of Digital Heritage (2003), establish a systematic CVCH model creation and documentation approach.

The innovation of this research lies in the establishment of scientific reference standards for 3D reconstructions, addressing four key areas:

1. Constructive Aspects – Ensuring geometric accuracy and structural integrity of 3D models.
2. Traceability – Documenting sources and evaluating the quality of historical reconstruction.
3. Accessibility & Interoperability – Enabling integration into digital platforms and ensuring data exchange compatibility.
4. Visualization – Defining high-quality graphical outputs to effectively communicate scientific content.

A comprehensive reference glossary has been developed to standardise terminology for hypothetical virtual 3D reconstructions, addressing the previous lack of a shared vocabulary in this field.

2.3 A Specialized Open-Access Repository

A digital 3D repository has been created to enhance the accessibility and dissemination of these models [18]. While previous platforms, such as the Inception Project [5], provided digital collections of European architectural heritage, our repository is the first to focus exclusively on lost or unbuilt buildings.

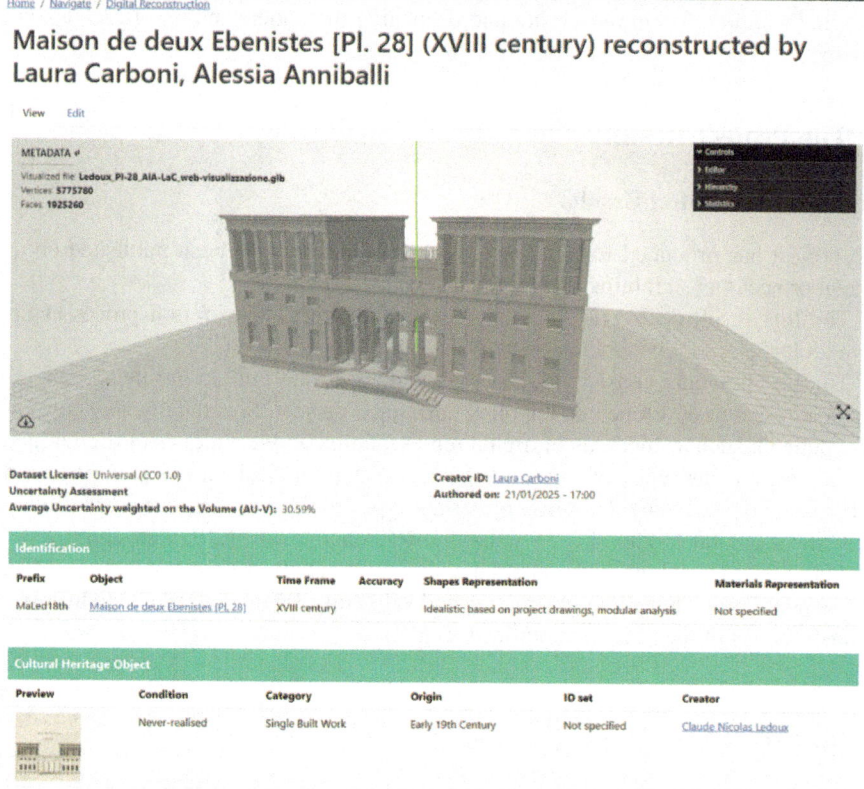

Fig. 1. CoVHer repository (https://repository.covher.eu/).

Unlike existing databases, this repository does not simply host 3D models; it also provides essential metadata and documentation for their critical evaluation. The platform serves two primary functions (Fig. 1):

- A scholarly resource – A reference hub where researchers, architects, engineers, art historians, and archaeologists can share, analyse, and download scientifically validated reconstructions alongside supporting documentation.
- A public archive – An open-access platform for non-specialists, fostering a broader appreciation and understanding of European architectural and cultural heritage.

2.4 Academic and Public Impact

The CoVHer project aims to generate a significant impact on both academia and public engagement. A key objective is to integrate dedicated teaching modules on CH virtual reconstructions into university curricula, equipping students with essential skills in digital heritage studies. Additionally, the project seeks to raise awareness among scholars, professionals, and the public about the scientific potential of digital reconstructions.

By promoting rigorous methodologies in virtual heritage, CoVHer aspires to contribute to the cultural and social cohesion of European citizens, reinforcing the role of digital technologies in preserving and deepening the understanding of architectural heritage.

3 The Project Results

3.1 The First Project Results

The project has produced four main results, all of which have been published on the official project website: https://www.covher.eu/.

The first result deals with methodologies, guidelines, cooperation processes and methodologies to outline operating standards for generating CVCH.

The first outcome consists of CoVHer guidelines that outline the theoretical and practical research developed and applied during the project. Specifically, key concepts were defined, such as methods of digital representation and techniques of digital modelling. The various types of 3D models used in hypothetical virtual reconstructions were also classified. The definition of certain types of reconstructive models, such as the Critical Digital Model [19] or Scientific Reference Model [20], were improved or introduced ex novo, along with potential workflows to apply in similar cases. Additionally, standard procedures for constructing and validating 3D models related to historical reconstructions of the past were outlined (Fig. 2).

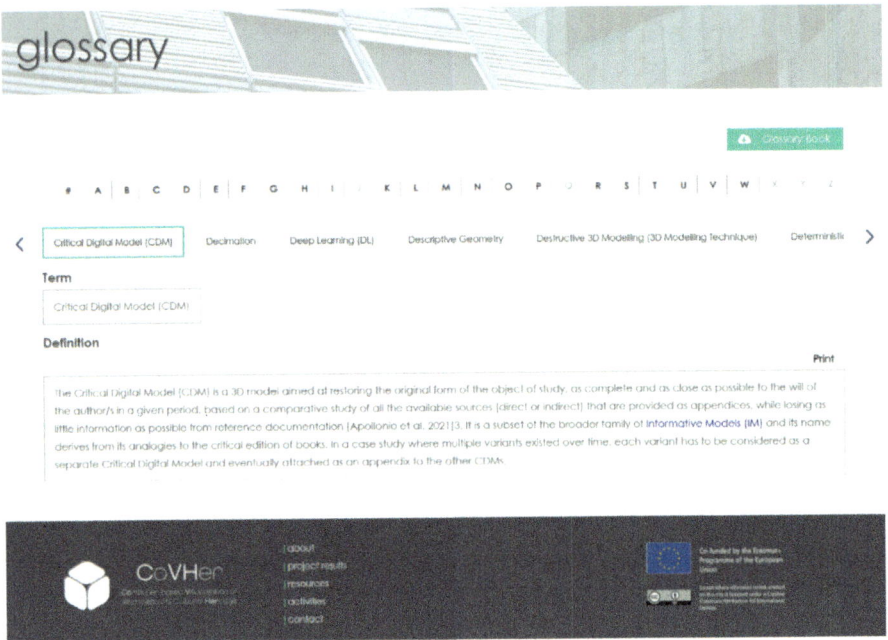

Fig. 2. Interactive CoVHer glossary (https://covher.eu/glossary/)

The second significant objective was the creation of an interactive CoVHer glossary, which is available online to facilitate easy and quick reference. This glossary provides the agreed-upon definitions for the most important terms used in the context of hypothetical virtual reconstructions. One of the key issues discussed throughout the project was the need to clarify certain concepts to improve the effectiveness and clarity of communication within the scientific community. For example, original terms were created and defined to clarify the types of 3D models and data used in virtual reconstructions.

3.2 The Raw Model and Informative Model

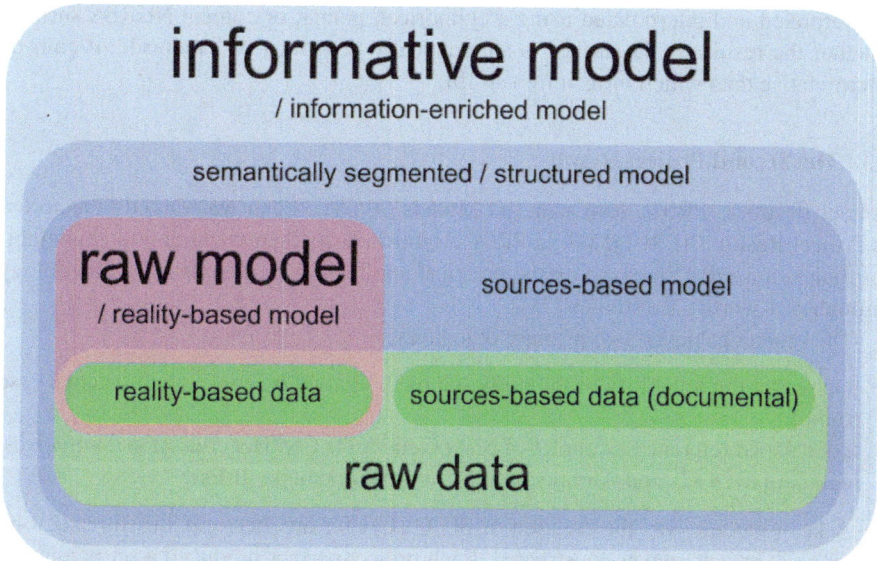

Fig. 3. Diagram of Informative and Raw Models related to the type of data used, first published in [17]

Among the novel terms introduced in the CoVHer glossary, the Raw Models (RM) and Informative Models (IM) are among the most relevant.

The Informative Model (IM) refers to a digitally enriched 3D model that includes accessible and relevant information. This term can also be applied to the concept of "Informed Models" or "Information-Enriched Models," though these variants differ slightly in meaning, as they do not necessarily require the information to be both available and accessible (Fig. 3).

An example of an IM is a virtual hypothetical 3D reconstruction based on architectural sources that are both documented and published. Another example would be an architectural survey that begins with raw data from a laser scanning campaign. This data is then processed automatically to generate an objective mesh model (RM), which is further refined, rectified, segmented, and redesigned by an author using CAD software to create the IM.

The key difference between RM and IM lies primarily in their conceptual nature. RM represents solely dimensional data (and sometimes colourimetric data) obtained directly from physical objects. In contrast, IM involves a complex interpretation of various sources generated through a reverse engineering process.

Technically, the RM is always discrete, typically represented numerically or polygonally. The IM, however, can be represented through different digital methods (either continuous or discrete) and constructed using a range of modelling techniques, including parametric, direct handmade, or polygonal modelling.

In summary, while the IM provides a wide range of information—such as metric, calorimetric, geometric, and source-based data—the RM primarily offers only metric and calorimetric information. For example, when a chunk of a point cloud from a survey is interpreted and interpolated using a cylindrical, planar, or conical NURBS surface, whether the resulting 3D surface is automatically generated or handmade, it embeds interpretative data which turns it into an IM.

3.3 The Second Project Result

Project Result 2 (PR02) dealt with 3D Models of CVCH and was directly connected to Project Result 1 (PR01). While PR01 established the theoretical and methodological foundation, PR02 focused on the practical application, validating the methodology through real-world case studies [21].

The project achieved two primary objectives:

- It assessed the reliability of the proposed methodology by applying it to actual case studies.
- It developed reference examples of best practices for CoVHer educational initiatives, including MOOCs and Architectural Drawing Workshops (ILPs).

A key outcome was the creation of 3D CVCH for architectural structures that no longer exist or were never constructed. Each project partner produced a set number of 3D models, selecting case studies in collaboration with local stakeholders.

The CVCH models were required to meet four scientific criteria:

- Constructive aspects – the accuracy of the 3D model's structure was ensured.
- Use of sources & historical reconstruction quality – traceability and reliability of the sources were verified.
- Platform compatibility, reusability, and interoperability – standardised formats were used to ensure compatibility across different platforms.
- Visualisation techniques – various modelling methods (mathematical and polygonal) were employed for both structural integrity and effective visual representation.

The project also integrated Virtual Reality (VR) to enhance the user experience, allowing students and the public to explore lost or unrealised architectures. This immersive approach improved spatial perception, evoked emotional engagement with historical architecture, and raised awareness of cultural heritage. For example, architects and engineers from different locations collaborated on virtual reconstructions of historical sites. This technology proved to be highly beneficial for archaeologists, art historians, and architects, especially in virtual courses focused on lost places.

The project envisioned virtual reconstructions becoming a standard tool in cultural heritage education and research, providing new ways to interact with and preserve architectural history.

The project deliverables, including the 3D models, were uploaded to the CoVHer platform: 3D Repository for Computer-based Visualisation of Architectural Cultural Heritage [22].

3.4 The Third Project Result

The third project result was focused on collecting 3D CVCH models of unbuilt or destroyed architectures. Unlike other repositories developed by previous projects, CoVHer's repository is uniquely focused on structures that were never realised or have been lost.

The key achievements of the CoVHer repository are:

1. Creation of a digital repository.

    The platform now hosts a growing collection of 3D reconstructions of historical architecture, making them accessible to researchers and the public.\
2. Integration of critical metadata & paradata.

    Each 3D model is accompanied by documentary sources, explanations of how sources were used (paradata), and technical details about the model's nature (polygonal, mathematical, or mixed).

    All entries documenting 3D models were developed on the basis of CIDOC CRM-based application ontology OntPreHer3D to align with Linked Open Data standards, ensuring interoperability and traceability of information.
3. Support for model reusability & modification.

    Users can upload, reuse, modify, and submit updated versions of 3D models directly on the platform. Whenever possible, both mathematical and numerical models have been provided. Each reconstruction is available in two formats: Native format and Universal interchange format (e.g., OBJ/FBX/GLB for polygonal models, 3DM for mathematical models)
4. Ensuring accessibility & licensing compliance.

    Metadata and paradata facilitate traceability, reusability, and access through clarified Creative Commons licensing.
5. Two dedicated user experiences.

For scholars in fields like architecture, engineering, history, and archaeology, the platform serves as a scientific research tool. For laypersons, the platform can be seen as a tool that provides a user-friendly experience to promote European architectural and cultural heritage, allowing non-experts to explore lost or never-built structures.

The CoVHer platform now stands as a pioneering digital resource, bridging academic research and public engagement in the field of architectural heritage visualisation, and it is available at the following link: https://repository.covher.eu/.

3.5 The Fourth Project Result

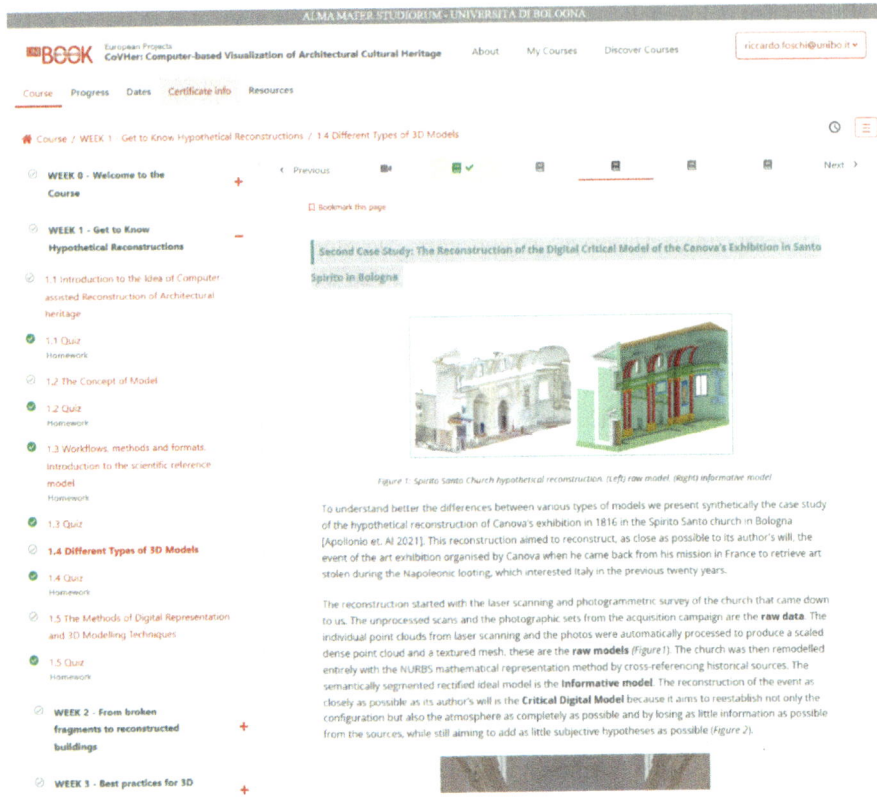

Fig. 4. CoVHer Massive Open Online Course (MOOC).

The primary accomplishment of the Fourth CoVHer project was the development and launch of the Massive Open Online Course (MOOC) titled "CoVHer: Computer-based Visualization of Architectural Cultural Heritage" [23]. Now available on the University of Bologna's e-learning platform, this course is accessible worldwide, providing individuals with an opportunity to engage in digital heritage education. It stands as the first comprehensive online resource dedicated to the creation and evaluation of 3D CVCH models (Fig. 4).

Through the creation of the MOOC, four objectives have been achieved.

First, the launch of the CoVHer MOOC represents a pioneering effort in digital heritage education, offering an in-depth exploration of 3D CVCH model creation. Structured into four distinct modules, the course covers:

- Week 1: Introduction to Hypothetical Reconstructions.
- Week 2: From Broken Fragments to Reconstructed Buildings.
- Week 3: Best Practices for 3D Modeling and Visualization.

- Week 4: Documenting, Sharing, and Reusing 3D Models.

The course's availability on the University of Bologna's platform ensures global accessibility, allowing learners worldwide to engage with advanced topics in digital heritage.

Secondly, the MOOC provided the implementation of blended learning modules in University curricula. A significant achievement of the CoVHer project was the integration of innovative teaching modules into architecture and engineering courses across partner universities. By combining the MOOC's resources with traditional academic lectures, the project fostered a hybrid learning approach that benefited both local and Erasmus students. This blended learning model is now embedded in the curricula of the participating institutions, enriching the educational experience.

Third, the MOOC offered the development and teaching of a shared standard methodology for the creation of 3D CVCH Models. By defining clear scientific and educational criteria for 3D CVCH models, the project contributed to establishing a shared standard that ensures consistency and reliability in the digital representation of architectural heritage. These standards have been integrated into the CoVHer digital platform, ensuring compatibility with existing digital heritage repositories.

Fourth, it supported student engagement and impact. Student participation played a crucial role in the project's success. The MOOC's open accessibility enables a global reach, potentially engaging thousands of students. During the development and testing phase, approximately 250 students from partner universities actively participated in the blended learning modules during the first semester of the 2024/2025 academic year. Feedback gathered through student evaluations and final exam results has been instrumental in refining and enhancing the course content and delivery.

Through the CoVHer MOOC and blended learning modules, the project has set a new benchmark in digital heritage education, offering a structured, accessible, and standardized approach to the study of computer-based visualization of architectural cultural heritage. The course is accessible at the following link: https://book.unibo.it/.

4 Conclusion

The CoVHer project has made substantial contributions to advancing digital heritage research and education, establishing itself as a pivotal initiative in the Computer-based Visualization of Cultural Heritage (CVCH) field. Through interdisciplinary and international collaboration, the project has successfully tackled key challenges related to the digital reconstruction of lost or unbuilt architectural heritage, ensuring methodological rigour, accessibility, and broad dissemination. The four main project results have not only addressed existing gaps in the field but have also provided concrete solutions that we hope will have a lasting impact on both academic research and public engagement.

The first major achievement of the project has been the development of comprehensive methodologies and guidelines for the creation, documentation, and evaluation of 3D CVCH models. By defining clear theoretical frameworks and classification criteria, CoVHer has established a standardised vocabulary and workflow for digital reconstructions. The introduction of key concepts such as Raw Models (RM) and Informative Models (IM) has improved clarity in differentiating levels of data processing and interpretation in digital modelling. These guidelines, grounded in scientific rigour, offer references for researchers, architects, and cultural heritage professionals, ensuring the traceability and reliability of digital reconstructions.

Building on this methodological foundation, the second key result of CoVHer has been the creation and validation of 3D models of lost or unbuilt architecture. The project applied its proposed methodologies to real-world case studies, assessing the accuracy, traceability, and interoperability of the digital reconstructions. The case studies explored topics in architecture [24] and archaeology [25].

The results have demonstrated that the developed framework is not only applicable but also essential for ensuring the scientific credibility of CVCH models. By integrating Virtual Reality (VR) technologies, the project has enhanced the experiential dimension of digital heritage, allowing users to engage with reconstructed environments in an immersive way. This innovation has been particularly beneficial for educational and research applications, fostering new ways to explore and analyse historical structures.

A crucial third outcome of the project has been the establishment of a dedicated 3D model repository designed specifically for storing and sharing scientifically validated reconstructions of lost or never-built architecture. Unlike existing digital heritage platforms, CoVHer's repository ensures that each uploaded model is accompanied by critical metadata and paradata, providing transparency regarding sources, modelling techniques, and historical interpretations. By adopting Linked Open Data standards and integrating CIDOC CRM-based ontologies, the repository guarantees interoperability, allowing seamless data exchange with other digital heritage initiatives. Additionally, the platform supports model reusability and versioning, enabling scholars and professionals to refine and expand upon existing reconstructions while ensuring proper attribution and licensing.

The fourth and final key achievement of the project has been the development and launch of the CoVHer MOOC (Massive Open Online Course), which stands as the first comprehensive online educational resource dedicated to the creation and evaluation of 3D CVCH models. Hosted on the University of Bologna's e-learning platform, the course provides a structured learning path covering fundamental aspects of digital heritage visualization. By integrating the MOOC into blended learning modules across participating universities, the project has successfully enriched academic curricula, equipping students with essential skills in digital modelling, documentation, and historical reconstruction. The open accessibility of the course ensures a broad impact, allowing not only university students but also professionals and enthusiasts worldwide to engage with the latest developments in digital heritage studies.

As a result of these four key achievements, the CoVHer project has the potential to establish a new benchmark in the field of digital heritage. By bridging the gap between academic research, technological innovation, and public engagement, it could contribute to the development of a sustainable framework for the study and dissemination of lost and unrealized European architectural heritage. The methodologies, resources, and tools developed within the project may continue to influence the future of cultural heritage visualization, facilitating the accessibility, comprehensibility, and scientific validation of historical structures—whether lost to time or never built—for future generations.

Acknowledgments. CoVHer (Computer-based Visualisation of Architectural Cultural Heritage) is an Erasmus Plus Project (ID-KA220-HED-88555713). It is a 36-month project, and it started in February 2022. There are seven principal partners from five different European countries. The partners are University of Bologna (Bologna, Italy), Hochschule Mainz (Mainz, Germany), Politechnika Warszawska (Waraw, Poland), Universidade Do Porto (Porto, Portugal), Universitat Autonoma de Barcelona (Barcelona, Spain), Tempesta Media SL (Barcelona, Spain), Interessengemeinschaft für semantische Datenverarbeitung e.V (München, Germany). For more detailed information, compare the two websites: www.CoVHer.eu and https://erasmus-plus.ec.europa.eu/projects/search/details/2021-1-IT02-KA220-HED-000031190.

Disclosure of Interests. Author Contributions Conceptualisation, F. Fallavollita; methodology, F. I. Apollonio, F. Fallavollita, R. Foschi; validation, F. I. Apollonio, F. Fallavollita and R. Foschi; formal analysis, F. I. Apollonio, F. Fallavollita and R. Foschi; investigation, F. I. Apollonio, F. Fallavollita and R. Foschi; data curation, F. Fallavollita and R. Foschi; writing—original draft preparation, F. Fallavollita; writing—review and editing, F. I. Apollonio, F. Fallavollita and R. Foschi; visualisation, F. Fallavollita and R. Foschi; project administration, F. Fallavollita; funding acquisition, F. Fallavollita. All authors have read and agreed to the published version of the manuscript.

References

1. Lutteroth, J., Kuroczyński, P., Bajena, I.P.: Digital 3D reconstructions of synagogues for an innovative approach on Jewish architectural heritage in East Central Europe. Virtual Archaeol. Rev. **16**(32), 144–160 (2025). https://doi.org/10.4995/var.2024.22542
2. Apollonio, F.I.: The three-dimensional model as a 'scientific fact': the scientific methodology in hypothetical reconstruction. Heritage **7**(10), 5413–5427 (2024). https://doi.org/10.3390/heritage7100255
3. Denard, H.: The london charter. for the computer-based visualisation of cultural heritage, Version 2.1. London, UK, King's College (2009). https://www.londoncharter.org. Accessed 5 March 2025/
4. Principles of Seville. 'International Principles of Virtual Archaeology'. Ratified by the 19th ICOMOS General Assembly in New Delhi (2017), https://link.springer.com/article/10.1007/s00004-023-00707-2. Accessed 5 March 2025
5. Inception Homepage. https://www.inception-project.eu/en. Accessed 9 March 2025
6. Timemachine Homepage. https://timemachine.eu/. Accessed 9 March 2025
7. CrossCult Homepage. https://cordis.europa.eu/project/id/693150. Accessed 9 March 2025
8. Dariah Homepage. https://www.dariah.eu/about/dariah-in-nutshell/. Accessed 9 March 2025
9. V4Design Homepage. https://cordis.europa.eu/project/id/779962. Accessed 9 March 2025
10. Koszewski K.: Visual representations in digital 3D modeling/simulation for architectural heritage. In: Niebling F., Münster S., Messemer H. (eds.) Research and education in urban history in the age of digital libraries. Second International Workshop, Communications in Computer and Information Science, pp. 87–105. Springer, Cham (2021). ISBN 978-3-030-93185-8
11. Charter on the Preservation of the Digital Heritage. Ratified at the 32nd General Conference of UNESCO on 17 October 2003, https://unesdoc.unesco.org/ark:/48223/pf0000179529. Accessed 3 March 2025
12. Wilkinson, M., Dumontier, M., Aalbersberg, I., et al.: The FAIR Guiding Principles for scientific data management and stewardship. Sci. Data **3**, 160018 (2016). https://doi.org/10.1038/sdata.2016.18

13. Grellert, M., Wacker, M., Bruschke, J., Beck, D., Stille, W.: IDOVIR – a new infrastructure for documenting paradata and metadata of virtual reconstructions. In: Ioannides, M., Baker, D., Agapiou, A., Siegkas, P. (eds.) 3D Research Challenges in Cultural Heritage V. Lecture Notes in Computer Science, vol. 15190. Springer, Cham (2025). https://doi.org/10.1007/978-3-031-78590-0_9
14. DFG Research Network Homepage. https://www.gw.uni-jena.de/en/14530/dfg-netzwerk-3d-rekonstruktion. Accessed 9 March 2025
15. Münster, S., et al.: Handbook of digital 3D reconstruction of historical architecture. Springer Nature (2024). https://doi.org/10.1007/978-3-031-43363-4
16. Foschi, R., Fallavollita, F., Apollonio, F.I.: Quantifying uncertainty in hypothetical 3d reconstruction—a user-independent methodology for the calculation of average uncertainty. Heritage 7(8), 4440–4454 (2024). https://doi.org/10.3390/heritage7080209
17. Fallavollita, F., Foschi, R., Apollonio, F.I., Cazzaro, I.: Terminological study for scientific hypothetical 3D reconstruction. Heritage 7(9), 4755–4767 (2024). https://doi.org/10.3390/heritage7090225
18. Bajena, I., Kuroczyński, P.: WissKI 3D Repository as a tool for the preservation and exploration of 3D models of cultural heritage. In: Proceedings of eXploЯA Conference on Virtual Journeys to Discover Inaccessible Heritages, Rome. PUBLICA (in Edition, expected date 2025)
19. Apollonio, F.I., Fallavollita, F., Foschi, R.: The critical digital model for the study of unbuilt architecture. In: Niebling, F., Münster, S., Messemer, H. (eds.) Research and Education in Urban History in the Age of Digital Libraries. UHDL 2019. CCIS, vol. 1501. Springer, Cham (2021). https://doi.org/10.1007/978-3-030-93186-5_1
20. Kuroczyński, P., Apollonio, F.I., Bajena, I.P., Cazzaro, I.: Scientific reference model—defining standards, methodology and implementation of serious 3D models in archaeology, art and architectural history. ISPRS Int. Arch. Photogramm. Remote Sens. Spat. Inf. Sci., XLVIII-M-2-2023, 895–902 (2023)
21. Bajena, I.P. et al.: Documentation and publication of hypothetical virtual 3D reconstructions in the CoVHer project. In: Ioannides, M., Baker, D., Agapiou, A., Siegkas, P. (eds.) 3D Research Challenges in Cultural Heritage V. LNCS, vol. 15190. Springer, Cham (2024). https://doi.org/10.1007/978-3-031-78590-0_10
22. 3D Repository for Computer-based Visualization of Architectural Cultural Heritage Homepage. https://repository.covher.eu/. Accessed 9 March 2025
23. UniBO OPEN KNOWLEDGE Homepage. https://book.unibo.it/. Accessed 9 March 2025
24. D'Addario, N., Garrido de Oliveira, C.: Redesigning Bramante's rounded perspective: digital speculations on the unbuilt cloister of the Tempietto. Virt. Archaeol. Rev. (2025). https://doi.org/10.4995/var.2024.22605
25. Tzerpou, E., et al.: 3D hypothetical reconstruction of a Neolithic hut from the waterlogged site of La Draga (Banyoles, Spain). Virtual Archaeol. Rev. (2025). https://doi.org/10.4995/var.2024.22557

New Interoperable Solutions for Cultural Heritage Protection: The ANCHISE Toolset

Axel Kerep[1(✉)], Valentina Vassallo[2,4], and Benjamin Omer[3]

[1] Solutions pour la protection des biens, PARCS, 39 rue Michel Ange, 91080 Évry-Courcoronnes, France
axel.kerep@parcs-pro.com
[2] APAC Labs, Science and Technology for Archaeology and Cultural Heritage (STARC), The Cyprus Institute, K. Kavafi 20, 2121 Nicosia, Cyprus
v.vassallo@ciy.ac.cy
[3] École française d'Athènes, Didotou 6, 10680 Athens, Greece
benjamin.omer@efa.gr
[4] Department of Archaeology and Ancient History, Lund University, Helgonavägen 3, 22362 Lund, Sweden

Abstract. The illicit trafficking of cultural heritage represents a significant global challenge, exacerbated by digital technologies that facilitate unauthorised trade while offering new protection opportunities. The ANCHISE project addresses these challenges through a suite of six innovative, complementary tools designed to enhance the detection, prevention, and investigation of cultural property trafficking. This paper presents these integrated tools, combining monitoring, authentication, analysis, matching, data fusion and standardisation technologies, with a strong focus on interoperability, and their real-world implementation across varied operational environments. The paper details the technological architecture of each tool, discuss implementation challenges across varied operational environments, and evaluate their performance through stakeholder feedback. Developed through collaborative efforts between law enforcement agencies, cultural heritage professionals, and technical experts, the ANCHISE toolset demonstrates promising capabilities in transforming dispersed, heterogeneous data into actionable intelligence and resources for protection of cultural heritage. The paper concludes with an assessment of the technological readiness levels achieved and outlines future development pathways to enhance the interoperability of these digital solutions for safeguarding our collective cultural heritage.

Keywords: Cultural Heritage Protection · Illicit Trafficking of Cultural Property · Object Authentication · Provenance · Archaeology · Satellite Surveillance · Heritage Database · Spectral Fluorescence · Image Matching · Data Interoperability

1 Introduction

The illicit trafficking of Cultural Heritage is a pressing hazard that endangers the preservation of global cultural identities and the integrity of historical knowledge. Indeed, beyond the immense economic value caused by the theft of cultural goods [1] their loss diminishes our collective past and important information to understand and reconstruct it.

In the last few years, Cultural Heritage faces significant and increasing threats from illicit trafficking globally [2], with digital technologies enabling trafficking networks [3]. The looting of cultural heritage sites initiates a chain reaction that extends far beyond the initial theft. Stolen objects are transported, stored, and advertised online through private forums and social media groups to stimulate demand [4]. These items are then smuggled across borders, laundered, and eventually reintroduced into the legitimate market [5].

International efforts are put in place by various stakeholders to combat these illegal procedures and protect such a valuable world cultural heritage[1]. However, the complexity and transnational nature of cultural goods' crimes together with the facilitation given by these new illegal routes, often cause failing the traditional law enforcement methods and require more sophisticated and innovative approaches in line with those used by looters and smugglers.

In this vein, the current advancements in technology have boosted the development of new digital strategies and tools to counteract these illicit activities and offer new protection opportunities. Several solutions developed in the last years have shown promise, yet significant challenges remain. Current obstacles include fragmented data about looted cultural goods across institutions, heterogeneous formats and lack of systematic and holistic organization, hindering effective law enforcement response. The disconnected nature of these systems creates information silos that traffickers exploit, while technical barriers often prevent seamless information exchange between stakeholders.

The EU-funded project ANCHISE[2] aims to build a comprehensive answer to meet these challenges for the effective protection of cultural heritage in Europe (and beyond), addressing both antiquities and modern cultural goods through sustainable, replicable and interoperable digital solutions. Predicated on a bottom-up procedure, ANCHISE develops an all-encompassing approach at each phase of analysis (prevention, stoppage and discovery) through an integrated suite of six complementary tools. Together, these tools—spanning monitoring, authentication, analysis, matching, data fusion and

---

[1] Recent international efforts to combat illicit trafficking of cultural property have gained significant momentum through several key legislative and regulatory developments. The United Nations Security Council Resolution 2347 (2017) marked the first resolution exclusively focused on cultural heritage protection in the context of armed conflicts, specifically addressing trafficking as a potential source of terrorist financing. In the same year, the Council of Europe adopted the Nicosia Convention, representing the first comprehensive criminal law treaty specifically targeting the illicit trafficking of cultural property. The European Union strengthened its regulatory framework with Regulation 2019/880 on the introduction and import of cultural goods, establishing stricter controls on cultural goods entering the EU market.

[2] ANCHISE – Applying New solutions for Cultural Heritage protection by Innovative, Scientific, social and economic Engagement. A project funded by the European Union's Horizon Europe Framework Programme under grant agreement No 101094824. https://www.anchise.eu/

data aggregation capabilities—create a comprehensive protection ecosystem connecting diverse stakeholders (e.g., law enforcement, heritage professionals, museums) and transform dispersed data into actionable intelligence [6].

This paper will present the current situation at European level concerning the initiatives and technologies developed and used for the fight against the illicit traffic of cultural goods, and it will highlight the current gaps and challenges especially in terms of data and knowledge interoperability. In this perspective, the paper will offer the vision of the ANCHISE project and the description of an interoperable toolset proposed for an effective solution to mitigate this anthropogenic threat through digital technologies. Moreover, the paper will discuss the necessity of a continuous collaboration with the actors of the fight against illicit trafficking of cultural property for the assessment of their needs and the testing and implementation of digital technologies for fighting the illicit trade. Specifically, the paper is structured as follows. Section 2 examines both previous projects and initiatives in the field of cultural heritage protection, as well as existing tools and technologies. Section 3 discusses the interoperability challenges and limitations of current approaches. Section 4 presents the solution proposed by the ANCHISE project with its toolset, describing each of the six complementary tools that compose it. Section 5 concludes the paper by identifying critical success factors for the ANCHISE project and the application of its toolset, and exploring future perspectives for cultural heritage protection.

2 State of the Art

2.1 Projects and Initiatives

Recent years have seen several EU-funded projects and initiatives attempting to address the previously mentioned issues. Some of them worked on the development of stakeholders' networks for information sharing; others focused on the development of different (digital and analytic) solutions or tools for data sharing.

The POLAR (*Police et archéologues face au trafic d'antiquités, 2015–2016*) *project, led by Ecole nationale supérieure de la police (ENSP), in collaboration with Maison de l'Orient et de la Méditerranée Jean Pouilloux and Office central de lute contre le traffic de biens culturels* (OCBC), focused on sharing knowledge and professional good practices to better fight the illicit trafficking of cultural property[3]. Innovative in approach, the POLAR project successfully established a foundational network among stakeholders, creating valuable connections that would later evolve into more extensive collaborations. The project laid essential groundwork by facilitating knowledge exchange through discussion forums, though it concluded before developing a permanent digital infrastructure for continued knowledge sharing. Nevertheless, many of the professional relationships formed during POLAR became instrumental in subsequent collaborative initiatives in the field.

---

[3] POLAR - Policiers et Archéologues face au trafic d'antiquités. École Nationale Supérieure de la Police (ENSP). https://www.ensp.interieur.gouv.fr/Recherche/Les-axes-prioritaires-de-rec herche/Systemique-entre-sciences-humaines-et-sociales-et-sciences-de-l-information-et-des-technologies/POLAR-Policiers-et-Archeologues-face-au-trafic-d-antiquites2.

The NETCHER (NETwork and digital platform for Cultural Heritage Enhancing and Rebuilding, 2019–2021)[4] project aimed to establish a Europe-wide information network and charter of best practice for the preservation of cultural heritage. Funded by Horizon 2020, it brought together a consortium of seven European entities structured into seven work modules. Faced with the proliferation of often unconnected initiatives in the protection of endangered heritage and the fight against illicit trafficking, NETCHER adopted a participatory approach to harmonise these efforts by creating a social platform bringing together various stakeholders (international organisations, governments, researchers, NGOs, foundations). The project resulted in two products: a charter of best practices and a social platform, thus constituting a first step towards an effective international and inter-sectoral fight against the trafficking and looting of cultural property. Nevertheless, despite these promising developments, the platform's impact remained limited after the project's conclusion, with minimal ongoing activity and limited integration into operational practices of law enforcement and heritage protection agencies, highlighting the challenge of sustaining digital initiatives beyond their initial funding period.

The PREVISION project (Prediction and Visual Intelligence for Security Information, 2019–2021)[5], funded under Horizon 2020, marked a significant advancement in data-driven law enforcement capabilities by developing cutting-edge technologies for processing large-scale, heterogeneous data streams. While not specifically targeted at cultural heritage protection, its integration of artificial intelligence, big data analytics, and knowledge graph technologies enabled law enforcement agencies to establish connections between seemingly unrelated information. Key contributions included dynamic knowledge graphs for visualising entity relationships, predictive analytics for forecasting criminal activities, cross-source data fusion, and tools for analysing dark-net marketplaces where illegal transactions occur. PREVISION provided the framework that enabled the development of Arte-Fact©, a specialized tool subsequently deployed as an operational programme for French Police and Customs agencies. Arte-Fact© has proven effective in the fight against illicit trafficking of cultural goods and continues to be enhanced within the ANCHISE project, demonstrating the successful transition from research innovation to practical law enforcement application.

In recent years, the European Commission has adopted a strategic approach to combat illicit trafficking of cultural goods by funding complementary projects that address different aspects of this challenge. This strategy aims to develop both analytical and digital solutions with innovative societal impact, promoting complementarity across initiatives. Within this framework, two projects are being developed alongside ANCHISE as part of the same Horizon Europe cluster: AURORA and ENIGMA[6]. The AURORA project

---

[4] NETCHER - NETwork and digital platform for Cultural Heritage Enhancing and Rebuilding. https://netcher.eu/

[5] PREVISION - Prediction and Visual Intelligence for Security Information. https://prevision-h2020.eu/

[6] ANCHISE, AURORA and ENIGMA are projects funded under the Cluster 2: Culture, Creativity and Inclusive Society of the Horizon Europe programme. European Commission. https://research-and-innovation.ec.europa.eu/funding/funding-opportunities/funding-programmes-and-open-calls/horizon-europe/cluster-2-culture-creativity-and-inclusive-society_en.

focuses on establishing robust digital identities for cultural artifacts through deep chemical composition analysis, developing non-destructive anti-counterfeiting markers coupled with miniaturized tracking devices and blockchain-based verification tools. Complementarily, the ENIGMA project introduces the Unique Authenticity Identifier (UAI) concept while integrating earth observation techniques with Geographical Information Systems (GIS) for heritage site protection [7], leveraging machine learning for cultural heritage object clustering, and analysing metadata to interlink disparate data sources through a comprehensive decision-support platform. Together with ANCHISE, these sister projects represent the European Union's coordinated effort to develop effective technological solutions for cultural heritage protection.

2.2 Existing Systems and Tools

Currently, the landscape of the existing tools for combating illicit trafficking of cultural property encompasses several distinct categories of systems, each with specific functions but often operating in isolation from one another.

Law enforcement agencies have developed specialised databases and tools to track stolen cultural property. At national levels, several countries maintain their own specialised databases. France's TREIMA II (*Thesaurus de Recherche Électronique et d'Imagerie en Matière Artistique*), managed by the Office Central de lutte contre le trafic des Biens Culturels (OCBC)https://www.legifrance.gouv.fr/jorf/article_jo/JORFARTI0 00001444302, contains detailed records of stolen art and cultural objects within French jurisdiction. Similarly, Italy's Leonardo database, developed and operated by the Carabinieri Tutela Patrimonio Culturale (TPC), is complemented by the mobile application ITPC to facilitate field identification of stolen Italian artefacts [8]. These national systems, while sophisticated, often face challenges in sharing data across international boundaries, creating potential blind spots in transnational trafficking routes.

To address these cross-border challenges, INTERPOL's Works of Art Database was established as a centralised international solution that aims to unify information from various national databases[7]. Based on the Object ID standard [9]—the same framework used by many national databases—this system represents one of the most prominent international efforts to create interoperability between disparate national systems. The database contains records of stolen cultural property reported by member countries, enabling law enforcement agencies worldwide to cross-reference suspected items against an international registry. This coordinated approach has been further enhanced through the development of the mobile application ID-ART, which allows field agents and the general public to search for stolen objects through a simplified interface, though with limited functionalities compared to the full database[8].

A second category comprises databases focused on legal frameworks rather than specific objects. UNESCO's Database of National Cultural Heritage Laws (NATLAWS)[9]

---

[7] INTERPOL: Stolen Works of Art Database. https://www.interpol.int/en/Crimes/Cultural-heritage-crime/Stolen-Works-of-Art-Database.

[8] INTERPOL: ID-ART mobile application. https://www.interpol.int/Crimes/Cultural-heritage-crime/ID-Art-mobile-app.

[9] UNESCO: Database of National Cultural Heritage Laws. https://www.unesco.org/en/cultnatlaws.

compiles national legislation relating to cultural heritage protection from Member States worldwide. Although invaluable as a reference tool, it functions primarily as a repository of legislative documents rather than an operational instrument for enforcement.

ArThemis[10], developed by the Art-Law Centre at the University of Geneva, provides a database of case notes about cultural property disputes settled through various dispute resolution methods. While offering important insights into legal precedents, it focuses on resolved cases rather than supporting active investigations.

Both these systems provide essential legal context but remain largely disconnected from the operational databases used by law enforcement, creating a gap between legal knowledge and practical application in the field.

A third approach focuses on facilitating collaboration and information sharing among stakeholders. The ICOM Observatory on Illicit Traffic in Cultural Goods[11] offers a cooperative platform designed to gather information and resources from various contributors. As previously mentioned, the NETCHER project also contributed to this collaborative approach by developing specific digital tools for knowledge sharing, including a social platform and a charter of best practices, creating connections between heritage professionals, law enforcement agencies, and technical experts.

Similarly, UNODC's SHERLOC (Sharing Electronic Resources and Laws on Crime)[12] system includes modules on cultural property crimes, but operates largely as a knowledge repository rather than an active monitoring tool.

3 Discussion

3.1 Interoperability Challenges

Several standardisation initiatives have attempted to address this critical barrier to effective information exchange. For instance, Object ID, the international standard developed under the auspices of the J. Paul Getty Trust and managed by ICOM, established a minimum set of information needed to identify cultural objects, facilitating recovery in case of theft. Other initiatives, such as the UNESCO's thesauri and controlled vocabularies[13], offer additional standardisation frameworks specifically tailored to cultural heritage documentation.

Despite these efforts, implementation remains inconsistent across institutions, creating a fundamental interoperability gap that directly impacts the effectiveness of the tools dedicated to the illicit trafficking combat. Many cultural organizations and museums continue to use proprietary classification systems or simplified catalogues that lack the detailed information necessary for unique identification. Museum documentation

---

[10] University of Geneva, Art-Law Centre: ArThemis - Art and Cultural Heritage Dispute Settlement Database. https://plone.unige.ch/art-adr/about-a-propos.

[11] ICOM: International Observatory on Illicit Traffic in Cultural Goods. https://icom.museum/en/heritage-protection/international-observatory-on-illicit-traffic-in-cultural-goods/

[12] UNODC: SHERLOC - Sharing Electronic Resources and Laws on Crime. https://www.unodc.org/icsant/en/sherloc.html.

[13] UNESCO: UNESCO Thesaurus - Hierarchical lists of terms used in subject analysis and document retrieval. https://vocabularies.unesco.org/browser/en/about.

systems, while comprehensive, operate with metadata schemas not fully compatible with those of the law enforcement databases. This technical fragmentation mirrors and reinforces the institutional silos mentioned earlier.

The lack in the use of common metadata standards significantly impacts operational capabilities in several ways. First, it complicates cross-database and tools searches, making it difficult to track objects across systems when they enter illicit markets. Second, it hampers authentication processes, as inconsistent documentation creates uncertainty about provenance and in general about artifacts information. Third, it limits the potential of advanced technologies like image recognition and AI-powered matching, which rely on consistent, high-quality data to function effectively. This inconsistency creates significant barriers to interoperability and hinders the effectiveness of cross-institutional cooperation in combating illicit trafficking.

These standardisation and interoperability challenges represent a fundamental obstacle that any comprehensive solution must address. The ANCHISE project's integrated approach directly responds to these challenges by implementing semantic solutions aligned with the FAIR principles (Findable, Accessible, Interoperable, and Reusable) [10] to integrate tools and harmonise data across diverse sources.

3.2 Limitations of Current Approaches

Current approaches to protecting cultural heritage face other critical limitations:

1. **Limited Real-Time Capabilities**: Most existing systems operate on historical data rather than providing real-time alerts and monitoring capabilities essential for rapid response.
2. **Accessibility Barriers**: Many sophisticated tools remain inaccessible to field agents and front-line staff who interact directly with potentially trafficked items.
3. **Fragmented Information Landscape**: The dispersal of data across multiple platforms with limited interoperability creates significant information gaps.
4. **Technical Sophistication Gap**: There exists a notable disparity between advanced technological capabilities (AI, machine learning, image recognition) and their practical implementation in cultural heritage protection. This gap is further widened by the insufficient adoption of existing standards such as Object ID, which impedes interoperability between systems and undermines the effectiveness of technological solutions.
5. **Resource Constraints**: Many cultural institutions and even law enforcement agencies lack the resources necessary to implement and maintain sophisticated technological solutions. This limitation is compounded by restricted access to digital resources due to inadequate digitisation efforts, creating additional barriers to comprehensive cultural heritage protection.

These limitations create a clear need for innovative approaches that can integrate diverse data sources, leverage advanced technologies in user-friendly interfaces, and create a more cohesive ecosystem for cultural heritage protection. The ANCHISE project directly addresses these gaps through its suite of complementary tools designed to enhance detection, prevention, and investigation capabilities across the entire protection ecosystem.

4 The ANCHISE Toolset

The ANCHISE Toolset is composed of six different tools aimed at operating at the three axes of the illicit traffic combat: prevention, stoppage and discovery. Each of these tools develops specific features for the protection of cultural goods subject to looting and illicit traffic. From the monitoring of archaeological sites and sensitive areas, to the authentication, analysis, matching, data aggregation and retrieval, the developed tools will operate under the same ecosystem. The ANCHISE Toolset is composed of the following digital and analytical instruments: the Site Monitoring and Protection Tool, Kiku-Mon, the Cultural Good Detection and Characterization by Fluorescence Emission tool, Arte-Fact©, ART-CH and GUARDIAN – CH.

4.1 The Site Monitoring and Protection Tool

The Site Monitoring and Protection tool [11], developed by Iconem[14], is a digital platform designed to enhance the surveillance and protection of archaeological sites. It integrates satellite imagery, archaeological and archival data, with high-resolution 3D scans of selected looted sites across Europe. By combining satellite imagery analysis with 3D photogrammetry, the system identifies suspected looting patterns and documents them spatially and temporally. This helps prioritise protection measures and archaeological interventions in the most affected areas. The Monitoring Toolset includes: a satellite imagery comparison tool with blending modes for detecting illicit excavations; a high-definition satellite data facilitator for advanced remote sensing analysis; an interactive visualisation platform allowing measurement, annotation, and overlay of georeferenced data, integrating archival documents, satellite imagery, and successive 3D scans for comparative detection and collaboration; a practical guide for large-scale 3D site digitisation, providing methodologies for producing high-quality models suited for volumetric analysis. This tool enhances continuous and efficient monitoring of sensitive sites, providing crucial insights into looting activities and enabling proactive cultural heritage protection.

4.2 Kiku-Mon

Kiku-Mon, developed by Fraunhofer[15] SIT, is an automated monitoring tool for tracking and identifying stolen objects on online marketplaces. KIKu-Mon is developed as a web application, built on advanced crawling technologies and deep learning-driven image matching. Through a user-friendly web interface, users can easily upload object information, manage stolen artifacts, customise monitoring parameters, and submit monitoring tasks. Its advanced crawling tools enable automatically collecting items from different online sales platforms based on keyword searches and can handle multiple monitoring tasks submitted by different clients in parallel. Its image matching tool identifies stolen

---

[14] Iconem is an innovative startup that specialises in the digitisation of endangered cultural heritage sites in 3D (https://iconem.com/).

[15] Fraunhofer - Fraunhofer Gesellschaft zur Forderung der Angewandten Forschung E. V., is an organisation of institutes of applied research in Germany, undertaking contract research on behalf of industry, the service sector and the government (https://www.fraunhofer.de/en.html).

objects by visual comparison, minimising the need for subsequent manual inspections. This solution extends the scope of web searches for stolen cultural goods, automating the monitoring process and reducing the manual workload while providing a comprehensive solution for tracking and identifying stolen objects, thereby enhancing the recovery efforts of law enforcement agencies.

4.3 The Cultural Good Detection and Characterization by Fluorescence Emission Tool

The Cultural Good Detection and Characterization by Fluorescence Emission tool, developed by INOV[16], is a sophisticated fluorescence spectroscopy diagnostic method for analysing paper. This method uses a compact and robust spectrometer to provide information-rich spectral fluorescence signatures (SFS). It employs a modern technique that uses lamp-induced fluorescence to analyse the spectral density of fluorescence emission, providing a comprehensive analysis of paper documents and supporting more accurate authentication. The tool includes machine learning software capable of interpreting SFS spectra and providing production dates for paper documents, enhancing authentication efficiency and accuracy. Designed to be portable and self-contained, with a spectrometer, mini-computer, and battery for power, the system ensures usability in various settings, including airports and borders, by non-experts. This tool effectively addresses the illicit trafficking of manuscripts and cultural objects by providing a reliable method for artefact authentication, enabling law enforcement agencies and cultural heritage professionals to identify and authenticate cultural goods with greater confidence.

4.4 Arte-Fact

Arte-Fact©, developed by PARCS[17], is an object typology matching AI application that enhances existing datasets of looted objects to a digital and AI level. This tool facilitates the identification of objects at borders and connects border agents with dedicated experts. By extending the data volume and region of the Arte-Fact© application, which has already been successful with Libyan and Egyptian collections, the tool provides rapid and accurate object identification, reducing investigation time and process. It includes object typology matching that provides a facilitated link to dedicated experts, ensuring that the right expert is reached for the right typology, reducing response time and preventing the saturation of experts with irrelevant inquiries. The user-friendly Arte-Fact© mobile application features an intuitive interface supporting quick and efficient identification

---

[16] INOV - Instituto de Engenharia de Sistemas e Computadores Inovação - is one of the largest national technological infrastructures in the field of Information and Communication Technologies (ICT) and Electronics in Portugal. It is a private institute that fosters relations between Higher Education Institutions and society and the economy, with a view to increasing their competitiveness (https://www.inov.pt/).

[17] PARCS - Protection Avancée contre le Recel - is a French company supported by Cercle K2, a multidisciplinary working group, section Art and Heritage. It offers integrated solutions which supplied services under different forms (prevention, recording, insurance and police declarations, research, restitution, and analysis) around an Internet application and databases (http://www.parcs.solutions/fr/).

for field agents in border and police control. The system implements expert-connect technology allowing law enforcement agents to quickly consult with specialists, while also providing access to regulations on the export of cultural goods from the origin country of the suspected object with links to official documents directly in the app. This comprehensive solution supports field agents by enabling rapid and accurate object identification, allowing them to take swift action against illicit trafficking of cultural goods.

4.5 ART-CH

ART-CH [12], developed by the Institute of Communication and Computer Systems[18], combines anticipation and investigation capabilities focused on identifying criminals' modus operandi, illegal marketplaces, and flows of cultural goods. This tool uses advanced algorithms to analyse data and detect patterns and anomalies within the fused data, providing deeper insights and intelligence that enhance market analysis and the detection of black market patterns on the merchant web. It brings a unique combination of anticipation and investigation capabilities that support more effective law enforcement efforts, while its data fusion engine focuses on refining fusion algorithms to enhance the accuracy and efficiency of data integration, ensuring more robust performance and supporting the analysis of a broader number of data sources. The tool incorporates advanced machine learning techniques to automate the detection of patterns and anomalies within the fused data, providing deeper insights and further intelligence. By enhancing market analysis and the detection of black market patterns on the merchant web, this tool enables law enforcement agencies to take proactive measures against illicit trafficking of cultural goods, offering a comprehensive solution for the identification and disruption of illegal trade networks.

4.6 GUARDIAN – CH

GUARDIAN-CH, developed by the Cyprus Institute[19], is a shared database infrastructure based on a unique domain ontology (Object ID-based) for combating illicit trafficking and on the use of the digital twin concept for artifacts. This tool aims to aggregate data from different stakeholders engaged in the fight against illicit trafficking. The database structure facilitates the organization, acquisition, and exploitation of data, ensuring interoperability and effective data sharing among stakeholders. The database

---

[18] The Institute of Communication and Computer Systems - ICCS, is a Greek non-profit Academic Research Body established in 1989 by the Greek Ministry of Education. ICCS aim is to carry research and development activities in the fields of all diverse aspects of telecommunications and computer systems, as well as their application in a variety of areas (https://www.iccs.gr/enact/).

[19] The Cyprus Institute - CYI- is a Cypriot non-profit research and educational institution with a strong scientific and technological orientation. It is a regional Centre of Excellence, addressing issues of regional interest but of global significance, with an emphasis on cross-disciplinary research and international collaborations. CYI is being developed as an international science and technology organization to strengthen the research community of Cyprus and to help transform its economy to a knowledge-based economy (https://www.cyi.ac.cy/).

structure is built on semantic solutions that harmonise data from different sources, ensuring that information is findable, accessible, interoperable, and reusable, aligning with the FAIR principles [10]. The implementation of digital twins for artifacts provides a comprehensive digital representation of physical objects, enhancing the understanding and management of cultural heritage data and supporting more efficient data sharing and analysis. GUARDIAN-CH promotes the use of standardised metadata schemas, ensuring consistency and facilitating interoperability between different databases. This tool significantly improves data sharing among stakeholders engaged in the fight against illicit trafficking, harmonising information from different sources and ensuring effective coordination, which is crucial for unified efforts to combat the illicit trafficking of cultural goods.

As mentioned above, all these tools will work together under the same framework. Indeed, the GUARDIAN - CH will not only aggregate data, but will also be the access point for and to all the other tools, ensuring an interoperable environment for information retrieval and analysis.

4.7 Deployment of the ANCHISE Toolset

All ANCHISE tools are currently in active development stages, undergoing rigorous field testing through organized demonstrations across diverse operational environments including border checkpoints, museums, and archaeological sites within the European Union. These field deployments are strategically designed to evaluate tool performance under real-world conditions and are conducted by various stakeholders including law enforcement agencies, cultural heritage professionals, and archaeologists. The implementation process faces several challenges, including technical integration complexities when connecting heterogeneous systems and data formats, practical deployment difficulties in varied operational settings, legal and jurisdictional complications arising from different national frameworks, authentication accuracy concerns regarding reliable identification while minimising false positives, and user adoption barriers. Performance evaluation incorporates multiple metrics including detection rates, processing speed, and accuracy measurements, with ongoing collection of stakeholder feedback to inform continuous improvements. Early demonstrations have revealed promising results in specific cases where the tools have contributed to successful identification of potentially trafficked artifacts. Moreover, they contribute to the further development of features to enhance interoperability, especially in terms of data harmonisation and tools integration. The complementary nature and the integration under the same umbrella of the six tools creates a comprehensive protection ecosystem stronger than any single solution.

5 Conclusions and Future Work

The success of the ANCHISE project hinges on several critical factors. Continued engagement and support from stakeholders are essential for the sustainability and widespread adoption of the developed tools. This includes financial backing, policy advocacy, and active participation in the project's initiatives. Furthermore, the adoption of common metadata standards is crucial for ensuring interoperability and effective data sharing among different platforms and organizations. This alignment with the FAIR principles facilitates collaboration and enhances the overall efficacy of cultural heritage protection efforts. Moreover, promoting interoperability between databases and tools enables seamless data exchange and integration, which is vital for coordinated efforts against illicit trafficking. Overcoming technical and organizational barriers to interoperability will strengthen the collective response to cultural heritage threats. The interconnection of the ANCHISE tools through the shared database constitutes a concrete use case of operational interoperability.

Currently, efforts to improve the interoperability of ANCHISE tools are not only taking place at project level, but also with those of AURORA and ENIGMA, the other two Horizon Europe Cluster 2 projects, as this subject is presently being discussed among the three projects and will soon lead to joint recommendations. Based on the lessons learnt from the initial deployments, this work includes addressing identified implementation gaps and exploring the potential adoption in different geographical and institutional contexts. These collaborative European initiatives represent coordinated efforts to address different yet complementary aspects of cultural heritage protection, with a particular focus on how these technological advances might influence future policy frameworks. Their development offers significant opportunities for methodological and technological integration.

Looking forward, artificial intelligence will undoubtedly emerge as a transformative force in the fight against cultural heritage trafficking. However, the advancement of AI applications in this domain cannot proceed in isolation from the humanities and social sciences. The effective development of intelligent systems requires not only sophisticated algorithms and robust datasets, but also a deep contextual understanding of the historical, cultural, and ethical dimensions that only interdisciplinary collaboration can provide. Future technological tools will necessarily integrate computational power with humanistic perspectives, creating solutions that are both technically sophisticated and culturally sensitive. This symbiotic relationship between technology and the humanities represents the most promising path forward in developing comprehensive approaches to safeguarding our collective cultural heritage.

Acknowledgments. This research was developed under the ANCHISE project, which has received funding from the European Union's Horizon Europe Framework Programme under the grant agreement No 101094824. Views and opinions expressed are however those of the author(s) only and do not necessarily reflect those of the European Union. Neither the European Union nor the granting authority can be held responsible for them. Additionally, the authors would like to thank Titien Bartette (Iconem), Armando Fernandes (INOV), Huajian Liu (Fraunhofer) and Nikos Peppes (ICCS) for kindly providing relevant information on their tool, crucial to this article.

Disclosure of Interests. The authors have no competing interests to declare that are relevant to the content of this article.

References

1. UNODC: False Trades: Uncovering the scale and scope of trafficking in cultural property. Knowledge gaps and future directions for research, pp. 7–10. United Nations Office on Drugs and Crime, Vienna (2022)
2. UNODC: False Trades: Uncovering the scale and scope of trafficking in cultural property, op. cit., p. 11
3. Brodie, N.: How to Control the Internet Market in Antiquities? The Need for Regulation and Monitoring. Antiquities Coalition Policy Brief, no. 3. Antiquities Coalition, Washington DC (2017)
4. Al-Azm, A., Paul, K.A.: Facebook's black market in antiquities. trafficking, terrorism and war crimes. ATHAR Project (2019)
5. Mackenzie, S., Yates, D.: What is grey about the "Grey Market" in antiquities. In: Beckert, J., Dewey, M. (eds.) The Architecture of Illegal Markets: Towards an Economic Sociology of Illegality in Economy, pp. 70–86. Oxford University Press, Oxford (2017) https://doi.org/10.1093/oso/9780198794974.001.0001
6. ANCHISE Project: ANCHISE Toolset Flyer. https://www.anchise.eu/_files/ugd/694c76_295d87fe89034ed1926351d5a1f489e1.pdf. Accessed 21 March 2025
7. Caspari, G., et al.: Semi-automatic identification of cultural heritage looting activities through Earth observation. In: Proceedings of the SPIE 13212, Earth Resources and Environmental Remote Sensing/GIS Applications XIII, 1321202. SPIE, Bellingham (2022). https://doi.org/10.1117/12.3037070
8. Lukács, D.: The italian law enforcement system used to protect cultural properties, with particular reference to databases and mass media. Criminal justice issues. J. Crim. Just. Secur. **18**(5–6), 243–250 (2018)
9. Thornes, R., Dorrell, P., Lie, H.: Introduction to object ID: guidelines for making records that describe art, antiques, and antiquities. J. Paul Getty Trust, Los Angeles (1999). https://www.getty.edu/publications/virtuallibrary/0892365722.html
10. Wilkinson, M.D., et al.: The FAIR guiding principles for scientific data management and stewardship. Sci. Data **3**, 160018 (2016). https://doi.org/10.1038/sdata.2016.18
11. ANCHISE Project: preserving our past: a review of modern technologies for remote site monitoring to prevent looting. https://www.anchise.eu/post/preserving-our-past-a-review-of-modern-technologies-for-remote-site-monitoring-to-prevent-looting
12. Alexakis, T., Peppes, N., Adamopoulou, E., Demestichas, K.: ART-CH: an advanced reasoning tool for fighting trafficking of cultural heritage. In: Research and Innovation Symposium for European Security and Defense, SECURITY AND DEFENSE 2023 Conference, p. 7170. Rhodes, Greece (2023)

Heritage Buildings and Objects' Digitisation and Visualisation Within the Cloud (HERITALISE)

Alan Miller[1(✉)], Catherine Anne Cassidy[1], Sharon Pisani[1], Mikel Borras[2], Drew Baker[3], and Jacquie Aitken[4]

[1] Computer Science, University of St Andrews, St Andrews KY8 4QH, Scotland
{ahr1,cc274,cc259}@st-andrews.ac.uk
[2] Innovation, Ingeniería Medio ambiente y Arquitectura, Barcelona, Spain
mborras@idp.es
[3] Heritage, Cyprus University of Technology, Limassol, Cyprus
drew.baker@cut.ac.cy
[4] Museum, Timespan Museum, Helmsdale, Scotland
jacquie@timespan.org.uk

Abstract. HERITALISE mission is to research and develop advanced digitisation techniques and solutions for documenting and representing diverse Cultural Heritage assets, giving a full comprehension of the diverse Cultural Heritage features, visible and non-visible. In addition, AI-powered tools including Machine Learning (ML) will be developed for improved and optimised data post-processing and integration based on standard and expanded methodologies. All this will be connected through a knowledge graph environment that allows the individual aspects known about the CH object to be related and retrievable. As with Wikipedia, by following links it will be possible to learn more about a particular object, what research has been done, and what results have been derived from it. HERITALISE will provide the upcoming European Collaborative Cloud for Cultural Heritage with an interoperable web-based Ecosystem, advanced input data from improved digitisation methodologies and preservation supporting tools, which will be achieved by meeting the projects general objectives.

Keywords: heritage · digitisation · HHBIM · memory twin · virtual museums · ECCCH

1 Heritage Buildings and Objects' Digitisation and Visualisation Within the Cloud

The HERITALISE mission is to research and develop advanced digitisation techniques and solutions for documenting and representing diverse CH assets, giving a full comprehension of the diverse CH features, visible and non-visible. In addition, AI-powered tools including Machine Learning (ML) will be developed for improved and optimised data post-processing and integration based on standard and expanded methodologies. All this will be connected through a knowledge graph environment that allows the individual aspects known about the CH object to be related and retrievable. As with Wikipedia, by following links it will be possible to learn more about a particular object, what research has been done, and what results have been derived from it (Fig. 1).

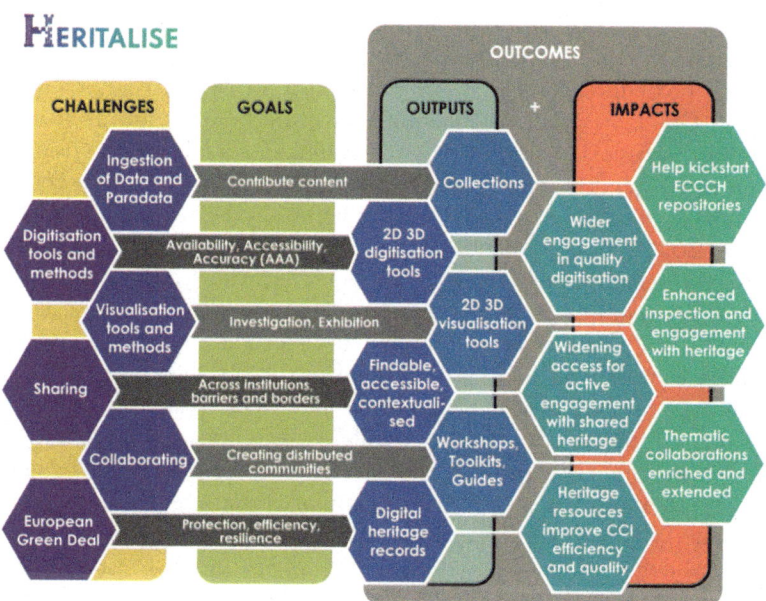

Fig. 1. Challenges, Goals, Outputs and Impacts for the HERITALISE project.

2 Context

Cultural Heritage (CH) is a complex ecosystem, involving institutions and actors that continuously produce and utilised multifaceted data and knowledge related to various types of CH objects. These objects can range from movable assets, architectural heritage [1], archaeological contexts, and natural environments, and may be of different nature and materials, whether tangible or intangible, which can be represented in a digital format. Complex and very diverse data are required to effectively document, study and support the preservation of such artifacts. New potential is enabled by recent technologies for data survey, analysis and sharing. In addition, data about the CH context and environment are often critical to complement their proper understanding and protection.

The digital recording of CH is an essential step in understanding and preserving the values of memory of the past. It creates an accurate digital record for the future and provides a means to transmit and communicate the knowledge and value of the material objects to society. Therefore, the main goal is to understand and appreciate the various values and meanings of the CH object - artistic, historical, scientific, aesthetic, social, and economic. This understanding can only be achieved if the individual aspects can be related to each other and are always available to users as a knowledge graph that allows traversing from one aspect to another seemingly. The creation and maintenance of this knowledge graph requires compliance with certain standards and best practices. Both aspects as well as the technical realization of the knowledge graph are the focus of HERITALISE. However, there is no internationally accepted framework, methodology or standard procedure for specifying the quality of detail, completeness, and accuracy in CH digitisation. Documentation projects are typically determined on a case-by-case basis using the many available methods and often require significant multi- and interdisciplinary cooperation. An object needs to be carefully examined, studied, and inspected to define the best available digitisation options for 2D/3D data acquisition and processing, visualization, and usage. Therefore, the recording of tangible CH requires a thorough understanding of the stakeholder requirements, the necessary technical specifications, the existing environmental conditions, the intended use of the final 3D digital model, its metrical accuracy and fidelity to the physical CH. Selection of the optimal human resources and digitisation technology are usually related to the size, complexity, material, texture, location, accessibility, Intellectual Property Rights of the CH artefact. For visible characteristics, nowadays consolidated technologies exist for 2D/3D digitization, e.g., laser scanning, structured light systems, and photogrammetry techniques. However, the use of artificial intelligence and other advanced technologies opens new possibilities. In addition, the heritage sector demands for the asset digitisation the aggregation of new types of data such as advanced hyper/multi-spectral and panoramic detection, data uncertainty local assessment, or detection of non-reachable surfaces by tomography. The use and improvement of these new techniques for CH still require further research, and furthermore, the fusion of all this information requires new data pre- and post-processing software (SW) tools that make use of the latest innovations on Information and Communication Technologies (ICT).

3 Aims and Objectives of the HERITALISE Project

HERITALISE will provide the upcoming ECCCH with a interoperable web-based Ecosystem, advanced input data from improved digitalisation methodologies and preservation supporting tools, which will be achieved by meeting the following General Objectives (GO) and setting the conditions for a wide-scale replicability and scalability across European CH institutions/organisations across European CH institutions/organisations:

GO1: State-of-the-art review of current digitisation standards and methodologies defining the data requirements for CH tangible and intangible objects' digitisation and sharing, identifying the gaps, and defining objectives and protocols for HERITALISE.

GO2: Improve 3D/2D Data acquisition methods and technologies, to increase the capability of traditional and well-consolidated one and covering a wide array of data typology such as visible/non-visible, and large/small scale characteristics. Development of specific dimensional and calibration procedures for panoramic acquisition of digitised data.

GO3: Data post-processing methods and technologies will be adopted, including new AI-powered digitisation methods and the development of data fusion techniques to mix various multi-modal digitisation approaches (multi sensory, multiscale, multi-spectral, external, and internal). CH sector professionals will benefit of this smoother and faster workflow to better curate, analyse and monitor visible or hidden characteristics of complex assemblies. Non-tangible data like temperature, humidity, light, sound, or flow of visitors, will be integrated.

GO4: Development of methodologies and solutions as Hardware (HW) and/or Software (SW) services (3D printing techniques, Monitoring & Analysis/preservation platform -to cope with the phenomena of deterioration Geo-HBIM based DTE, VR/AR/XR Game engine) that make use of previously mentioned CH data (including data modeling) that enable a wide range of CH organisations to draw upon CH in different ways.

GO5: Development of ECCCH-compliant open interoperability components enabling connecting and sharing data and modular services in a distributed web-based architecture. Such components will streamline the upload and sharing of data, including those data resulting from the new survey and processing methodologies, as structured and documented (with metadata and paradata) data.

GO6: Increasing the Impact of current and developing digitisation technologies of objects and buildings by overcoming the common problems related to technology transfer to museums, touring companies, and dissemination to individual end users. This includes the implementation of standardized web platforms of digitised assets and virtual touring. In this regard, HERITALISE brings in 4 different Use Cases as Proof of Concept.

These objectives will be translated into technical objectives addressing the following areas.

To define methodologies and guidelines for user-friendly digitisation and visualization, to enable the adoption of developed tools by the Heritage sector.

To develop new user-friendly tools for CH sector professionals (researchers, curators and conservators) to better study 3D assets (like objects or architectural details) and 2D assets (like paintings) by i) adding multiscale data fusion where macro detail data (geometry) combines with microscale data (scratches and cracks); and ii) adding multispectral data fusion by combining visible and non-visible spectrum (infrared, UV and X-ray) that also allows to better understand the deterioration processes tackling it through automation under the precepts of active preventive conservation.

To address in the CH sector important metrology concepts such as measurement uncertainty, accuracy, completeness, radiometric (colour) calibration, wide angle lenses panoramic reconstruction, and internal reconstruction of assets with computer tomography.

Advance the state of the art in 2D/3D post-processing methods using new technologies such as Artificial Intelligence and Algorithmic scripting for point-cloud processing, final digital asset data cleaning, segmentation and automatic categorization, to improve efficiency in massive digitisation scenarios.

To apply developed tools to improve the Home museum concept and enhanced CH analysis/management opportunities to allow general people access world CH for study or recreational purposes, and experts to multiscale enhanced data, through Digital Twin Environments (DTE) including Geo-HBIM models, Augmented and Virtual Reality as well as Game Engine technologies underpinned by relevant standard APIs and data encoding standards.

To increase Findability, Accessibility, Interoperability and Reusability (FAIR) of the Heritage information and by standardization of components, tools, procedures, metadata, visualization, and data structures, to incorporate results within the European Collaborative Cloud for CH (ECCCH).

To demonstrate developed tools and methodologies by 4 case studies in real uncontrolled scenarios, with a focus on the actual needs of the current CH sector professionals and users. The four case studies will be, West Highland Museum and the Timespan Museum in the Highlands of Scotland, Reggia di Venaria Reale in Torino and Villa Portelli in Malta.

4 Methodological Approach

HERITALISE will enable new improved management (restoration, documentation and maintenance, monitoring, tourism, and education) of CH. The project will develop improved digitisation of CH (GO2), including visible, nonvisible, hidden information and enhanced descriptions (GO3). F.A.I.R. management of data following standards, Open exchange protocols and semantic technologies will ensure machine-readable, consistent, open and secure communication of the information about CH in an enhanced ecosystem including all the related information (environmental, geographical, cultural context) (GO5). Such information will be effective input to new.

HERITALISE advanced methods and tools for processing and analysis (AI, data validation and integration) and use of data (GeoHBIM, Digital Twins, Augmented, Virtual, eXtended Reality, gaming) (GO4). Starting point are requirements from representative demo cases (covering diverse kinds of heritage and different use cases and conditions) (GO1), in which the solutions will be iteratively tested in close connection with stakeholders (GO6).

The work methodology, as shown in the following figure, is divided into four pillars/GOs: 1) HERITALISE Requirements and Methodology; 2) CH data acquisition techniques; 3) CH data processing/post-processing; 4) Services based on CH data; 5) ECCCH-compliant and interoperable ICT Ecosystem; and 6)

TRL 5–6 Validations to enable European scale scalability and replication. Therefore, the first pillar begins with research and definition of a methodology for digitising CH objects (and premises) focusing on HERITALISE Demo Sites and Use Cases. Then, in the second pillar, digital technologies are defined and further developed to improve CH tangible and non-tangible data. In the third pillar, AI-powered SW is developed and customized to enhance the processing and post-processing of data acquired whereas pillar 4 aims at developing HW and SW services that make use and boost the usability of all this CH data acquired and processed/post-processed. In between, Pillar 5 is responsible for the development of the ECCCH-compliant and interoperable ICT Ecosystem enabling FAIR CH data, paradata, and metadata exchange amongst CH stakeholders in accordance with defined user roles, rights, and data privacy/ethics aspects. Finally, overall validation is carried out in 4 diverse demo sites in Pillar 6, aiming at further scalability and replication across European CH institutions (Fig. 2).

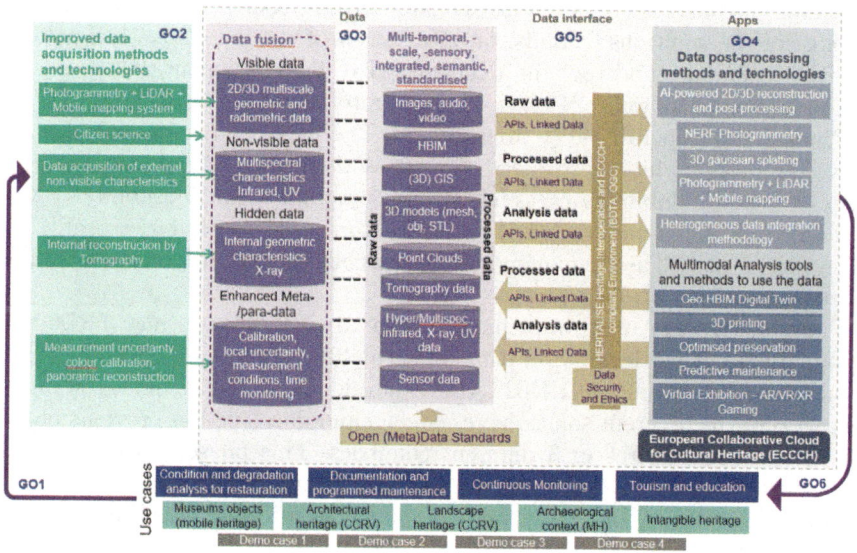

Fig. 2. Four pillars of the HERITALISE methodology.

5 Phases

The projects work will be organised into six phases.

Phase 1: CH Digitisation requirements and methodology definition: This phase aims at the definition of the basic requirements for the development and implementation of HERITALISE solutions, technologies and, further the ICT tool development passing along the data concepts (standards, ontologies), AI techniques, ... that will serve later to enable the tools and services deployment. This Phase is corresponding to the Pillars of development 1 and 2.

Phase 2: Digitisation tools' development and testing at lab scale: This phase, along with Phase 3 will represent the core technology research activity of the project. CH digitisation tools/components for enhanced data acquisition will be developed. All the activities will be carried out by strongly coupling numerical and experimental development according to an iterative process, benchmarking the results at each stage of development with the KPIs defined in Phase 1 [2].

Phase 3: CH data processing and post-processing: This phase complements the previous phase in technology research activities, taking as inputs the data sets gathered by the technologies involved in Phase 2. Innovative data processing, and post-processing tools will be developed by implementing latest technologies powered by Artificial Intelligence and scripting for automation, useful for large data scenarios. This phase corresponds to Pillar 3 [3].

Phase 4: CH data Services development: This phase is key to achieve one of the main objectives of HERITALISE: the development of a set of services combining the potential of different CH data streams, considering the complexity and cost of the solutions. Finally, an integration of the innovative technologies and ICT techniques and tools in a centralised ICT environment will be carried out, underpinned by webAPI services, leading to Phase 5 [4].

Phase 5: Interoperable ICT architecture: The developed methodologies and processing tools within the project, as well as the produced data, will need to comply to the Findability Accessibility Interoperability and Reusability (FAIR) principles. Thus, a standard-based data structures and vocabularies profile will be developed, as well as recommendations and components supporting FAIRness of developed pieces of SW [5].

Phase 6: HERITALISE implementation at Real Use Cases and TRL6 validation, aiming at EU level replication and scalability strategies: This phase represents the core outcome of HERITALISE development and includes the implementation of the different solutions researched and developed in previous phases in 4 demonstration sites in 3 different countries. This phase will also include the evaluation of the solutions to define the advancement up to TRL6 overall (with a different range of TRL depending on the solution/services) after project ends [6].

6 Use Cases and Pillars

There will be four use cases in the HERITALISE project. These are focussed on the West Highland Museum and Timespan Museum in Scotland, the Reggia di Venaria Reale, in Torino Italy, and the Villa Portelli, Malta [7]. Table 1 describes the heritage and goals for each use case. There will be four use cases in the HERITALISE project. These are focussed on the West Highland Museum and Timespan Museum [8] in Scotland, the Reggia di Venaria Reale, in Torino Italy, and the Villa Portelli, Malta [7]. Table 1 describes the heritage and goals for each use case.

Through this work Heritalise aims to advance the state of the art in the following areas.

6.1 Digitisation Standards

CH digitisation is currently a very dynamic field, each CH item requires a careful planning of the digitization workflow according to the dimension, materials, movability, fragility, and degradation state of the item itself. CH digitisation is largely unregulated and lacking generally accepted definitions on relevant aspects. The combination of range in digitisable artefacts and accelerating pace of relevant technological advances makes the definition of standards and general methodologies nontrivial. A comprehensive review in the relevant state of the art with consideration to the use cases and relevant solutions and technologies with be used to define the requirements and methodologies which will be used. CT scan and 3D printing: A combination of artefact specifics, in terms of features, and technical capabilities in terms resolution will define and dictate the achievable requirements and methodology that will be applied and used.

Defining requirements and methodologies for the utilization of CT scans and 3D printing in CH is crucial. It sets the guidelines for data acquisition, processing, and replication, ensuring accuracy and authenticity in preserving cultural artifacts. The process involves reviewing the relevant state of the art, close collaboration with CH experts and stakeholders to establish the specific data needs, formats, and preservation goals. By defining robust methodologies, including scanning techniques, material selection, and printing parameters, we ensure that the digitization process remains faithful to the original artefacts and highlights hidden or important features. Ultimately, these requirements and methodologies serve as the foundation for responsible CH preservation, facilitating access and research while safeguarding our shared history for future generations.

6.2 Digitisation Tools

Digitisation techniques have gathered during the last years the interest of experts in the field of CH. The creation of a 3D model of artefacts, without doubt, brings several advantages. Firstly, the possibility of fully documenting an item and creating a trustworthy digital replica, which includes data regarding the over all aspect, geometry, colour, texture, and morphology of the asset. Secondly, digital twins of artefacts can be archived to virtually preserve an artefact and monitor its state of preservation over time, in consideration of future degradation or non-predictable damage or loss. 3D models can be employed as an active tool for the study of an artifact by documenting and monitoring the morphology and aspect of an item, along with its conservation or during interventions, as traditionally done with 2D technical imaging, but with the advantage of having a model that can be virtually manipulated. Moreover, a virtual replica also finds applications among the public, enabling virtual access to items from all over the world. Eventually, 3D models can even be employed to create 3D-printed replicas

Table 1. HERITALISE Use Cases

Demo Site	Type of Heritage	Use Case Goals
West Highland Museum [8]	Cultural landscape, including objects, buildings, scenes, and intangible heritage	Digitise highland cultural landscape related to Gaelic Intangible heritage. Digitise artefacts, building and scenes, ingest into ECCCH and implement museum at home, game engine solution
Timespan	Object Collections (archaeological, working tools, artwork, textiles); Vernacular Fishing Village Architecture; Archaeological Landscapes; Intangible Heritage	i) Create themed content in ECCCH connected with the exploration of visualization; ii) Create digital twins of landscapes, buildings, objects, and scenes, based on GeoHBIM DTE including VR/AR/XR experience; iii) Record and collect intangible CH, songs, stories, and poetry, to tell stories of climate change and colonialism; iv) Develop metadata and para data which enables connections to be established and replicated within visualisation scenarios
Reggia di Venana Reale	Mobile objects (statues, paintings, furniture), Architecture, Landscape and historical gardens	i) Multiscale and multisensor data integration for the digitization of both the outdoor historical gardens and the indoor environments with also the cultural objects; ii) 3D data completion and integration-development of an HBIM [9] model standardized and able to collect monitoring data for the planned maintenance and preventive conservation plan; iii) Application of tomography on artefacts for study, research and touristic purposes, including CT scan and 3D printing
Villa Portelli	CH site-Villa and Gardens, Artefacts, intangible heritage	GeoHBIM digitization based on LiDAR/photogrammetry [10] 3D model of the villa to be used for documentation purposes, before and after restoration and reuse; ii) Creating a virtual site that can be explored using VR/unreal gaming engine - will also include a virtual museum of the site. iii) Creation of digital outreach test products related to CH interpretation; iv) Create a DT which shows how the site looked before the landscape around the Villa changed; v) Exploring the digitization of cultural intangible CH through collecting memories of people who have worked in or around the villa itself. The creation of a XR tool which will allow visitors to explore the site with the help of an AI powered avatar. The concept of digital twin will be extended to memory twin, where the digital twin acts as a gateway to intangible as well as tangible heritage [11]

of an artefact that can be exploited to create more inclusive tactile exhibitions or for innovative displays.

6.3 Data Processing Supported by AI

The innovative elements, beyond the state-of-the-art, of the proposed solution are: i) Combination of NeRFs, semantic segmentation, decay identification and recognition for complete and semantically enriched 3D models; ii) Data fusion with the integration of the internal parts of CH (such as statues) with the external one, thanks to tomography [12]; iii) Creation of standards and guidelines on data acquisition and expected accuracy based on the different types of instruments and sensors used; iv) The introduction of new indicators on the quality of the data acquired and processed thanks to the characteristics of the sensor and statistical methods. This will allow you to have a new awareness of the quality of the data; and v) Automatic interpretation, starting from multi-sensor techniques, of 3D models for the identification and recognition of the types of degradation.

6.4 Services Development

Digital Twins are one of the most relevant trends presently found among digitalization across all the sectors. In the same way scale models has been used since humanity started to use tools, their evolved Digital counterparts could offer the same benefits and beyond. From health1 to environment2, Digital Twinning appears as an unstoppable wave although they are often targeting just one of the most relevant benefits attached to the Digital Twin Environments: to be an effective PLM (Product Lifecycle Management) tool3 focused on CH buildings and objects. By avoiding data silos among stakeholders across any complex workflow, DTs allow a better decision taking based on comprehensive (not necessary complex) and updated information. Moreover, DTs allow another inherent benefit, the predictive purpose, which is by itself more than enough to justify the effort of developing Digital Twins of any connected physical object. Ambition 2 In the case of the CH sector, virtual experiences are being increasingly offered, according to home museum concept, based on digital replicas of CH buildings/objects and the integration of tools such VR/AR/XR into this CH DTE [13]. Ambition 3: Consistent integration methodology of multisource data will be developed starting from the project use cases requirements. HBIM, documenting detailed construction elements, will be used to represent architectures and building behaviours, supporting documentation, operation, and maintenance. GIS data, including data coming from integration and conversion from the HBIM, will relate each CH object (either tangible or intangible) into its context, enabling holistic and GIS-based queries and analysis, besides an enhanced Home Museum potential. Additional data (e.g., sensor data, environmental data, imagery) will be used to enhance the analysis potential and support further use cases. Linked data and the OGC RAINBOW are key technologies for the semantic integrations.

6.5 AR/VR Visualisation

Methods of visualising 3D digitised heritage artifacts can be applied to different types of heritage artifacts and can be presented in different use cases. Heritage Objects may be pieces of art, artifacts such as vases, monuments, buildings or archaeological sites. With improved graphics and processing powers it is now increasingly practical to represent landscapes, sea scapes and city scapes. This gives us three scales of digital heritage objects; each scale shares many characteristics. We will refer to these scales as artefact, scene and vista. Augmented Reality and Virtual Reality can be thought of as a sliding scale. At the augmented end our interactions with the real world are augmented digitally. At the Virtual Reality end, we are immersed in "complete" virtual representations. In cross or X reality we can interact simultaneously with the virtual and augmented world.

6.6 Digital Twins

These take a digital representation at any of the artifact, scene and vista scales, and supplement it with data which describes the relationship between the digital representation and the real world. Digital twin applications themselves can cover a wide spectrum from real time control applications through to digital objects with descriptions and interactions attached. In the context of tools for ECCCH, we are interested in developing applications which enable digital twins to be developed from digital models at each of the scales to be deployed in web, mobile and museum contexts.

Ambition: Through building on existing applications developed by project partners and deploy them within use cases. This will play the basis for design of tools for the ECCCH which enable museums to develop mobile, web and kiosk applications of digital twins at the scale of collections of artefacts, digital scenes and vistas.

6.7 Cultural Heritage Conservation Module

Engage stakeholders in conservation and preservation to gain insights, perspectives, and support for their preservation purposes. Develop specific, measurable, achievable, relevant, and time-bound goals for the proposed CH preventive conservation technology. Prioritize actions that need to be taken to achieve the identified conservation and preservation goals. Create a method outlining the actions required to achieve the goals for integrate the CH conservation technology/tool of HW/SW into an integrated ITC ecosystem.

Related KPIs: 4 CH sites in three countries that includes different categories of CH objects (monuments/artefacts, tangibles/intangibles) and engage a heterogeneous group of stakeholders and experts in the field with expertise in a representative variety of CH typology and historical periods.

6.8 CT SCAN Based 3D Printing

From educational institutions to museums, the combination of CT scan data processing and 3D printing can become an indispensable tool in unlocking the secrets and preserving the beauty of our shared human history. 3D printing has become significantly more accessible both by individuals for personal use, and in addition to institutions. This work aims to establish the methods by which the data can be processed and made widely available for reuse, hence realising the potential of these technologies in CH.

7 Impact

Cultural Heritage practitioners in Europe, including curators, conservators and researchers of CH, use a common set of new innovative tools and methods for the digitisation and visualisation of CH objects (3D and enhanced 2D). Our collective work will elevate the precision, accuracy, speed and consistency with which digitisation can take place. HERITALISE will also develop innovative tools supporting new ways of visualising heritage objects.

The European Collaborative Cloud for CH (ECCCH) provides CH institutions and professionals with enhanced technological and methodological capabilities to study CH objects, to share related data of their visible and non-visible properties and characteristics, and to develop new forms of collaboration. Contribution from provide innovative tools that redefine and extend the way we engage with CH. Is, we will add value to the way museums can engage with both their collections and audiences.

By connecting digital objects with Sustainable Development Goals [14] and tasks we will contribute to the role of museums in education, economy and society.

A digital ecosystem open to all stakeholders' professions and activities will enable interaction with each other contributing to a new digital commons through extending the ECCCH ecosystem with interoperable tools and using open standards we will ensure the tools and outputs of this project extend the new digital commons to include the creation of a best use tool box made up of the different case studies and plot projects and research from the project - which can be used by any CH organisaton engaged in digitisation and visualisaiton.

Through improving the accuracy and reliability of digitisation, we will make it possible for digital twins to be better mirror real world heritage objects. This will improve authenticity in application that make use of digital twins, improving their effectiveness in heritage organisations and in the creative and cultural industries. At the same time improvements in ease of use, development of support infrastructures and development of communities of practice will increase the quantity of digital twins. This will in turn boost tourism, the creative industries, and quality education. As more digital representations of heritage are made available across Europe this will contribute to the strengthening of European Identity as well as contributing to the preservation, restoration and promotion of CH. Through improving the accuracy, consistency of digitised CH we will make resources available to museums and to the cultural and creative industries that will enable engagement with CH resulting in the following impacts: 1) Provides the perspective to embrace the green transition by re interpreting the relationship between cultural and natural heritage, 2) Sustain social cohesion by engaging citizens, researchers, and experts within heritage communities. 3) Protects and transmits tangible cultural assets [15].

Contribute to the Green Deal (GD) goals and support an economy that works for people: To achieve the EU GD goals, the heritage sector has a huge role in monitoring, adaptation, mitigation, and communication, promoting climate action to address the climate emergency. Digitisation heritage artifacts creates a record of the current state of heritage which will be important in monitoring and tracking climate change.

8 Summary

The HERITALISE project brings together a consortium of SMEs, Heritage organisations and knowledge institutions with the aim of developing and sharing tools which take the state of the art for the digitisation and visualisation of heritage forward. Contributing to the European Collaborative Cloud for Cultural Heritage ECCCN HERITALISE will help CH practitioners realise the potential of emerging technologies for the promotion and preservation of heritage [16] (Fig. 3).

Fig. 3. HERITALISE project project number 101158081, funded from Call HORIZON-CL2-2023-HERITAGE-ECCCH-01 as an RIA action.

References

1. Noardo, F.: Architectural heritage semantic 3D documentation in multi-scale standard maps. J. Cult. Heritage **32**, 156–165 (2018). https://doi.org/10.1016/j.culher.2018.02.009
2. Kortaberria, G., Mutilba, U., Gomez-Acedo, E., Tellaeche, A., Minguez, R.: Accuracy evaluation of dense matching techniques for casting part dimensional verification. Sens. (Switz.) **18** (2018) https://doi.org/10.3390/s18093074
3. Chiabrando, F., Sammartano, G., Spanò, A., Spreafico, A.: Hybrid 3D models: when geomatics innovations meet extensive built heritage complexes. ISPRS Int. J. Geo-Inf. **8** (2019). https://doi.org/10.3390/ijgi8030124

4. Casacuberta, J., Sainz, F., Madrid, J.: Evaluation of an inclusive smart home technology system. In: Bravo, J., Hervás, R., Rodríguez, M. (eds.) IWAAL 2012. LNCS, vol. 7657, pp. 316–319. Springer, Heidelberg (2012). https://doi.org/10.1007/978-3-642-35395-6_43
5. Getchell, K., Miller, A., Allison, C., Sweetman, R.: Exploring the second life of a byzantine basilica. In: Petrovic, O., Brand, A. (eds.) Serious Games on the Move. Springer, Vienna (2009). https://doi.org/10.1007/978-3-211-09418-1_11
6. Brown, K., et al.: Report on a policy round table by EU-LAC-MUSEUMS held at the European Commission offices, Brussels, 29 April 2019. Zenodo (2019). https://doi.org/10.5281/zenodo.3368301
7. Formosa, S., Sciberras, E., Charles, G.: Applied geomatics approaches in the maltese Islands - SpatialTrain II (2022)
8. Mccaffery, J., Miller, A., Vermehren, A., Fabola, A.: The virtual museums of caen: a case study on modes of representation of digital historical content. Technical report (2015)
9. Alonso, R., Borras, M., Koppelaar, R., Lodigiani, A., Loscos, E., Yöntem, E.: Sphere: BIM digital twin platform. Proceedings **20**, 9 (2019). https://doi.org/10.3390/proceedings2019020009
10. Sebar, L.E., et al.: 3D multispectral imaging for cultural heritage preservation: the case study of a wooden sculpture of the Museo Egizio di Torino. Heritage **6**, 2783–2795 (2023). https://doi.org/10.3390/heritage6030148
11. Martinez-Rodriguez, S., et al.: Practices for the Underground Built Heritage Valorisation. Second Handbook (2023). https://doi.org/10.48217/MNGSPC03
12. Vigorelli, L., et al.: Comparison of two ancient Egyptian middle kingdom statuettes from the Museo Egizio of Torino through computed tomographic measurements. J. Archaeol. Sci.: Rep. **44**, 103518 (2022). https://doi.org/10.1016/j.jasrep.2022.103518
13. Cassidy, C.A., et al.: Digital pathways in community museums. Technical report (2019)
14. Zipsane, H.: On the special preconditions for open air museums in times of the sustainability agenda
15. Loscos, M.E.: Sphere from BIM representation to functional simulation and real time advanced control. Technical report (2021). https://sphere-project.eu/
16. OGC 3D-IoT platform for smart cities engineering report. Technical report (2020). http://www.opengeospatial.org/

Florence4D's Interdisciplinary Workflow for Research-Based 3D Models: A Palazzo Medici Case Study

Fabrizio Nevola[1(✉)], Anna McGee[1,2], and Luca Brunke[1,2]

[1] University of Exeter, EX4 4PY, Exeter, England
f.nevola@exeter.ac.uk
[2] National Gallery, WC2N 5DN, London, England

Abstract. This paper considers best practices for research-based 3D modelling in art and architectural history, proposing a refined Florence4D workflow for the integration of 'traditional' scholarly research with digital visualisation methods in a way that is transparent, stable and verifiable. The case study through which these issues are explored is the digital reconstruction of the *camera terrena* of Florence's Palazzo Medici, as it appeared in *c*.1492. The goal is to revisualise and test out hypotheses for the interaction between furniture, architectural space and artworks (including Paolo Uccello's *Battle of San Romano* panels) in this exceptional Renaissance interior during a key moment in its history.

Keywords: Research-based 3D modelling · research and reconstruction workflow · Renaissance art and architecture · Florence4D

Research-based 3D modelling holds significant potential for art and architectural history, allowing objects to be reconnected with their original material and spatial contexts and helping the scholar to develop and transmit new hypotheses. However, for these visualisations to be of value, the underlying research must be both connected to it and readily accessible; after all, an argument without evidence cannot be tested. This article focuses on a new early modern Florentine case study to explore best practices for effectively communicating this kind of research output within the academic community and beyond [20, 35]. By refining the Florence4D workflow, we aim to enhance the integration of research with visualisation, ensuring that scholarly interpretations remain transparent and verifiable.

Creating a 3D model operationalises research by integrating advanced digital technologies with traditional methods like archival study, library research, and site surveys. This inherently interpretative process follows an iterative workflow, moving from an initial hypothesis to visualisation and back to refinement (Fig. 1). Conceptualising this workflow as two intersecting paths that converge in the final output is useful. The upper path focuses on reality-based reconstruction, gathering extant evidence through site surveys, which is then processed and optimised to model the current state of the object or building. Simultaneously, the lower path draws upon historical and secondary sources to hypothesise prior states. The final step merges these two strands, structuring the underlying data and ensuring that both the model and its evidentiary basis remain accessible and interconnected.

This visualisation project – which is ongoing – takes as its case study the *camera terrena* of the Palazzo Medici as it appeared around 1492. The research is a collaboration between Anna McGee, who focuses on traditional art-historical data, and Luca Brunke, who is developing the 3D model. Their combined efforts can ensure the model was grounded in rigorous research, integrating both reality-based data and historical interpretation. This case study also highlights the need for a multidisciplinary approach in research-based 3D modelling, where success depends on synthesising diverse skills and information to create a model that visualises historical hypotheses while remaining firmly connected to its source data.

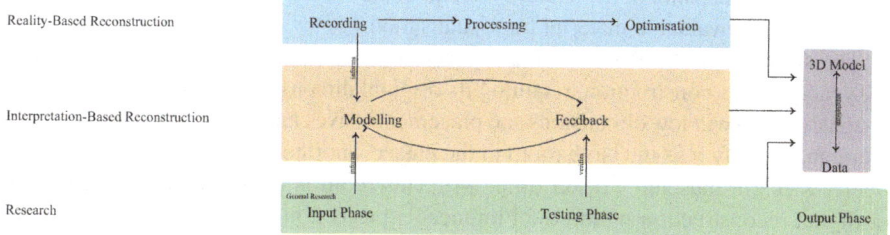

Fig. 1. Diagram of Florence4D's hybrid research-based 3D modelling process, combining reality- and interpretation-based reconstruction workflows, and adapted to reflect the wrap-around workflow of the *camera terrena* case study.

1 An Archetypal Space in the 15th-Century Florentine Palazzo

The ground-floor rooms of privately owned palazzi were becoming increasingly important parts of the home in the 15th century [25, 33, 34]. A new room type developed as the focal point for activity in this newly prominent ground floor: a luxurious *camera terrena* for the head of the household.[1] The Palazzo Medici *camera terrena*, a large space at 10 by 7.5 m, was accessible from both the cortile and the palace garden, and was adjoined by a *stufa* (heater or heated space) and the manservants' sleeping quarters, from which it could be serviced. The head of the Medici household would probably have hosted in the *camera terrena* their most esteemed guests and allies, as well as some of the many petitioners who visited daily in the hope of an audience [10, 18, 19, 28]. The *paterfamilias* was also likely to have slept there on occasion [1, 22].

An inventory of the contents of Palazzo Medici taken in 1492 reveals that its *camera terrena* was filled with luxurious furniture and artworks, showcasing Medici wealth and

---

[1] A more in-depth analysis of the *camera terrena* in 15th-century Florentine palazzi forms part of Anna McGee's forthcoming doctoral thesis.

refinement in this bustling part of the home.[2] Some of the paintings the inventory records in this space can be identified as still-extant masterpieces: the three panels depicting the Battle of San Romano by Paolo Uccello, now separated between London's National Gallery (NG583), the Uffizi (1890 n. 479) and the Louvre (MI 469) [MAP, ASF, 165, fol. 6r, see 5, 30, 31]; Piero del Pollaiuolo's portrait of Galeazzo Maria Sforza, which has also made its way into the Uffizi's collection (1890, n. 1492) [MAP, ASF, 165, fol. 6r, see 30, 31]; and the large tondo depicting the Adoration of the Magi, by Fra Angelico and Filippo Lippi, today in Washington's National Gallery of Art (1952.2.2.) [Ibid.]. In addition, there were three other large panels, depicting "battles and [of?] lions and dragons", the "story of Paris", and "a hunt", along with a portrait of the Duke of Urbino and two smaller images of saints [Ibid., 14]. In terms of furnishings, the inventory lists a canopied bed on a plinth, intarsiated *spalliera* panelling, a *lettuccio* (padded bench) with built-in cupboards, and a table and chairs [Ibid.]. Of course, the 1492 inventory captures only a snapshot of the *camera terrena* at the moment in which it was taken, yet it still provides invaluable material for visualisation.

The structure of the Palazzo Medici *camera terrena* survives largely intact nearly 600 years after its construction, retaining its original dimensions, vaulting, and corbels, though door and window dimensions and placements have changed. Seventeenth-century floorplans identify it as the large room in the palace's northeast corner, now the Palazzo Medici Riccardi museum's ticket office [4]. This room is therefore an ideal test case for digital reconstruction within the Florence4D project: not only do its rich political, social, and artistic history makes it a compelling subject, its surviving structure, detailed inventory and extant artworks make producing a 3D model actually feasible.

2 Visualising the *Camera Terrena*

The 1492 inventory provides detailed descriptions of the objects found in the room, often including references to their dimensions, their component parts and the materials used. However, attempting a visual reconstruction of the *camera terrena* reveals just how much the written word does not specify, just how many assumptions and interpretative decisions are necessary to conjure fully the putative appearance of the furnished room in 1492. In particular, the inventory entries make only one or two references to the location of objects within the space – and these are relative to other objects, rather than absolute.

Two visualisation attempts of this room have previously been made by scholars. The first, by Anna Maria Amonaci and Andrea Baldinotti in 1992, consists of two simple reconstructive line drawings, broadly outlining the positions of the largest artworks and key furnishings [2]. These were not stand-alone images but relied on an accompanying essay to highlight uncertainties and justify interpretative choices. Then, in 2004, Gabriele Morolli led a team to produce a digital model of the room, building on the earlier research.[3] However, this detailed simulation presents an illusion of completeness,

---

[2] "L'inventario dei beni e delle masserizie esistenti nel palazzo di via Larga", 1492 (1512 copy), Archivio Mediceo avanti il Principato (MAP), Archivio di Stato di Firenze (ASF), filza 165. For transcription, see [30] and for English translation, see [31].

[3] The digital reconstruction, executed for Morolli by the Florence-based modelling and videography company 3dSign, was first made public in February 2004 as part of an installation called the "Laboratorio di Lorenzo" at the Palazzo Medici Riccardi museum.

smoothing over omissions and blending fact with assumption – everything seems in its proper place. Moreover, unlike the earlier reconstruction, this version lacks scholarly commentary that could indicate degrees of certainty, cite evidence for the appearance or placement of a particular feature, or admit to areas of creative licence.

The model we are developing with Florence4D builds on these earlier projects, aiming to integrate the sort of discursive reconstruction made possible in 1992 by the inclusion of written commentary with the opportunities for visualisation provided by current digital technologies. Crucially, though, and unlike these precursors, our model is primarily intended as an analytical tool, a virtual space for testing out reconstructive hypotheses. Unknowns and uncertainties should no longer be seen as hindrances to the development of a complete model [7]. Rather, they can generate new research questions, not only about the case-study objects but also more widely, about the interrelationship between furniture and paintings, and the spatial dynamics of domestic interiors.

The following section discusses the modelling work in progress for this case study. As the project is ongoing, this discussion relates to process and experimentation rather than seeking to showcase definitive technical procedure or draw specific art-historical conclusions. We will focus here on the reconstruction of the east wall, which comprised the vaulting and corbels, a door leading to the manservants' quarters, the *spalliera* panelling and three large paintings. Of these elements, some have survived to this day, some have been modified and some have disappeared entirely and are known only through documentary evidence. Therefore, here we are combining reality-based and interpretation-based reconstructions, and, in so doing, working to refine the Florence4D workflow.

3 The Modelling Process

Reality-based reconstruction begins with the building in its current state. For the surviving architectural structure of the *camera terrena*, spatial data is obtained through LiDAR scanning, which produces a scaled point cloud of the room.[4] This must be reduced and converted into a polygon mesh, then optimised via retopology using Cloud Compare and Blender. Retopology regularises the model by removing extraneous details, making it easier to work with. A key step is removing modern ticket office furnishings. Manual retopology closes gaps left behind by extrapolating from the existing mesh. Some elements, such as the original doorway on the east wall, must be preserved as separate objects. While optimisation slightly alters the scan, the process is documented, with both raw and refined versions archived. The final base mesh provides a clean architectural shell for further reconstruction.

For smaller details, photogrammetry is more effective. This method captures both geometry and texture, useful for elements like the *pietra serena* corbels supporting the vaulting along the east wall. Two full and two partial corbels are photographed from multiple angles using a DSLR camera, then processed into 3D models. These can be optimised using decimation, remeshing, and baking. However, due to their high

---

[4] The Leica BLK360 laser scanner was used, with additional reference photographs taken with the CANON EOS 5D Mark III camera.

placement and obstruction, photogrammetric results vary, with gaps in the upward-facing surfaces.

Scanning, meshing, and photogrammetry generate large amounts of data, requiring suitable repositories for storage and management [24]. It is useful to have one repository for the active development of 3D models and datasets, and a separate repository that can hold and distribute the finalised data. The former mimics a local file system, where each workflow step is a separate project, while also providing version control, remote access, and collaboration features. It stores raw project data and intermediate processing steps, allowing future adjustments. The latter repository will facilitate the citation of different states, persistence and identifiers upon distribution.[5]

In order to proceed to a research-based reconstruction, analogue data, primarily gleaned from the 1492 inventory, needs to be modelled and integrated into this born-digital version of the *camera terrena*. The challenge is that even the most detailed written description cannot directly translate into a visual object, yet Blender (or any other 3D modelling software) requires precise instructions to generate a model. Researchers must therefore start by dissecting the inventory and other sources to create fully dimensioned templates of the objects, making clearly documented interpretative assumptions where necessary.

The *spalliera* panelling is described in particular detail in the inventory: some fourteen metres long, made of cypress wood and walnut intarsia, with built-in cupboards, two parts cut out to accommodate the room's doorways behind, and a nearly eight-metre-long *cassa* incorporated into the front [MAP, ASF, 165, fol. 6r, see 30, 31]. Though it has not survived – nor have any 15th-century *spalliere* of its kind – we can look to contemporary paintings of domestic interiors for a general sense of the furnishing we aim to replicate.[6] We can then sketch a visualisation and input data into Blender. The *spalliera* (13.92 m, 24 *braccia*) can be arranged along the *camera terrena*'s east wall (10.1 m), with the remainder covering part of the north wall. Its surface can be divided into modules, with cutouts positioned over the doors. The *cassa* (8.75 m, 15 *braccia*) fits below the east wall panelling, between the door and the south wall. For 2D characteristics such as wood tone and intarsia, the model can either incorporate a placeholder texture or remain a generic block colour, prioritising either the verisimilar yet misleading or the honest yet unconvincing. Dimensions not specified in the inventory – such as depth, *cassa* height, and others – require educated guesses based on research, with given and speculative values distinguished in the sketch.

The *spalliera*'s overall height is its most crucial unknown, as it affects the positioning of paintings above it. Following deductions by Amonaci and Baldinotti, we might assume

---

[5] We are currently researching and implementing different repositories that are self-hosted, to give ourselves more control over their configuration and the data we store in them. Rather than having to develop a bespoke solution, it would be preferable for the data repository to already exist and be well established. In general, a dedicated data repository would give our finalised digital data better structure and maintainability in both the short and long term.

[6] Often cited is the panelling depicted Domenico Ghirlandaio's *The Birth of the Virgin* fresco (c.1485–90) in the church of Santa Maria Novella. Extant wooden furnishings with a different function from the *spalliera*, but of the same period, are further sources worth consulting (e.g. the choir stalls for the Palazzo Medici chapel) [29, 32].

it was at least as high as the door apertures behind it (1.98m) [2]. Since the panelling left for the doors was just 1.89m high, the *spalliera* likely stood on a low platform, raising it by 9cm. Additionally, given the 20cm-wide door surround on the east wall, a cornice of similar width likely sat atop the *spalliera*, aligning it horizontally with the architectural elements. We can therefore estimate the *spalliera*'s height at 2.2m.

To arrange the three paintings above the *spalliera* on the east wall, we start with three assumptions: (1) of the six paintings listed above the *spalliera* and *lettuccio*, the three San Romano panels by Uccello ran along the east wall; (2) they survive today as the versions in London, Florence, and Paris; and (3) they were arranged left to right in that sequence. These assumptions are widely accepted in scholarship [15]. The paintings themselves can be reconstructed with high accuracy, using high-resolution images to texture 3D models.[7] The paintings' exact positioning, however, remains unknown, as does their relationship with the *spalliera*, the wall, vaulting, and corbels. The inventory states that each painting was 200cm (3½ braccia) high, but their current height is 182 cm. Since there is no evidence they were cut down after 1492, the missing 18cm likely accounts for their gold frames, making them 9 cm wide. This means the combined height of the *spalliera* and paintings would have been approximately 4.2 m.

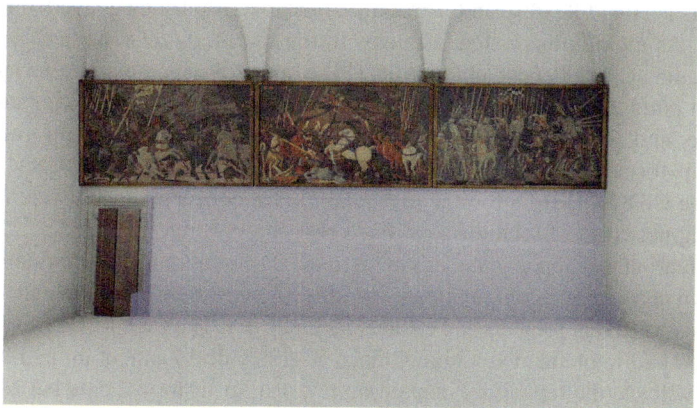

Fig. 2. Preview of the Florence4D digital model of the *camera terrena* east wall (unfinished).

Using these annotated sketches, interpretation-based data on the *spalliera* and paintings can be integrated into the reality-based reconstruction (Fig. 2). In Blender, 3D objects are built with Geometry Nodes, a parametric modelling system that allows iterative construction. A one-metre section of the *spalliera* can be replicated along the east wall, streamlining the process while enabling easy updates or modifications. This approach facilitates multiple versions during prototyping and future revisions. A model created in this way enhances precision in reconstructing the east wall, revealing spatial

---

[7] At this stage, we are using San Romano painting images from collection websites. These vary in resolution and lack details on capture, processing, orthorectification, and do not provide the raw data needed for colour adjustments. Image permissions for published models would need to be addressed.

constraints for the San Romano panels. The corbels, at 3.8 m high, sit below the calculated painting height of 4.2 m. Additionally, if the frames are correctly estimated, the gap between corbels at that level is too narrow for the panels. This suggests an overlap between paintings and corbels. Volker Gebhardt noted this issue but dismissed it, stating that the corbels would not have significantly obstructed the panels [13, 17]. However, our visualisation makes this conflict explicit, showing that three-dimensional elements cannot simply be ignored. Next, we will assess how digital reconstruction can help explore solutions for this apparent incompatibility.

Having gathered all our data in digital form, we can now create an interrogable digital model. Research-based 3D models can be stored similarly to reality-based models, but the data informing them should be kept separately in a dedicated repository for structured and textual information. For this purpose, the Florence4D project has used the web-publishing platform Omeka S [12]. This approach allows for more complex relationships between objects and their data, avoiding the limitations of embedding research data directly within the 3D model, which often only supports simple key-value pairs. Keeping data in a separate, centralised database simplifies updates and reduces the risk of 3D models circulating with outdated research information.

To ensure that unstructured information from inventory and art-historical research conclusions is stored flexibly and is machine-readable, it must be converted into structured data. As a preliminary step, all items in the inventory are dissected in a spreadsheet, assigning each a Persistent Identifier (PID) and providing separate entries for their constituent parts, historical figures involved in their creation, evidence regarding their appearance, and any art-historical commentary. This semi-structured information can then be transformed into a fully structured language using the CiDOC CRM ontology [6, 21]. The CiDOC CRM's formal vocabulary helps conceptualise this knowledge by establishing networks of relationships. Each real object connects to coded information about its creation and appearance, linking it to its 3D counterpart, an information object with its own network and computational workflow. This system enhances data interoperability across different projects and ensures its longevity. The CiDOC CRM schema can be imported and implemented within Omeka S. A key development in the Florence4D workflow will see the repository containing not just art-historical data but also details about the technical infrastructure, including the contents and locations of other digital files related to an object.

We are currently exploring user-friendly navigation between the 3D visualisation and these associated sources and explanations (Fig. 3). In previous iterations of the Florence4D workflow, the case-study model was imported into a 3D web viewer linked to the research repository, allowing users to click on modelled objects and view brief descriptions along with links to the corresponding Omeka S item pages. This method effectively connects research data to the 3D model, but lacks sufficient integration for users to interrogate and manipulate the data within the same application as the model itself. A promising prototype in development employs a self-developed Blender add-on to download and link research data, exposing specific values to Blender's internal components. This allows users to perform conditional operations or modify data as needed [11]. The advantage of this system lies in its integration with existing software within our workflow, leveraging Blender's native features instead of requiring users

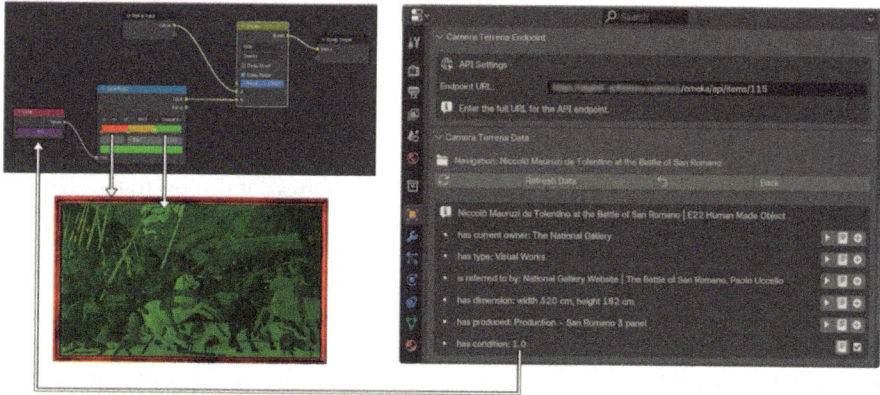

Fig. 3. Shader setup up in Blender that overlays a colour driven by data from the Omeka S repository. The data is received by a custom add-on and made available for any operation within Blender (here, green signifies high certainty/existence, red signifies low certainty/non-existence).

to implement every function from scratch. Our goal is to simplify the recreation and adaptation process by enabling users to access and input documentation directly in Blender's interface, without having to log into the database's web interface and enter the data manually.

We are also investigating how Blender can visualise uncertainty and experiment with different object arrangements in the space. In addition to written notes on evidence quality now accessible in Blender, we can encode and communicate the degree of certainty within the model using conditional rendering [16]. Within the remote data repository, we assign values to specific object features, and in Blender, prepare shader instructions that overlay colours based on these values from Omeka S. For instance, colour overlays might indicate which structures are reality-based versus those based on interpretation. Using the same value assignment system, we can set up instructions in Blender to include or exclude certain *camera* features. Users can encode factors beyond uncertainty, such as artist, conservation status, or current location. Because all data resides in a structured database, users can alter the type of data controlling the colour, provided the correct value mapping instructions are stored in the shader.

The user does not have to stop at highlighting uncertain features; they can also test out alternative hypotheses by manipulating these features in the model. This can be achieved through parametric modelling. For uncertain objects or parts, an input field in Blender allows users to enter different values within set parameters (e.g. maximum and minimum heights of artwork on a wall). This capability is valuable for scholars seeking feasible arrangements for the San Romano panels or illustrating specific theories to their audience. Several other factors are fixed based on their evidence strength, such as the required location of the San Romano panels on the east wall, above the *spalliera*, in a specified sequence with defined dimensions [3, 23]. If a scholar wishes to reduce the height of the *spalliera*, mindful of potential obstruction, parametric modelling adjusts it proportionally rather than simply stretching it. Alternatively, scholars might experiment with frame structures or test theories, such as the suggestion that panels were angled forward to avoid corbels, allowing for modelling and measurement of that angle.

4 Conclusions

While the *camera terrena* model remains a work in progress, it demonstrates how and why researchers should develop shared methodologies and approaches that operate across the fields of art history and digital humanities, rather than separately, in distinct 'silos'. A research-based model requires input from a diverse range of sources and skillsets, and needs to be developed iteratively and with shared objectives. To ensure that the final outputs from such collaborations are valuable research resources, the model and the data from which it derives must be made accessible, though challenges remain regarding the technical standards to be applied to the storage, availability and reusability of such data.

Defining and refining how 3D modelling can operate as a robust research environment, with data that is independent from and outlasts any particular visualisation produced from it, is important if models are to offer an enduring contribution to art-historical practices. Stable outputs based on machine readable datasets will ensure that 3D models can be properly cited, and, just as crucially, be subject to commentary and future revision within the field. At the same time, we should not lose sight of the value of visualisations as a means of communicating research, to the peer community as well as to wider audiences.

Acknowledgements. Florence4D began as a research project funded by the Getty Foundation and led by Fabrizio Nevola (University of Exeter) and Donal Cooper (University of Cambridge) and currently continues through the work of a number of researchers, including the co-authors of this article, Luca Brunke and Anna McGee, whose research is funded by the Arts and Humanities Research Council, UK, in collaboration with the University of Exeter and the National Gallery, London. See [8, 9, 26, 27] for recent Florence4D projects and publications. Throughout its development, this research has been presented at, and received feedback from, various forums, including: the Renaissance Society of America Annual Conference (April 2022), the 'Future of the Virtual Past' International Conference at the University of Cambridge (June 2022) and the University of Exeter Digital Humanities Laboratory Seminar Series (January 2023).

References

1. Ajmar-Wollheim, M., Dennis, F. (eds.): At Home in Renaissance Italy. V&A Publishing, London (2006)
2. Amonaci, A.M., Baldinotti, A.: La "chamera grande terrena" di Lorenzo in Palazzo Medici: ipotesi di ricostruzione. In: Morolli, G., Acidini Luchinat, C., Marchetti, L. (eds.), L'architettura di Lorenzo il Magnifico, pp. 126–128, Silvana, Florence (1992)
3. Baily, J.: Using Geometry Nodes as a Modifier for True Proceduralism. Blender Base Camp. blenderbasecamp.com/home/what-are-geometry-nodes-in-blender/
4. Bulst, W.A.: Die ursprüngliche innere Aufteilung des Palazzo Medici in Florenz. Mitteilungen Des Kunsthistorischen Institutes in Florenz. **14**, 369–392 (2018). https://doi.org/10.11588/MKHI.1970.4.41607

5. Caglioti, F.: Nouveautés sur la Bataille de San Romano de Paolo Uccello. Revue du Louvre. **51**, 37–54 (2001)
6. CIDOC CRM. cidoc-crm.org/
7. Cohen, M.: Visualizing the unknown in the digital era of art history. Art Bull. **104**, 6–19 (2022). https://doi.org/10.1080/00043079.2022.2000271
8. Cooper, D., Capulli, C.: Perugino nei perduti contesti fiorentini. In: Pierini, M., Picchiarelli, V. (eds.) Il meglio maestro d'Italia: Perugino e il Suo Tempo, pp. 334–345. Dario Cimorelli Editore, Milan (2023)
9. Cooper, D., Nevola, F., Capulli, C., Brunke, L.: Hidden Florence 3D and experiments in reconstruction. In: Nevola, F., Rosenthal, D., Terpstra, N. (eds.) Hidden Cities: Urban Space, Geolocated Apps and Public History in Early Modern Europe, pp. 231–248. Routledge, London (2022). https://doi.org/10.4324/9781003172000-15
10. DePrano, M.K.: "Chi Vuol Esser Lieto, Sia": objects of entertainment in the Tornabuoni palace in Florence. In: Campbell, E., Miller, S., Consavari, E. (eds.) the Early Modern Italian Domestic Interior, 1400–1700, pp. 127–142. Routledge, London (2013). https://doi.org/10.4324/9781315615813
11. Demetrescu, E., Ferdani, D.: From field archaeology to virtual reconstruction: a five steps method using the extended matrix. Appl. Sci. **11** (2021). https://doi.org/10.3390/app11115206
12. Digital Scholar: Omeka S. www.omeka.org/s/
13. Gebhardt, V.: Some problems in the reconstruction of Uccello's "Rout of San Romano" Cycle. Burlingt. Mag. **133**, 179–185 (1991)
14. Gombrich, E.: The early Medici as patrons of art. In: Norm and Form: Studies in the Art of Renaissance, pp. 35–57. Phaidon, London (1978)
15. Gordon, D.: The Fifteenth Century Italian Paintings. Yale University Press, London (2003)
16. Hermon, S., Nikodem, J.: 3D modelling as a scientific research tool in archaeology. In: Layers of Perception: Proceedings of the 35th International Conference on Computer Applications and Quantitative Methods in Archaeology, pp. 1–6. Habelt-Verlag, Bonn (2008). https://doi.org/10.15496/publikation-3066
17. Joannides, P.: Paolo Uccello's "Rout of San Romano": a new observation. Burlingt. Mag. **131**, 214–216 (1989)
18. Kent, F.W.: Palaces, politics and society in fifteenth-century Florence. I Tatti Stud. Ital. Renaissance **2**, 41–70 (1987). https://doi.org/10.2307/4603652
19. Kent, F.W., James, C.: Princely Citizen: Lorenzo de' Medici and Renaissance Florence. Brepols, Turnhout (2013). https://doi.org/10.33137/rr.v38i4.26391
20. Kuroczyński, P., Apollonio, F.I., Bajena, I., Cazzaro, I.: Scientific reference model – defining standards, methodology and implementation of serious 3D models in archaeology, art and architectural history. In: The International Archives of the Photogrammetry, Remote Sensing and Spatial Information Sciences, XLVIII-M-2-2023, pp. 895–902 (2023). https://doi.org/10.5194/isprs-archives-xlviii-m-2-2023-895-2023
21. Kuroczyński, P., Hauck, O., Dworak, D.: 3D models on triple paths – new pathways for documenting and visualizing virtual reconstructions. In: Münster, S., et al. (eds.) 3D Research Challenges in Cultural Heritage II: How to Manage Data and Knowledge Related to Interpretative Digital 3D Reconstructions of Cultural Heritage, pp. 149–172. Springer, Berlin (2016). https://doi.org/10.1007/978-3-319-47647-6_8
22. Lindow, J.: The Renaissance Palace in Florence: Magnificence and Splendour in Fifteenth-Century Italy. Ashgate, Aldershot (2007)
23. Liberotti, R., Gusella, V.: Parametric modeling and heritage: a design process sustainable for restoration. Sustainability. **15**, 1317 (2023). https://doi.org/10.3390/su15021371
24. Münster, S.: Advancements in 3D heritage data aggregation and enrichment in Europe: implications for designing the Jena experimental repository for the DFG 3D viewer. Appl. Sci. **13**, 9781 (2023). https://doi.org/10.3390/app13179781

25. Nevola, F.: Home shopping: urbanism, commerce, and palace design in renaissance Italy. J. Soc. Archit. Hist. **70**, 153–173 (2011). https://doi.org/10.1525/jsah.2011.70.2.153
26. Nevola, F., Cooper, D., Capulli, C., Brunke, L.: Immersive renaissance florence: research-based 3-D modeling in digital art and architectural history. Getty Res. J. **15**, 203–227 (2022). https://doi.org/10.1086/718884
27. Nevola, F., Cooper, D., Capulli, C., Brunke, L.: Research-based 3D modelling of Santa Maria degli Innocenti: recovering a context for the Quattrocento altarpieces. In: Terpstra, N. (ed.) Lost and Found: Locating Foundlings in the Early Modern World, pp. 109–133. I Tatti Research Series 6, Villa I Tatti and Istituto degli Innocenti, Florence (2023)
28. Preyer, B.: Planning for visitors at Florentine palaces. Renaiss. Stud. **12**, 357–374 (1998). https://doi.org/10.1111/J.1477-4658.1998.TB00415.X
29. Schiaparelli, A.: La casa fiorentina e i suoi arredi nei secoli XIV e XV. Sansoni, Florence (1908)
30. Spallanzani, M., Gaeta Bertelà, G.: Libro d'Inventario dei beni di Lorenzo il Magnifico. Associazione Amici del Bargello, Florence (1992)
31. Stapleford, R.: Lorenzo de' Medici at Home: the Inventory of the Palazzo Medici in 1492. Penn State University Press, Philadelphia (2013)
32. Thornton, P.: The Italian Renaissance Interior 1400–1600. Weidenfeld & Nicolson, London (1991)
33. Trexler, R.: Public Life in Renaissance Florence. Cornell University Press, Ithaca (1980). https://doi.org/10.7591/9781501720277
34. Vigotti, L.: The Origin of the Renaissance Palace: Domestic Architecture during the Florentine Oligarchy, pp. 1378–1432 (2019)
35. Wilkinson, M., Dumontier, M., Aalbersberg, I., et al.: The FAIR guiding principles for scientific data management and stewardship. Sci. Data **3**, 160018 (2016). https://doi.org/10.1038/sdata.2016.18

A Question of Competence, Quality & Infrastructure: The EUreka3D Initiative

Valentina Bachi(✉) and Antonella Fresa

PHOTOCONSORTIUM, Via della Bonifica 69, 56038 Peccioli, Italy
valentina.bachi@photoconsortium.net

Abstract. The paper aims to discuss three main questions that are related to the successful implementation of digitisation actions in the cultural heritage sector, namely: competence, quality and infrastructure. The three questions are strictly interrelated, but equally urging to enable a factual response of the cultural heritage sector to the 2021 Recommendation of the European Commission about promoting and accelerating the digitisation of cultural heritage. The objectives of the Recommendation are very ambitious – "to digitise by 2030 all monuments and sites that are at risk of degradation and half of those highly frequented by tourists" –. To be ready to cope with these objectives it is necessary to accelerate the pace of digitisation, which is challenging, in particular, for the case of 3D digitisation.

3D digitisation is a very complex task that requires competences that must be shared with the European cultural heritage institutions, with a special attention to the small ones. Furthermore, standards, methods, tools must be promoted, to guarantee high quality digitisation, to avoid that investments are wasted in low quality or perishable collections that are outdated and unusable in few years.

Finally, a robust digital infrastructure is needed to secure that contents produced by European institutions remain in Europe. The infrastructure should cover the whole digitisation process being accessible from the stakeholders that provide contents until the users that take advantage of these contents.

The EUreka3D initiative, started with co-funded project EUreka3D (2023–2024) and continuing with EUreka3D-XR (2025–2026) provides answers to these questions and contributes to the current digital transformation of the CH domain with a range of competences, resources, tools and services that are immediately available for use and tested in real-life environments. Future work may consider to further improve capacity in 3D cultural heritage across Europe, developing a common language to enable the collaboration among multiple disciplines, enhancing the understanding of media transformation, acknowledging the role of artistic reflection and human creative process, networking, establishing cooperation agreements and adopting bottom-up approaches.

Keywords: 3D digitisation · cultural heritage · data sharing · digital infrastructures · XR cultural experiences

1 Introduction

The EUreka3D project [1] began on 1 January 2023 as a data space supporting project funded by the European Commission's Digital Europe Programme. It is now followed by its continuation project named EUreka3D-XR, started in February 2025. Both projects aim to support the digital transformation of the cultural heritage sector, with a specific focus on 3D digitisation and management, and XR scenarios development for compelling narrative and reuse of cultural assets in digital format. This work is in line with the recent EC Recommendation 2021/1970 of 10 November 2021 on a common European data space for cultural heritage [2], that demands Member States and cultural institutions make an urgent effort to digitise heritage in 3D and to make it available online for reuse. However, cultural heritage institutions face various challenges concerning the creation, storage, visualisation and preservation of 3D models of cultural heritage, which are significantly more complex than 2D collections, and with their use and reuse for the benefit of different stakeholders communities such as collections and sites visitors, educators, researchers, conservators and other stakeholders in neighbour sectors like tourism and creative industry.

In this light, the EUreka3D initiative addresses the growing need of enabling the digital transformation of the Cultural Heritage sector, offering competences, resources and tools to support big and small institutions to take the challenge and succeed.

The digital transformation comes from a decades-long process of basing museum (and also in general Galleries, Libraries, Archives and Museums-GLAMs) operations on solid information-sharing infrastructures, forcing an overall rethinking of the underlying work processes and business models. However, not all institutions have achieved the same level of maturity towards the new digital environment they need to embrace, and despite the Covid19 crisis, which acted as an accelerator of the process for nearly everyone in the sector, much work still needs to be done, especially for smaller Cultural Heritage Institutions (CHIs). Museums, galleries, libraries, archives and archaeological sites need to review and modernise, if not to create from scratch, their internal processes from digital capture to end-user access and re-use. They need to re-train their personnel to cope with the new digital responsibilities and roles; to review their infrastructure capacity, in particular with regard to the ability to process 3D contents and reuse them; to generate a novel holistic documentation of the digital objects.

The vision of a common European data space for cultural heritage as a participatory playfield for all the actors involved (cultural institutions, technology partners, multi-disciplinary experts, creative industry, scientific researchers, end-users) moves in this direction, and requires CHIs of any size to enter the challenge of advanced digitisation (especially 3D digitisation in high-quality), holistic representation of CH information and re-use approaches. The existing services of the Europeana platform, as core part of the common European data space for cultural heritage, are a good starting point to support sharing and re-use, but integration with more advanced, powerful and secure services is needed to meet the demands of small institutions, as well as modern workflows and increased digital capacity on the part of CHIs.

From a technical viewpoint, CHIs need to move away from former ICT generations that focused on Web presence, specialised catalogue databases, isolated digitisation processes and virtual exhibitions, to a comprehensive, integrated, cloud-based

IT infrastructure that extends beyond the boundaries of individual centres and focuses on network services and interoperability within the common European data space for cultural heritage, crossing also with other Data Spaces that are under construction and evolution.

In this sense, the EUreka3D initiative consists in a centre of competence that CHIs of any size can refer to, which aims at improving the digital capacity of the cultural sector by enriching the offer of services available on the data space, such as access to high quality and high value datasets, cloud services, technical know-how references, tools for sharing and reusing collections in XR scenarios, consultancy and other knowledge sharing services, to support digitisation, preservation and online access to digital cultural heritage assets.

2 Authenticity, Metadata and Paradata

Since the dawn of a scientific approach to the digitisation of heritage artefacts, clear challenges emerged in capturing and storing authentic digital representations of physical objects. In this context, a digital media asset is considered authentic if it represents a true representation of the original artefact and is unaltered since its inception. Artworks, for example, can vary widely in appearance when digitised under different conditions. Differences in lighting, camera equipment, and even subtle environmental factors like temperature can all affect the outcome. These inconsistencies make it difficult to assess artefacts scientifically and to compare digital reproductions over time. These problems become apparent when searching the web for iconic artworks such as Leonardo da Vinci's Mona Lisa or Pieter Bruegel's Tower of Babel. Discrepancies in colour, contrast, and even proportions can complicate the viewer's understanding of the original piece. Copies and parodies are not always easy to identify.

Authenticity of the digital representations of physical objects becomes even more relevant in the 3D digitisation process.

The EUreka3D project aimed to address these concerns by promoting the consistent capture and preservation of what is known as 'paradata'—detailed information describing the conditions and settings of each digitisation event. This paradata includes information about the camera settings, lighting setup, environmental conditions and the specific equipment used. Capturing these details ensures that digital representations are more reliable and comparable over time. Recording this information allows historians, scientists and the public to trace a digital record back to its source conditions. In the EUreka3D framework, preserving paradata alongside digital images is crucial for ensuring any future analysis of these digital records while accounting for variations resulting from variations in the capture conditions. While no unique standards and recording methods still exist in the cultural heritage sector, the importance of recording paradata to support scientific-based digitisation of heritage collections is becoming recognised in the CH sector. Such recognition is driving EU-wide initiatives like Europeana and the common European data space for cultural heritage to improving and extending metadata models, namely the EDM Europeana Data Model in specific [3], to accommodate such information for users to access it. Improved metadata models will contribute to enriching the ways in which users can assess the opportunities and possibilities of reuse for the digital reproductions for educational, scientific and other kinds of purposes, such as cultural tourism.

Therefore, the design of the EUreka3D platform is not limited to providing a technically capable infrastructure but also has to address the challenges of the management of these three categories of assets: the data (3D models, raw data, audiovisual content, etc.), the metadata (information about the models) and the paradata (information about the digitisation process). 3D metadata information has been studied for a long time, and many of the challenges involved have been minimised with the help of the EDM Europeana Data Model [7], which provides a common framework for the understanding of systems that exchange CH metadata. However, the situation is not so favourable as far as the paradata are concerned. Paradata information processing is a necessary yet not widespread practice amongst 3D content providers and is not currently addressed by EDM. Delivering the paradata information associated with 3D data provides key insights into how the digitisation process was carried out to obtain the data. Although there are different initiatives and efforts focused on the description of paradata, CH lacks a formal data model to express them, and this is one of the future enhancements planned for the Europeana Data Model.

This data-rich approach is especially important as digital reproductions increasingly serve as proxies for physical access to artefacts. By preserving paradata, EUreka3D aimed to bridge the gap between static digital captures and the dynamic, evolving reality of historical objects. For instance, through the accurate capture of paradata, one could theoretically track changes across multiple digitised versions of the same artefact, recognising alterations due to environmental factors, restoration efforts, or technological advances. Additionally, the growing role of artificial intelligence (AI) in digital media, both as a tool for enhancing images and as a source of potential manipulation, is an important factor in this discussion. AI driven tools are available to improve visual quality, for example by denoising, colorising or increasing the image resolution. However, such tools can introduce new information not present in the original work. While these developments provide valuable new possibilities, they further blur the line between authentic representations and digital alterations. The fact that those tools become more widely accessible poses challenges for distinguishing real artefacts from manipulated versions. AI-based detection methods are commonly used to identify generated and manipulated content. While such methods have lately become impressively accurate, the problem becomes an adversarial battle between AI tools. As detection tools improve, so do the methods used to create the content, leading to an ongoing game of 'cat and mouse'. As a sector, CHIs should work towards a future where provenance of digital media is precisely documented, starting from the creation of the media and continuing over the entire lifecycle.

To further safeguard the authenticity of digital heritage, paradata and metadata need to be securely linked to the media content by adopting cryptographic methods. To make this vision for the future a reality, interoperability and standardisation will be imperative. The JPEG Trust standard (ISO/IEC 21617) [4] aims to create a standardised framework for embedding and securing provenance data in digital media files. This initiative seeks to align efforts across organisations and technologies, allowing institutions worldwide to share and verify authentic cultural records more effectively.

EUreka3D exemplifies this proactive approach via the detailed documentation of paradata, and a programme of learning and capacity building events and resources that support CH professionals in innovating and improving their internal workflows in heritage documentation and sharing. EUreka3D's emphasis on both paradata and metadata as fundamental elements of digital preservation points toward a more transparent digital future, where provenance data ensures that cultural heritage remains reliable and accessible for generations to come.

3 Standards, Methods and Tools for 3D Cultural Heritage

Given the current efforts in the cultural sector towards 3D digitisation of heritage objects, sites and monuments, CHIs of any size and capacity are facing various challenges:

- first, to generate high quality digitisation data, that represent faithfully and accurately the Cultural Heritage Object (CHO) in question
- once the data file is created, to store safely such data in a way that various levels of access and editing rights are granted to CHI's staff members and possible partner organisations
- once the 3D models are created from raw data, to visualise them in the web, so that user communities can view the model via their own devices on the internet
- to accompany the 3D models with accurate metadata that describe the heritage object, and with in-depth information about the digitisation process that generated the 3D model, to converge in a paradata report
- to enable access and reuse of raw data and 3D models with their accompanying documentation, for user communities to use and reuse the content in different domains such as heritage research, education, cultural tourism and possible others
- to reuse such 3D and other digital contents to create new compelling narrative addressing visitors of the collections online and onsite, also creating XR experiences that engage users
- if wanted, to associate a Persistent Identifier (PID) to the objects published as public data collections, for granting digital preservation of such online content
- if wanted, to contribute the 3D collections in the common European data space for cultural heritage, via the publication in the Europeana Portal.

All these challenges are currently addressed by CHIs in an often disorganised manner, relying on in-house or outsourced services by different service providers, thus often resulting in duplication of efforts, redundancies and complex workflow management and orchestration. As a side, but not irrelevant point, cloud providers who also offer a 3D viewer are often private companies, often set outside Europe (one example is the Sketchfab service), which raises concerns about safe data management and storage.

The absence of an EU based, non for profit, federated and integrated solution for these challenges has created an evident need in the cultural heritage sector.

Additionally, there are many challenges associated with the ingestion, processing, aggregation and delivery of 3D content. These challenges stem from the nature of 3D content, current hardware limitations and the quality target, all elements set by the VIGIE Study 2020/654 on quality in 3D digitisation of tangible cultural heritage [5], which promotes guidelines to ensure the highest level of quality and the best possible outcome.

The current capabilities of consumer computers and networks impose limitations and challenges in the design of any CHI-oriented cloud platform that aims at supporting 3D collections. Quite often, processing of 3D data online is done on the client side, so the actual device used by the user plays a key role and must be considered when designing 3D experiences, which are affected by network limitations, computer memory or processing capacity.

The 3D initiatives have greatly evolved over the years but still lacks the standardisation level that 2D content has. This lack of standards for the use of 3D data makes it a challenge to decide on a universal 3D format. There is no complete alignment between the 3D software to process 3D data and the software to visualise or deliver 3D experiences to users. Herein, some content providers may use a format for the archival of 3D data, but this may not be the best choice for visualisation or delivery to end users. For example, OBJ is a widely known format, commonly accepted by 3D software and 3D visualisation libraries, but it is less space-efficient for data, making it a poor choice if the data to be sent over a network are too large. Such cases can benefit from a binary format such as PLY. The Nexus multi-resolution format [6], created by CNR-ISTI, delivers 3D data more efficiently over the network, but it is not supported by common software and current technical challenges make it unsuitable for 3D CAD data. Some algorithms and 3D formats focus on compression ratio, while others focus on performance. It is usually a trade-off: compression makes more efficient use of space (benefiting, for example, the storage or transfer of a file) but increases processing effort (both for compressing and decompressing the data). These are not intrinsic problems for 3D, as 2D content also suffers from them, but they are more prominent in 3D because 3D is more complex in nature, and 3D content requires extensively larger amounts of space than 2D content, which affects its storage, processing and transfer over a network.

In response to these challenges, EUreka3D project developed a suite of services and resources expressly dedicated to CHIs who need to store, manage, document and share 3D models relating to digitised or reconstructed cultural heritage assets. It is specifically intended to facilitate the sharing of such 3D cultural collections in the common European data space for cultural heritage, and it is now a fully functional platform, tested and running, that is named EUreka3D Data Hub.

4 EUreka3D Platform

The EUreka3D platform offers a comprehensive solution to CHIs involved in 3D digitisation, together with the direct entry-gate to the common European data space for cultural heritage. The platform offers a suite of services and resources for the management and sharing of cultural 3D assets over a European cloud for data, metadata and paradata storage, and for delivering 3D collections to users' platforms like Europeana. With regard to the publication process of the datasets in Europeana, this is coordinated by PHOTOCONSORTIUM, coordinator of the EUreka3D initiative, accredited aggregator for Europeana and partner in the common European data space for cultural heritage.

The EUreka3D platform is fully operative since 2023, featuring the following services:

- Secure authentication and authorisation mechanisms, to protect 3D objects from manipulation or unauthorised access;
- Storage of models in original formats (often with very large file sizes), and visualisation features that enable the object to be displayed online;
- Metadata model and paradata compatible with the Europeana Data Model;
- Interoperability with established tools and procedures;
- Harvesting functionality to provide the individual object or datasets to Europeana for publication.

The Fig. 1 below depicts the EUreka3D workflow, covering three big blocks: the digitisation process (capture), the upload and management of data in the platform (cloud) and the release of data and services to end users and external applications (delivery). The services to upload and manage data, metadata and paradata are accessible via the interface provided by the EUreka3D Data Hub.

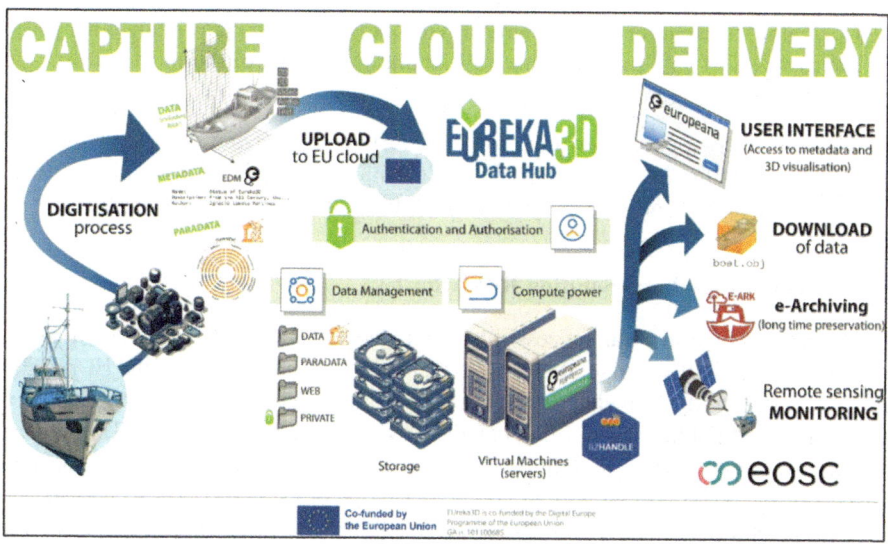

Fig. 1. EUreka3D Data Hub and workflow - general overview 2025. CC BY-SA EUreka3D-XR consortium.

4.1 Architecture and Underlaying Technology

The EUreka3D platform is technically supported by different components, among which the following stand out:

- The EGI Check-in service [8], the Identity and Access Management system that supports the processes of authentication (verifying who the user is) and authorisation (reporting what a user can do in a system). EGI Check-in allows users to authenticate with their home organisation (typically, a research institute participating in eduGAIN [9]) as well as with an academic account (e.g. ORCID), a social account (e.g. GitHub,

Google, LinkedIn, etc.) and others. EGI Check-in provides a simple and integrated method to ensure that EOSC users use EUreka3D services per their defined access policies.
- EGI Cloud Compute [10], which provides virtual servers in the cloud, on-demand. The virtual allocation of servers is done through Virtual Machines (VM), which are software components that run over physical hardware and emulate and provide the functionality of a physical computer system. One of the advantages of cloud technology is that the virtual infrastructure can be created directly through software instructions, without the need to physically access the servers. Moreover, this virtualisation greatly facilitates elasticity, a term used to describe the ability of a system to increase or decrease its resources to adapt to the current workload.
- The EGI DataHub [11], which provides a federated distributed system for data management and data publication that is used to support the EUreka3D Data Hub. It is directly used by EUreka3D end users and is therefore accessible through a user-friendly Web interface. Users can easily upload any type of data file, associate metadata to it in different formats, assign permanent identifiers to it and many other tasks. The tool is also able to communicate with the Europeana platform to perform the required content aggregation.

These three components form the core of the EUreka3D technical platform and will be complemented in the course of 2025–2026 with additional features and new tools expressly dedicated to reusing 3D and other contents in XR scenarios.

4.2 A "One-Stop-Shop" Solution Ready for Use

The EUreka3D platform was successfully developed and deployed as a pilot action and proof of concept in the course of 2023–2024 and the content partners of the EUreka3D initiative successfully uploaded their models and associated metadata and paradata, for aggregation and publication in Europeana and as open access collections. The interest shown by a number of CHIs that are external organisations who became associated partners of the project, often with the particular scope of using the EUreka3D solution for their 3D objects, is a clear signal of the fact that the EUreka3D solution is an answer to CHIs' challenges.

The EUreka3D platform offers a very welcome "one-stop-shop" solution to these challenges, allowing to store, manage, visualise and share 3D objects in an integrated environment with secured access. Moreover, the EUreka3D initiative provides added value granting data storage in servers located in Europe, permitting easier access to Europeana thanks to the full integration of the respective services. The platform serves multiple purposes:

- It offers a solution, accessible to CHIs that cannot or don't want to afford high costs to manage their own servers or storage.
- It contributes to the transformation of CH, enabling CHIs to use the cloud to store and manage their assets.
- It offers a European alternative, research oriented, to commercial products.
- It serves as an enabler for the publication of CH objects in Europeana.

The EUreka3D platform not only provides storage for the different 3D assets, but also metadata management, sharing, publication, and security to protect the data from unauthorised access. In addition to the suite of services and resources, other outcomes of EUreka3D can be of great interest to research communities. During the continuation project EUreka3D-XR (2025–2026) the current set up will be enriched with new functionalities and easily accessible, open tools that CHIs can use to create new compelling narratives that attract users, also leveraging XR, AR and other technologies to bring the cultural collections in the metaverse.

4.3 Functionalities for Users and Value Proposition

Through its innovative approach and resources, EUreka3D deployed the power of cloud services and tools in bringing together a wide range of organisations and professionals, who share a common goal and challenge of preserving CH in 3D for future generations. The project has set the basis for moving to the next phase of deploying its services and make them available for any CHIs to test it and use it.

In simple terms, CHIs can find in the EUreka3D platform is the following features:

- Upload different versions/formats of 3D models, to be shared with different authorization of access depending on user's need/preferences.
- Visualise the model online, in a viewer that is compatible with Europeana.
- Input metadata, already in the Europeana Data Model, via a simple metadata input form.
- Link contextual information and paradata to each model, to be shared to the public.
- Assign PIDs to the public objects to grant their long-term preservation online.
- Publish such openly accessible objects in the Europeana Portal.

In this light, the EUreka3D platform integrates various components to create a flexible and scalable "product" that could eventually be placed on the market of not-for-profit solutions, according to a sustainable planning aimed at covering the costs with competitive and affordable revenue streams and mechanisms. The value proposition identified in the project is to offer to CHIs an EU-based comprehensive solution for 3D data management and a direct entry-gate to the common European data space for cultural heritage. This clearly differentiates the EUreka3D platform from similar services for 3D data management, and showcases the competitive advantage of this solution, focusing more specifically on the needs of the "customers" (i.e. the European CHIs), in particular by making use of non-for-profit cloud providers based in Europe, federated to the EGI European Grid Initiative, and offering safe data management mechanisms and integrated tools. All these features make the EUreka3D platform not only specialised and competitive, but also more resilient in terms of scalability, adaptability and flexibility to future developments of the digital transformation of the cultural sector. In terms of costs, initial investigations have been done as part of the project's impact assessment task, to estimate the running cost of the platform in its current shape, identifying a requirement to be in line with the price applied by other services, often provided by private companies set outside EU, like for example Sketchfab, which in the past various CHIs chose for visualising and sharing their 3D collections ion absence of a reliable alternative. However, as mentioned, the EUreka3D platform is not comparable to these services, being a much more specialised infrastructure addressing the needs of the specific community of the CH sector. In this light, the EUreka3D platform, its Data Hub and a rich capacity building programme aim at offering a menu of tailor made services to the target customers, with integrated tools. CHIs would find these tools and services much more suitable to their needs than others, as EUreka3D is addressing specifically CHIs requirements rather than offering a generic platform for 3D contents, whatever is the target sector. Also, from a user perspective in the domain of cultural heritage, the EUreka3D infrastructure is much more efficient being directly integrated with Europeana and the common European data space for cultural heritage.

With the new services and tools to be developed in the course of the EUreka3D-XR project, the platform will be further enriched with features that finalize the lifecycle of 3D digitisation by supporting reuse of online collections in compelling narratives for user engagement.

5 EUreka3D-XR: A Step Further

EUreka3D-XR – European Union's REKonstructed content in 3D to produce XR experiences (2025–2026) is a project co-funded by the European Union to continue the work of EUreka3D project to support CHIs that want to innovate the way they approach 3D digitisation, access, storage, sharing and reuse in compelling and engaging narratives. The project is working to make available a set of tools for creating XR experiences with cultural content, deployed in concrete use cases for XR scenarios in France, Spain and Cyprus. The project also offers a capacity building and knowledge sharing programme, including demonstrations and hands-on experiments for the use of the tools and of the technical infrastructures.

The main research area of the new action in EUreka3D-XR is focused on transforming cultural contents such 2D, 3D, video, texts, maps, stories into compelling narratives and extended reality scenarios, and to deliver said scenarios to the common European data space for cultural heritage, to enrich the corpus of open access digital cultural contents online and to inspire others in experimenting new technologies.

EUreka3D-XR will deliver five open source digital tools that include online services and mobile apps to support innovative reuse and more compelling engagement with cultural 3D resources in various settings, collaboratively, with sustainable costs and efforts, leveraging XR and other advanced technologies applied to heritage collections.

EUreka3D-XR will handle three showcase scenarios, which will be available in the common European data space for cultural heritage as contents and documentation:

- The virtual visualisation of the middle-ages walls of the city of Girona
- The XR narrative of excavations in process in the Bibracte archaeological site
- The creation of a new life of Saint Neophytos Englystra in Cyprus in the virtual space

The deployment of tools and XR scenarios will guide the improvement of the services provided in the EUreka3D platform.

EUreka3D-XR will also promote capacity building and the re-use of digitalised cultural heritage to professionals in the cultural sector and in other domains such as education, tourism research and preservation. During the two years of 2023–2024, in its capacity building activities the project has reached hundreds of interested stakeholders from multiple countries from all over the world and this commitment continues in the next years, in the frame of the EUreka3D-XR project as part of the wider EUreka3D Competence Centre initiative.

6 Conclusion

The EUreka3D project concluded at the end of 2024 after two years of groundbreaking work in the field of 3D cultural heritage preservation and digitisation. One of the project's distinctive traits is the emphasis on the concept of 'Memory Twin' as opposed to the more traditional digital reproductions, or digital twins, of heritage collections, by integrating 3D digitised models and their associated metadata with extensive paradata. Paradata encompasses information about the origin, process, and creation of digital objects, as well as the tools and methodologies used. Paradata is crucial for transparency, reproducibility, and contextual understanding of digital heritage collections. EUreka3D project's shift from digital twins to memory twins through the inclusion of paradata represents a significant change in the approach to 3D digitisation in the cultural heritage sector. In this light, quality in digitisation and documentation has been a cornerstone of EUreka3D's approach, demonstrating that meticulous planning and execution are essential to capturing the complexity and dynamism of cultural objects. The need for improving the knowledge and the capacity of all CH operators and professionals to embrace this more advanced approach has been addressed in the project via a wide programme of training and learning activities and the production of open access resources, that will continue in the coming period in the context of the continuation project EUreka3D-XR.

A significant need in the cultural heritage sector is for sustainable and user-friendly platforms for uploading, storing, and hosting 3D models. The EUreka3D project responded to this challenge by developing the EUreka3D Data Hub. This platform provides a secure hosting space for 3D models from any cultural heritage institution, supports clear metadata and paradata management, ensures persistent identifiers and Linked Open Data, adheres to the Europeana Data Model, and makes these models accessible and viewable through the EUreka3D viewer. The EUreka3D Data Hub was conceived and created as an affordable non-commercial EU based platform that is interoperable with Europeana and supports the common European data space for cultural heritage. With the interest expressed from a number of external stakeholders and a guaranteed 3 year funding of the infrastructure, it is expected that the EUreka3D Data Hub will gain enough traction to be a self-sustainable solution for many CHIs who are currently blocked by the complexities of in-house infrastructures or dissemination to corporate based platforms based outside the EU.

The success of the EUreka3D project was thanks to careful planning, execution, and a genuine need from stakeholders for the knowledge and tools developed in the project: as a result, EUreka3D has been able to deliver and produce a methodology for high quality 3D cultural heritage.

Methods, tools, services, digital infrastructure, learning resources have been tested and assessed and they constitute the sound basis of the EUreka3D Competence Centre, a concrete and already running enterprise for 3D digital transformation in the cultural heritage sector. This approach has been documented into guidelines and backed up via several workshops, webinars and blog posts. Case study evidences, detailed by all the content partners who followed this digitisation best practice during the project, were recorded in the final publication of EUreka3D - Good practices for the 3D digitisation of Cultural Heritage [12].

Finally, the EUreka3D Competence Centre is also addressing the users of 3D content. This will be explored further in the 18 months continuation of the project, EUreka3D-XR, where stakeholders will be engaged in the development of XR scenarios based on 3D and other cultural contents. This new initiative promises to build on the foundations of EUreka3D and ensure sustainability, with a focus on extended reality (XR) technologies. EUreka3D-XR aims to enhance the accessibility and interactivity of 3D heritage collections, leveraging augmented and virtual reality to create even more engaging and immersive experiences.

In summary EUreka3D developed a best practice workflow, implemented a data hub, made available cloud computing and storage resources that are guaranteed to be accessible for the next 3 years, and delivered high quality 3D models promoted in front of the Ministries of Culture from all over the EU. The legacy of the project survives in the documented knowledge base and in its operational platform, and continues in EUreka3D Competence Centre.

Acknowledgement. The authors gratefully acknowledge the contributions made by the EUreka3D partners to the preparation of this paper. We wish to name in particular John Balean, Frederik Temmermans and Ignacio Lamata Martínez for their work on impact assessment, authenticity of digital cultural contents and technical development of the EUreka3D Data Hub.

References

1. https://eureka3d.eu/. Accessed 28 Feb 2025
2. https://eur-lex.europa.eu/eli/reco/2021/1970/oj. Accessed 28 Feb 2025
3. Isaac A., et al.: Making the Europeana Data Model a Better Fit for Documentation of 3D Objects. Springer (2024)
4. https://jpeg.org/jpegtrust/index.html. Accessed 28 Feb 2025
5. https://digital-strategy.ec.europa.eu/en/library/study-quality-3d-digitisation-tangible-cultural-heritage. Accessed 28 Feb 2025
6. https://vcg.isti.cnr.it/nexus/. Accessed 28 Feb 2025
7. https://pro.europeana.eu/page/edm-documentation. Accessed 28 Feb 2025
8. https://www.egi.eu/service/check-in/. Accessed 28 Feb 2025
9. https://edugain.org/. Accessed 28 Feb 2025
10. https://www.egi.eu/service/cloud-compute/. Accessed 28 Feb 2025
11. https://www.egi.eu/service/datahub/. Accessed 28 Feb 2025
12. https://eureka3d.eu/wp-content/uploads/2024/12/EUreka3D-FinalBooklet.pdf. Accessed 28 Feb 2025

An Integrated and Open-Access Plugin for Uncertainty Assessment of the Hypothetical Virtual Reconstruction of Architecture

Fabrizio Ivan Apollonio, Federico Fallavollita, and Riccardo Foschi(✉)

Alma Mater Studiorum University of Bologna, Viale del Risorgimento 2, 40136 Bologna, Italy
{fabrizio.apollonio,federico.fallavollita,
riccardo.foschi}@unibo.it

Abstract. In recent years, the field of virtual 3D reconstructions has witnessed growing interest in developing solutions to enhance the accessibility, clarity, shareability, transparency, and overall reusability of these models within scientific contexts. These efforts have been particularly evident in several large-scale recent European projects. Notably, the CoVHer Erasmus + project focused on lost or never-built architecture, emphasising that the production and publication of comprehensive and transparent paradata and metadata are indispensable for scientifically accurate reconstructions. This detailed documentation is often disseminated through scientific publications and accompanying visual materials, such as images and videos, with uncertainty represented through false-colour renderings. However, despite the scientific community recognising the importance of these best practices, no shared standards have yet been established, and 3D models are rarely made publicly available. This raises a critical question: why do we produce such 3D models if they cannot be compared, queried, studied, or reused by others? To contribute to addressing this issue, this research introduces an innovative open-source digital tool, developed for seamless integration into a widely used open-source 3D modelling and rendering software (Blender), aimed at simplifying the process of uncertainty analysis. This initiative aspires to encourage the application of best practices for the creation of high-quality 3D models making them more easily shareable, interrogable, and reusable; fostering the development of structured uncertainty assessment based on a versatile and unambiguous uncertainty source-based 7-level false-colour scale complemented with analytic formulas capable of synthesising the average uncertainty of the 3D model with the two coefficients AU_V and AU_VR; and advocate for the publication of 3D models to enhance their reusability on shared open platforms.

Keywords: Digital Reconstruction · Cultural Heritage · Blender Plugin · Uncertainty Assessment

1 Introduction

Hypothetical virtual 3D reconstructions (e.g. Fig. 1) are widespread tools in the academic field aimed at simulating, visualising, and disseminating possible hypotheses of lost cultural heritage artefacts from the past. The process of hypothetical reconstruction is based on sources of various types (e.g., textual, graphical, pictorial, sculptural, oral) and can have different levels of accuracy, completeness, consistency, quality, and readability. Depending on the sources used, the reconstruction process embeds a certain level of uncertainty, because no matter how accurate and complete they are, there is always a certain level of interpretation that the author of the hypothetical reconstruction needs to introduce to translate the sources into three dimensions [2]. To complete a three-dimensional model of a lost architecture from the past, it is crucial to comprehend and solve every one of its aspects and find a solution for every connection and node, which requires accessing a level of detail that is often not present in the authorial historical direct/primary sources alone. Thus, the use of secondary/sources and personal interpretation is always necessary. This complex process, based on inferences and subjective choices, must be published and communicated in the most transparent way possible in order to allow others to verify and validate the results, and most importantly, make the model reusable in scientific contexts [3].

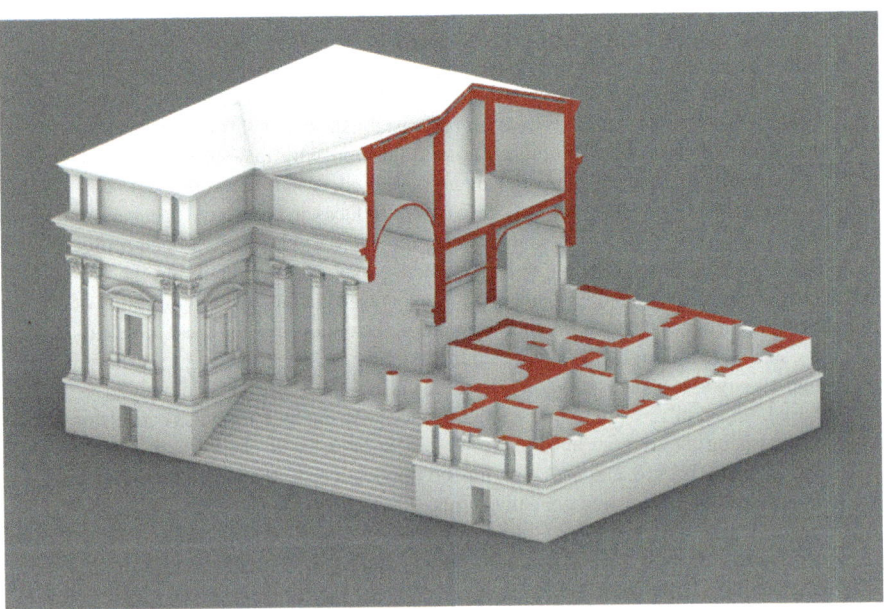

Fig. 1. Example of hypothetical virtual 3D reconstruction of a Palladian Villa made by the authors, from a never-built design by Andrea Palladio, dated to 1560 [1].

Despite most scholars nowadays knowing and agreeing with shared international charts and principles [4–7], foundational references in the field that trace guidelines that also involve hypothetical reconstructions, many 3D reconstructive hypothetical models are still lacking proper documentation and are not available for download, querying or direct investigation. One of the reasons might be the lack of time or budget, which prevents the scholars to organise and publish in a synthetic but complete and comprehensible way all the material gathered and used.

A possible solution to this problem might be the introduction of new and more efficient tools and workflows to help reduce the time and cost of the documentation, assessment, visualisation and publication steps. Thus, in this research we introduce a novel open-access plugin for the open-source polygonal modelling software Blender [8] that aims to simplify the uncertainty assessment workflow developed and improved in the context of the CoVHer project [9, 10], and enables some assessing features for the model proofing, which would speed up the workflow and would foster the adoption of our tested methodology aimed at producing high-quality transparent and reusable 3D reconstructive hypothetical models.

2 Digital Tools for Documenting and Publishing Hypothetical, Reconstructive 3D Models

Many researchers have developed, in recent years, novel tools and adopted various methodologies to simplify the organisation and dissemination of the reconstructive process. For example, the IDOVIR platform [11] was developed to improve the organisation and cataloguing of sources and the publication of related documentation. This tool is designed to be versatile and easy to use without compromising the quality of the documentation. It is particularly effective for architectural reconstructions with several variants and sources. It is an effective tool for the publication of the process of reconstruction, however, it does not allow the authors to upload and investigate the 3D models, and thus it is mainly based on images commented with short texts.

Concerning the publication of the 3D models, there are repositories aimed at surveyed heritage [12] and others that are also open to hypothetical reconstruction [13] or other institutional repositories and archives not accessible to the public.

Scholars sometimes also upload their 3D reconstructive models on commercial platforms [14], which are easier to use and more easily accessible. The commercial solutions are usually preferred because they usually guarantee longer-term support, but they base their business model on advertising, or require periodic payments for additional features or archival space, furthermore, they are usually not aimed at a specific type of reconstruction, thus the heritage models are lost in between other 3D models from various sources which makes it harder to interrelate analogous models and discern from quality 3D models to models built by amateurs.

A recent addition to the available tools that support the process of virtual hypothetical reconstruction is the CoVHer 3D repository [15] which was developed specifically for the publication of the 3D models of never-built or lost architectural heritage. This platform not only allows for the upload of 3D reconstructive models, but also provides an improved personalisation of the data, metadata, and paradata related to each project by putting effort into the creation of interrelations between different projects that share analogous data, paradata, and metadata.

Other tools aimed at improving the management and dissemination of the complexity of the reconstruction process exist. For example, a popular tool in the field of archaeology is the Extended Matrix tool. It is based on a Blender Plugin aimed at simplifying the application of the Extended Matrix workflow [16] which consists of a formal language which keeps track of virtual reconstruction processes intended to be used by archaeologists and heritage specialists to document their reconstruction.

3 A Novel Digital Tool for Uncertainty Assessment

Some of the mentioned tools are virtuous efforts that aim to simplify and standardise certain aspects of the hypothetical reconstruction process (e.g., production, documentation, dissemination), however, not all aspects of the reconstruction process still have proper custom-made tools, namely the uncertainty assessment based on the CoVHer 7-level scale. To be widely adopted, a methodology that aspires to be set as a standard must be as easy to use and as unambiguous as possible without loss of accuracy and robustness in every one of its steps.

Thus, for this reason, we introduce a novel digital tool aimed at simplifying the assessment of uncertainty for hypothetical virtual 3D reconstruction of lost or never-built architecture, based on the scale of uncertainty presented for the first time in [17] and improved in the context of the CoVHer project [18]. This tool is thought to be used after the 3D modelling process and before the publication of the 3D model. It helps to simplify and speed up the application of the proper uncertainty level to each element of the 3D model while assigning, at the same time, custom properties to the same elements. Furthermore, it simplifies the calculation of the average uncertainty through a novel procedure [19] developed in the context of the CoVHer project. Lastly, it speeds up the production of false-coloured views of the 3D model.

3.1 The CoVHer Scale of Uncertainty

The scale of uncertainty, to which the plugin refers, is made of 7 uncertainty levels plus one for abstention, and can be reduced to 5 or 3 levels for analysis that requires a reduced granularity without losing comparability to projects analysed with the 7-level scale. To each level, a colour, a numerical value, a percentage range, and a textual definition are assigned. The colour serves to easily recognise the elements in false-colour views; the numerical value is used to name each level and can be used when the colours are unavailable; the percentage range is used to calculate the average uncertainty; and the textual definitions serve to assign to each element of the 3D model a univocal level of uncertainty and are written in a way to minimise overlapping and ambiguity.

The definitions are based on the sources, their type, author, origin, quality, readability, and coherence. The scale was published in its last version in [18], where a flow chart that synthesises the scale and aids the users in assigning the proper level to each element was also published (Fig. 2).

This uncertainty scale was improved and updated over the years by testing it on hundreds of reconstructive projects of never-built buildings from Andrea Palladio, Antonio Guidi, Claude Nicolas Ledoux, Giovanni Antonio Antolini, Agostino Barelli and other

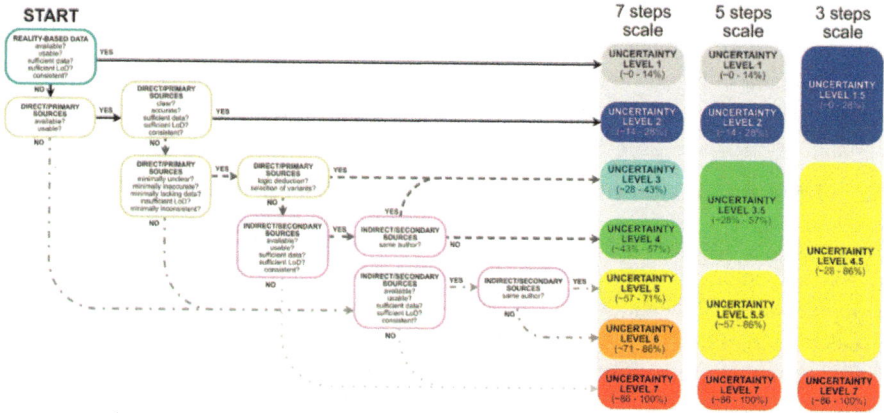

Fig. 2. Yes/No flowchart for the application of the CoVHer scale of uncertainty. Image first published in [18]

projects involving lost or never-built architecture (an example of hypothetical reconstruction visualised in false colours for clarifying the uncertainty is shown in Fig. 3). These projects were developed for research projects, commissions, museum exhibitions, workshops and didactic courses at university level.

colour	level	Uncertainty	Description
	1	0 to 14%	Physical remains
	2	14 to 28%	Direct sources
	3	28 to 43%	Indirect sources same author (Direct sources available but minimally lacking)
	4	43 to 57%	Indirect sources different author (Direct sources available but minimally lacking)
	5	57 to 71%	Indirect sources same author (Direct sources non-available)
	6	71 to 86%	Indirect sources the different author (Direct sources non-available)
	7	86 to 100%	Unreferenced sources
	\	\	Abstention

AU_V = 24.3%

AU_VR = 29,4% (Relevance classical orders = 20x)

Fig. 3. Uncertainty assessment and visualisation based on the scale of uncertainty [18] developed in the context of the CoVHer project [9, 10]. The assessment and visualisation of the project were made with the help of the Blender Uncertainty Calculation add-on [20].

Given the high amount of reconstructive models produced in the past years, to improve the comparability of these projects at a glance, we developed a methodology capable, through the use of a set of mathematical formulas, of calculating coefficients, aimed at representing the average uncertainty of each reconstruction, the Average Uncertainty Weighted on the Volume (AU_V) and the Average Uncertainty Weighted on the

Volume and Relevance (AU_VR). These two formulas represent the maximum synthesis of the uncertainty analysis and are thought to be complementary to the broader uncertainty assessment based on commented false-colour images and textual explanations. Refer to [19] for an in-depth explanation of how these formulas work.

3.2 AI-Aided Development of an Open-Source Plugin for Blender

The weighting with the volume, which characterises the two AU_V and AU_VR formulas, is a mathematical construct that was introduced to make the result independent from the segmentation of the model, and thus more user-independent and objective. However, the calculation of the volume of each architectonic element that composes the 3D model is unimaginable to be performed manually. For this reason, we developed an algorithmic approach in Grasshopper [19], which produced accurate results but has long computational times for the more granularly subdivided models due to Grasshopper limitations. Furthermore, most importantly, this tool was only accessible to those owning a Rhino licence.

As an alternative, we developed a novel open-access and open-source tool for Blender called Blender Uncertainty Calculator. It is a better-performing and more accessible solution that is available to download for free from GitHub [20]. Blender was chosen as the development platform because it is a widespread, donation-based modelling and rendering software that is nowadays an industry standard in many fields, including the academic field of hypothetical reconstruction, and it is available for free download for anybody.

A less trivial reason why to choose Blender was that, our tool was developed with the aid of AI chatbots for writing some parts of the Python code, and since Blender is an open software with plenty of documentation available online, this makes the AI chatbots much more effective into synthetising pieces of code for Blender compared to other commercial software packages that have a less active community or publicly available documentation. ChatGPT4 was used as the main scripting aid chatbot [21].

The tool was developed to work with every version of Blender from 2.8 onward and can be installed as an addon without requiring the installation of a custom Blender build. It was developed in a way that is easy to use for users who have basic knowledge of Blender and no knowledge of scripting.

3.3 Features of the Blender Uncertainty Calculator

The Blender Uncertainty Calculator add-on can be downloaded for free from GitHub [20] and can be installed by accessing the Blender add-ons installation interface in the preferences (Edit - > Preferences - > Add-ons - > Install from Disk) as shown in Fig. 4.

After the installation is completed, a new panel called "Uncertainty-7" becomes available in the sidebar next to the 3D viewport. In this panel, a series of tabs enables new tools for the uncertainty assessment. The tabs are subdivided into groups (Fig. 5).

The first group of buttons, "Assign" (Fig. 6), enables the application of the desired uncertainty level to each element. By hovering the mouse over each button, the standard textual definition for each level is shown. This is an aid to those who want to refer to the

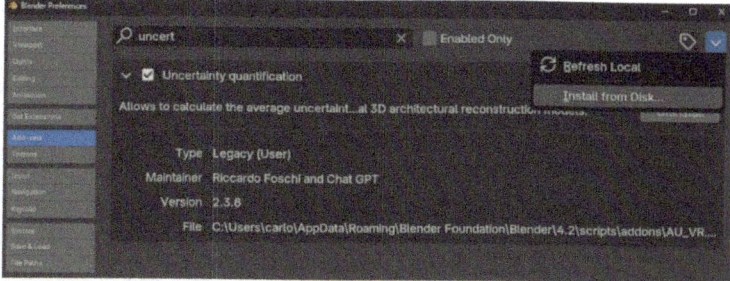

Fig. 4. Blender Uncertainty Calculator add-on Installation (Edit -> Preferences - > Add-ons - > Install from Disk)

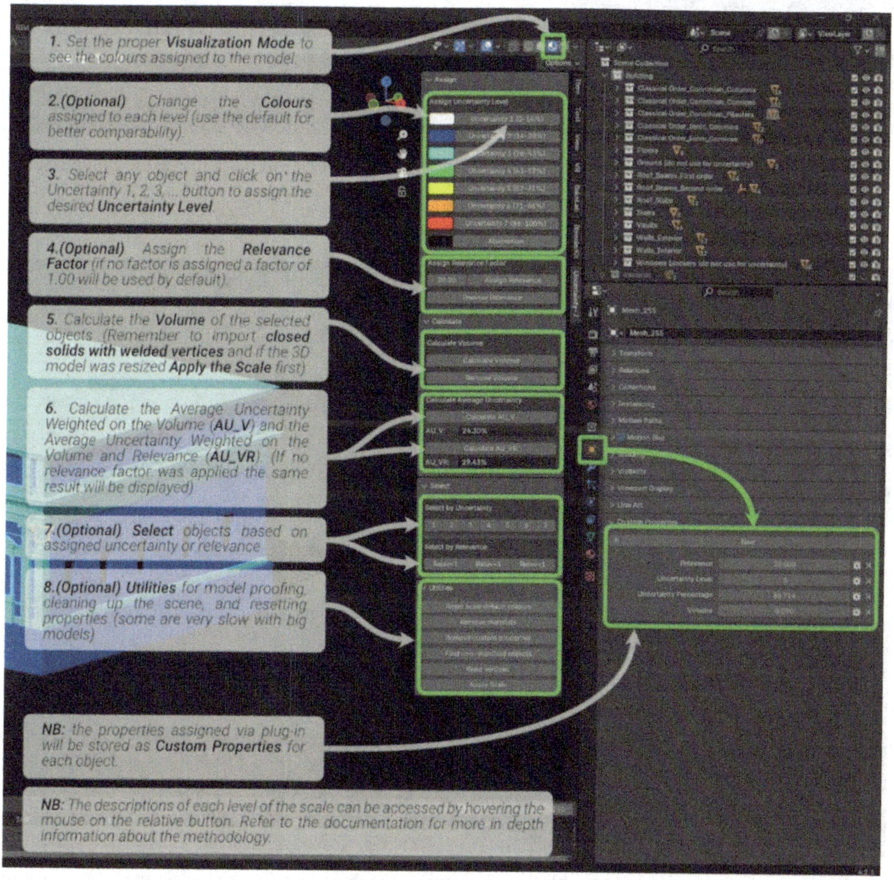

Fig. 5. Blender Uncertainty Calculator interface and synthesis of its functionalities

uncertainty scale used in [18], which is an uncertainty scale that was developed explicitly

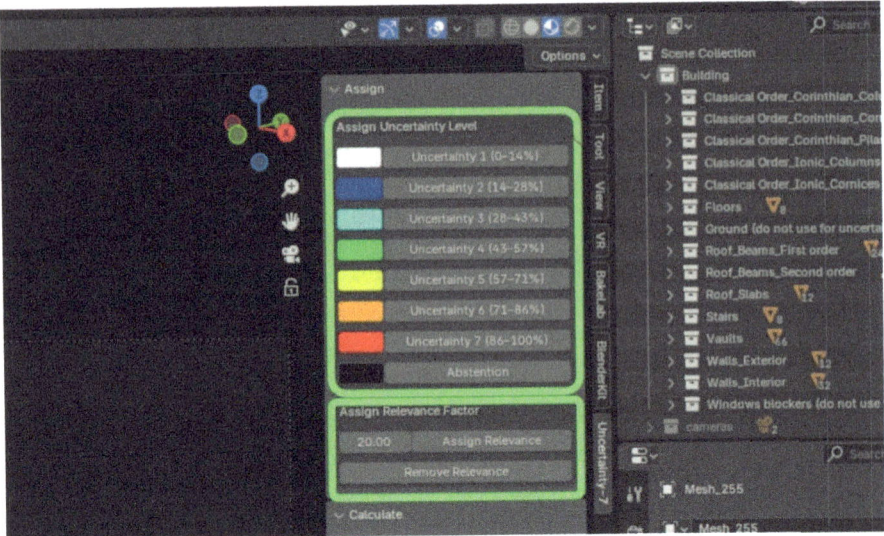

Fig. 6. The "Assign" panel, used to assign the uncertainty levels and a custom Relevance Factor to 3D objects or groups of objects

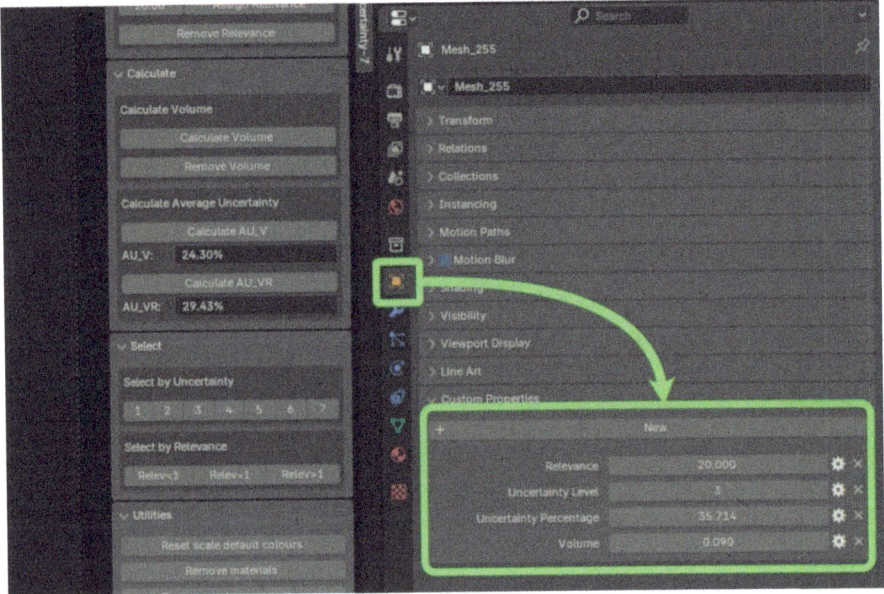

Fig. 7. Custom properties, accessible by clicking on each object that was assigned to a certain level of uncertainty

for never-built or lost architectural heritage reconstructed mainly from direct or indirect authorial sources. However different definitions can be used in case of need.

When clicking on one of these buttons, it will apply a coloured material to the selected elements together with a series of custom properties that can be accessed from the object property tab (Fig. 7). The colours can be personalised via the colour pickers placed on the left of the buttons.

In the "Assign" panel, there is also a group of buttons that is aimed at applying an optional relevance factor to individual objects or groups of objects. The relevance factor is used to assign a hierarchy to the elements of the 3D model and is used for the calculation of the AU_VR coefficient. The relevance factor is assigned by the operator and is aimed at obtaining a knowledge-enriched result (AU_VR) to be compared with the more user-independent AU_V result.

The "Calculate" panel sorts out all the commands that perform calculations of any sort (Fig. 8). First, the calculation of the volume of each of the selected elements, and, afterwards, the calculation of the AU_V and AU_VR coefficients.

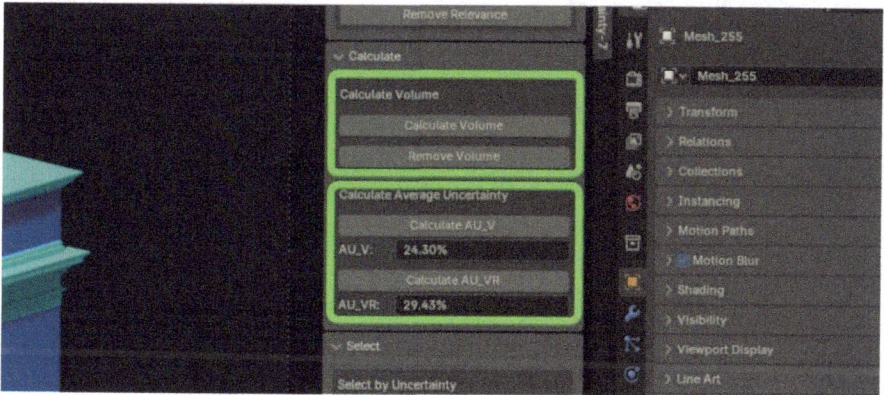

Fig. 8. The "Calculate" panel, used to calculate volumes and AU_V and AU_VR coefficients.

The panels' positioning in the interface follows from top to bottom the order of the workflow steps where they are supposed to be used. It is important to follow the correct order to avoid errors. For example, if no uncertainty value or volume is present as a custom property, the calculation of the AU_V and AU_VR will not output any result, and an alert message will be visualised.

The "Select" panel (Fig. 9) is useful for selecting at once groups of objects that were assigned to a certain level of uncertainty, and the objects with an applied relevance greater or smaller than 1 which is the default. Lastly the Utilities panel introduces a series of commands that can simplify certain operations that are often performed during the uncertainty assessment workflow, and that Blender cannot natively do with one single click.

The "Find non-manifold objects", "Weld vertices" and "Apply scale" tools are basic operations that are suggested for proofing the 3D models before proceeding with the analysis. "Find non-manifold objects" helps identify with one click which of the visible objects has some kind of geometric problem, which might cause a wrong calculation of the volume.

The use of these tools can be skipped if the user is confident that the model is properly modelled, however, their use is suggested to inexperienced users or when the model is imported from another software. The performance of some of these tools might not be optimal with models with many objects or errors, thus, it is preferable to isolate a few objects at a time before analysing or fixing them.

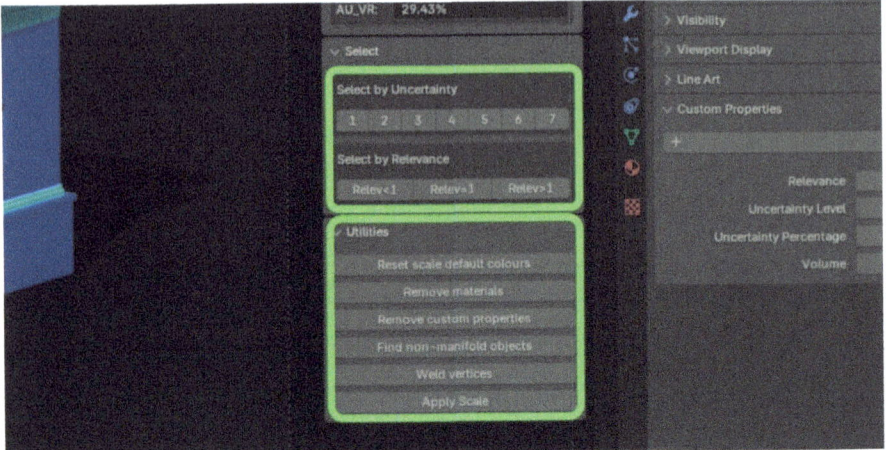

Fig. 9. The "Select" and "Utilities" panels.

3.4 Interoperability with Other Software Packages

If the 3D model is built outside Blender, the plugin can still be used, given that the 3D scene is imported into Blender correctly.

When exporting from another software, particular attention must be paid to exporting and importing closed watertight manifold solids. This is crucial because when meshes that are supposed to be solid have unwelded vertices or flipped normals, the volume calculation might give unexpected results. The volume calculation code is robust enough to output correct results even if not all edges are manifold, however, this is not always guaranteed, so to avoid any error, it is suggested to check carefully the imported result and eventually change import-export options.

For example, some possible exchange formats from Rhinoceros 8 to Blender 4.4 are the.fbx, the.obj and the.Glb (or.glTF). The fastest way to export an entire scene, preserving the hierarchical/layers structure is by using the.glTF or.Glb exchange formats. However, with these latter formats, Rhinoceros 8 exports the visualisation mesh and does not allow editing some of its parameters, thus, this might cause some problems in Blender. In particular, the Rhinoceros visualisation mesh presents split normals at sharp edges; thus, meshes that present sharp edges will not be watertight, closed, manifold, solid meshes when imported into Blender, which could cause errors in the calculation of the volume. Nevertheless, Blender can merge duplicated vertices at import (by using the settings shown in Fig. 10) and from empirical testing, we observed that the volume calculation in Blender will still be accurate most of the time, except when complex objects are present (e.g., Corinthian capitals or floral ornaments), where Blender's automatic vertices merge might fail.

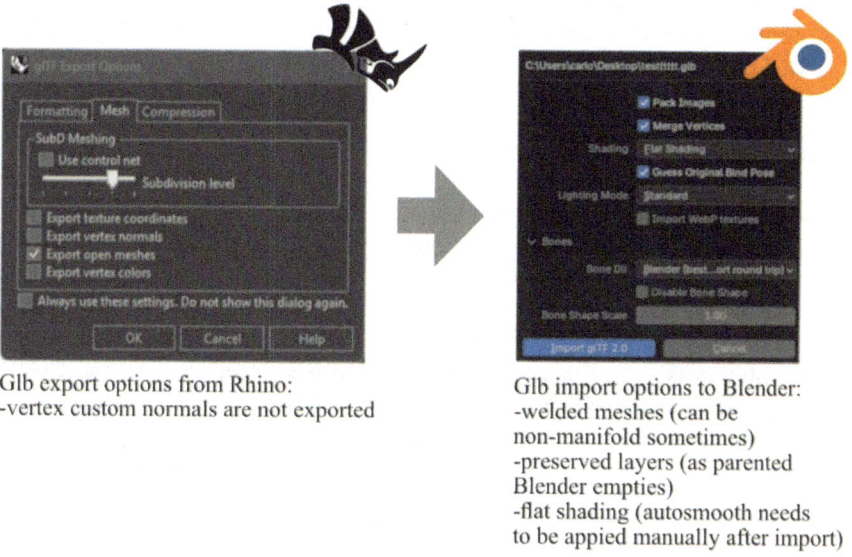

Fig. 10. Suggested options for import-export.Glb from Rhinoceros to Blender

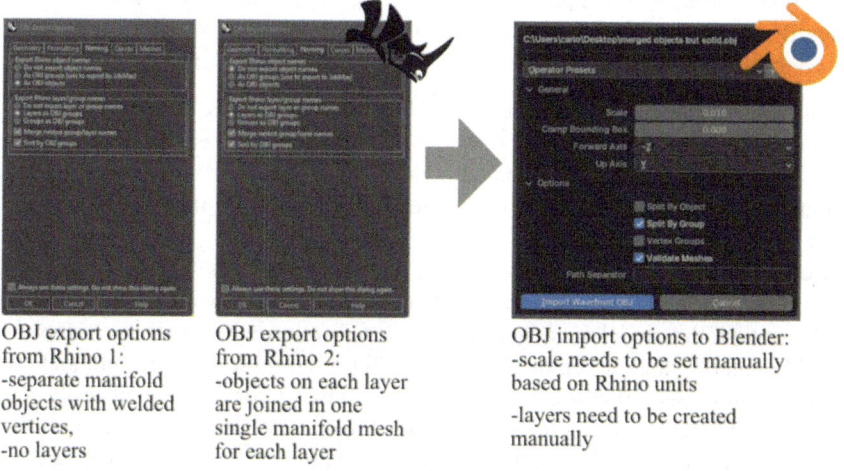

Fig. 11. Suggested options for import-export.obj from Rhinoceros to Blender

As an alternative, a more robust export-import format is the.obj format.

By following the options shown in Fig. 11, the meshes will be guaranteed to be closed, watertight solids (given that the original objects in Rhino are closed). The criticality of the .obj export from Rhinocers is that it will not preserve hierarchical structure and layers; thus, as a workaround, they can be exported layer by layer. Another criticality is that the .obj format does not import a properly scaled scene in Blender, thus the scene must be rescaled manually during or after the import.

4 Discussion and Conclusions

The Blender Uncertainty Calculator add-on was designed to simplify and enhance the process of uncertainty assessment for virtual, hypothetical 3D reconstruction, while being as easy as possible, but without compromising accuracy and scientific robustness. It is aimed at a specific step of the reconstruction workflow that was developed in the context of the CoVHer project.

The ambition is to see this tool used by those who want to adopt the CoVHer uncertainty assessment workflow to their hypothetical 3D virtual reconstruction projects.

The added value of using this methodology with this novel Blender add-on lies in five points:

1. It speeds up the assessment of the uncertainty for hypothetical reconstructive 3D models.
2. It simplifies the creation of false colour views for communicating the uncertainty assessment.
3. It simplifies the extraction of the AU_V and AU_VR coefficients to improve the comparability of different reconstructions.
4. It introduces basic model proofing tools to foster higher-quality 3D models.
5. The Blender file elaborated with this plugin can be shared with others and interrogated; the custom properties will be visible and accessible to any user.

The tool is still under development, so new tools might be added or changes in the interface might occur in future releases (the current release is 2.3.8). More model-proofing tools are already programmed in the future roadmap. Furthermore, currently the plugin supports only the 7-level scale, the possibility to use the 5-level and 3-level scales is also under development.

Despite being under development, this add-on encourages the creation of high-quality 3D models because in order to obtain a correct calculation of the volume all the elements of the model must be manifold closed solids, which makes it more easily shareable, interrogable, and reusable (e.g. for 3D printing, rendering, fluid and structural simulations and other uses). This add-on also fosters the development of a structured and well-organised uncertainty assessment based on a versatile and unambiguous uncertainty source-based 7-level false-colour scale complemented with analytic formulas capable of synthesising the average uncertainty of the 3D model with the two coefficients AU_V and AU_VR; which makes it easily sharable on open online repositories and comparable/relatable to other reconstructive models.

Acknowledgments. This research was funded by the CoVHer (Computer-based Visualisation of Architectural Cultural Heritage) Erasmus+ Project (ID-KA220-HED-88555713). For more information, refer to [9, 10].

Disclosure of Interests. Author Contributions Conceptualisation, R. Foschi; methodology, F. I. Apollonio, F. Fallavollita, R. Foschi; validation, F. I. Apollonio, F. Fallavollita and R. Foschi; formal analysis, R. Foschi; investigation, R. Foschi; data curation, R. Foschi; writing—original draft preparation, R. Foschi; writing—review and editing, F. I. Apollonio, F. Fallavollita and R. Foschi; visualisation, R. Foschi; project administration, F. Fallavollita; funding acquisition, F. Fallavollita. All authors have read and agreed to the published version of the manuscript.

References

1. Palladio, A.: Design for a villa: facade and plan, SC154/PALL/XVII/16 – RIB,A Ref No: RIBA125649 (1560). https://www.ribapix.com/design-for-a-villa-facade-and-plan_riba 125649. Accessed 21 Mar 2025
2. Münster, S., Pfarr-Harfst, M., Kuroczyński, P., Ioannides, M.: 3D research challenges in cultural heritage II: how to manage data and knowledge related to interpretative digital 3D reconstructions of cultural heritage. In: Lecture Notes in Computer Science, vol. 10025 (2016). https://doi.org/10.1007/978-3-319-47647-6
3. Bajena, I.P., Kuroczyński, P.: Challenges faced in documentation and publication of 3D reconstructions of Cultural Heritage: how to capture the process and share the data? In: Proceedings of the International Conference on Cultural Heritage and New Technologies (CHNT), 2–4 November 2021, vol. 26, no. Preview (2025)
4. Denard, H.: The London Charter. For the Computer-Based Visualisation of Cultural Heritage, Version 2.1; King's College, London, UK (2009). https://www.londoncharter.org. Accessed 05 Mar 2025
5. Principles of Seville. 'International Principles of Virtual Archaeology'. Ratified by the 19th ICOMOS General Assembly in New Delhi (2017). https://doi.org/10.1007/s00004-023-007 07-2. Accessed 21 Mar 2025
6. Charter on the Preservation of the Digital Heritage. Ratified at the 32nd General Conference of UNESCO on 17 October 2003. https://unesdoc.unesco.org/ark:/48223/pf0000179529. Accessed 05 Mar 2025
7. Wilkinson, M., Dumontier, M., Aalbersberg, I., et al.: The FAIR guiding principles for scientific data management and stewardship. Sci. Data **3**, 160018 (2016). https://doi.org/10.1038/sdata.2016.18
8. Blender webpage. https://www.blender.org/download/. Accessed 21 Mar 2025
9. CoVHer project webpage. www.CoVHer.eu. Accessed 21 Mar 2025
10. CoVHer Erasmus + project details on Europa.eu. https://erasmus-plus.ec.europa.eu/projects/search/details/2021-1-IT02-KA220-HED-000031190. Accessed 21 Mar 2025
11. Grellert, M., Wacker, M., Bruschke, J., Beck, D., Stille, W.: IDOVIR – a new infrastructure for documenting paradata and metadata of virtual reconstructions. In: Ioannides, M., Baker, D., Agapiou, A., Siegkas, P. (eds.) 3D Research Challenges in Cultural Heritage V. Lecture Notes in Computer Science, vol. 15190. Springer, Cham (2025). https://doi.org/10.1007/978-3-031-78590-0_9
12. Open Heritage webpage. https://openheritage3d.org/. Accessed 21 Mar 2025
13. DFG 3D Repository webpage. https://3d-repository.hs-mainz.de/browse. Accessed 21 Mar 2025
14. Sketchfab webpage. https://sketchfab.com/feed. Accessed 21 Mar 2025

15. 3D Repository for Computer-based Visualization of Architectural Cultural Heritage Homepage webpage. https://repository.covher.eu/. Accessed 09 Mar 2025
16. Extended Matrix tools webpage. https://www.extendedmatrix.org/em-framework/emtools. Accessed 09 Mar 2025
17. Apollonio, F.I., Fallavollita, F., Foschi, R.: The critical digital model for the study of unbuilt architecture. In: Niebling, F., Münster, S., Messemer, H. (eds.) Research and Education in Urban History in the Age of Digital Libraries. UHDL 2019. Communications in Computer and Information Science, vol. 1501. Springer, Cham (2021). https://doi.org/10.1007/978-3-030-93186-5_1
18. Apollonio, F.I., Fallavollita, F., Foschi, R., Smurra, R.: Multi-feature uncertainty analysis for urban-scale hypothetical 3D reconstructions: Piazza delle Erbe case study. Heritage **7**(1), 476–498 (2024). https://doi.org/10.3390/heritage7010023
19. Foschi, R., Fallavollita, F., Apollonio, F.I.: Quantifying uncertainty in hypothetical 3D reconstruction—a user-independent methodology for the calculation of average uncertainty. Heritage **7**(8), 4440–4454 (2024). https://doi.org/10.3390/heritage7080209
20. Blender Uncertainty Calculation add-on GitHub page. https://github.com/rikkarlo/Blender-Uncertainty-Calculator. Accessed 09 Mar 2025
21. ChatGPT 4.0 webpage. https://chatgpt.com/. Accessed 09 Mar 2025

Author Index

A
Aitken, Jacquie 138
Anderson, Janet 65
Apollonio, Fabrizio Ivan 77, 112, 175
Arnaud, David 46

B
Bachi, Valentina 163
Bajena, Igor Piotr 89
Baker, Drew 138
Bartalesi, Valentina 46
Borras, Mikel 138
Brunke, Luca 152

C
Cassar, Anthony 1
Cassidy, Catherine Anne 138
Crescenzo, Noël 46

D
de Koning, Jasper 102
Dimou, Anastasia 102
Drabczyk, Maria 102
Dubois, Arnaud 46

E
Eide, Øyvind 58

F
Fallavollita, Federico 112, 175
Foschi, Riccardo 112, 175
Fresa, Antonella 163

H
Haynes, Ronald 25
Huvila, Isto 15

K
Kerep, Axel 125
Kuroczyński, Piotr 77

M
Mackey, Stephen 65
Manfredini, Francesca 102
Manikaki, Vasiliki 46
Manitsaris, Sotiris 46
McGee, Anna 152
Meghini, Carlo 46
Miller, Alan 138
Moreno, Ines 46
Münster, Sander 35

N
Nevola, Fabrizio 152
Nikolaos, Partarakis 46

O
Omer, Benjamin 125
Ortega Gras, Juan José 46

P
Peeters, Ruben 102
Pisani, Sharon 138
Pratelli, Nicolò 46
Puche Forte, José Francisco 46

R
Rendina, Marco 102

S
Schlarb, Sven 65
Senteri, Gavriela 46
Svorc, Jiri 102

V
Vassallo, Valentina 125

Z
Zabulis, Xenophon 46

Made in the USA
Monee, IL
03 May 2026